The Chartered Institite of Marketing/Butterworth-Heinemann Marketing Series is the most comprehensive, widely used and important collection of books in marketing and sales currently available worldwide.

As the CIM's official publisher, Butterworth-Heinemann develops, produces and publishes the complete series in association with the CIM. We aim to provide definitive marketing books for students and practitioners that promote excellence in marketing education and practice.

The series titles are written by CIM senior examiners and leading marketing educators for professionals, students and those studying the CIM's Certificate, Advanced Certificate and Postgraduate Diploma courses. Now firmly established, these titles provide practical study support to CIM and other marketing students and to practitioners at all levels.

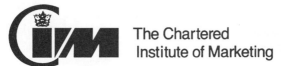
The Chartered Institute of Marketing

Formed in 1911, The Chartered Institute of Marketing is now the largest professional marketing management body in the world with over 60,000 members located worldwide. Its primary objectives are focused on the development of awareness and understanding of marketing throughout UK industry and commerce and in the raising of standards of professionalism in the education, training and practice of this key business discipline.

Books in the series

Market Focus

Achieving and sustaining marketing effectiveness

Rick Brown

*Published on behalf of
the Chartered Institute of Marketing*

Butterworth-Heinemann
Linacre House, Jordan Hill, Oxford OX2 8DP
225 Wildwood Avenue, Woburn, MA 01801-2041
A division of Reed Educational and Professional Publishing Ltd

A member of the Reed Elsevier plc group

OXFORD   BOSTON   JOHANNESBURG
MELBOURNE   NEW DELHI   SINGAPORE

First published 1993
Reprinted 1994, 1997 (twice), 1998

British Library Cataloguing in Publication Data
Brown, Rick
  Market Focus, - (Marketing Series)
  I. Series   II. Series
  658.8

ISBN 0 7506 0887 0

Printed and bound in Great Britain by
MPG Books Ltd, Bodmin, Cornwall

Contents

Contents

1 The market focus concept

Market orientation is increasingly becoming recognized as the basis and the starting point of effective business management. It has received extensive publicity in recent years, indeed the notion that businesses need to respond to markets and satisfy their customers now seems to be so widely accepted that it scarcely needs saying. The gradual acceptance of this simple principle of business has come about through the constant interviews given by prominent business leaders and management gurus, through newspaper and magazine articles, through television series, and a plethora of popular management books, videos and teaching packages. In recent years, it seems that the idea of marketing has been very well marketed indeed.

The notion that paying attention to markets and customers is the basis of business success is nothing new: as far back as 1977, Theodore Levitt expressed his view on the subject unequivocally.

> The purpose of an enterprise is to create and keep a customer. All other truths on this subject are merely derivative.

Levitt was taking issue with those who claim that the purpose of a business is to make a profit. While this assertion is self evidently true, the point is that profits only result when customers part with their money, because if they won't, there will be no profit and indeed no company. Thus, Levitt argued, the primary purpose of a business must be to create and keep *customers* profit can only accrue once sales revenue has been generated, hence his assertion that profit is 'derivative'. Former Jaguar chairman John Egan expressed the same sentiment in words which are rather easier to interpret.

> Business is about making money from satisfied customers. Without satisfied customers, there can be no future for any commercial organization.

Elements of market focus

Egan's words will strike a chord with many managers, after all, they are an eloquent statement of the obvious, an axiom with which nobody could seriously quarrel. Indeed, in textbooks, although ex-pressed in different words, Egan's axiom is accepted as the whole basis of marketing itself, the notion that meeting customer needs is fundamental to business success. Regrettably, however, making money by satisfying customers is not a simple matter; while im-possible to refute, this principle does not in itself constitute an actionable route to business success. The problem is that in the real world there are competitors, and they too are anxious to make money by satisfying customers. If two or more firms are trying to satisfy the same customer, the result is competition, and the weakest competitors get squeezed. Thus, firms can only make profits if they can create and keep customers, but in a competitive market, customers will only be created and retained if a company can satisfy them better than its competitors.

The purpose of market focus is to enable an organization to achieve superior customer satisfaction compared to the competition. The market focus concept is based on four key elements which come together in a focused operating marketing plan (see Figure 1.1). The first element is the ability to understand the customers very well, to know what their needs are, and thus be able to focus on the customers whose needs we can meet most effectively. Secondly, we have to focus on the competitors, and understand them very well, so as to be able to find a defensible market position relative to those with whom we do compete, and avoid those against whom it is better not to compete. In order to build a defensible position, we need to concentrate on the areas where we have the best chance of

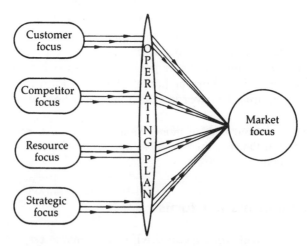

Figure 1.1 *Elements of market focus*

success, so the third element of market focus is to focus our resources onto those key priority areas. Finally, we need to find a winning strategy in the marketplace, thus the fourth element is to define a focused competitive strategy, dedicated to the achievement of a specified strategic goal. These four basic building blocks come together in the market focus planning process, which results in an actionable operating marketing plan, essential to the implementation of any marketing strategy.

This concept is reflected in the structure of this book: Chapter 2 is about customer focus and customer orientation, while Chapter 3 examines competitor focus through the concepts of segmentation and positioning. Effective positioning demands possession of a competitive advantage, and the most positive approach to offering something better is to do something different, something new; this involves innovation of one kind or another, the subject of Chapter 4. The next stage is to focus scarce resources onto key priority areas where the market is attractive and competitive advantage can be gained, and this is examined in Chapter 5. Chapter 6 looks at finding a focused competitive strategy (strategic focus), which forms the link between positioning (customer and competitor focus) and strategic priorities (resource focus).

These four key elements of market focus are the drivers of the operating marketing plan, thus Chapter 7 shows how the market focus planning process integrates the four elements to result in an actionable operating plan and the achievement of market focus. But once achieved, market focus will not last for ever: changes in the company's marketing environment will start to undermine it from day one. Responding to these external changes is the key to sustaining market focus, the subject of Chapter 8. Finally, Chapter 9 identifies twelve attributes which an organization needs to build in order to be able to achieve and sustain market focus. This chapter lays out a management agenda to assess, monitor and develop the characteristics of a truly market focused organization.

Basis for competitive success

Achieving and sustaining market focus requires intensive management effort, and in view of this, managers are entitled to ask what the benefits are likely to be. Fundamentally, market focus is the route to superior competitive performance, it is the basis of competitive success. One can do no better than quote the best known marketing guru of all, Philip Kotler, author of the world's best selling marketing text book.

Market Focus – No company can operate in every market and satisfy
every need. Nor can it even do a good job within one broad market:
even mighty IBM cannot offer the best solution for every computer
need. Companies do best when they define their target markets
carefully.

Kotler goes on to outline the example of Japanese car makers, who
have attacked the US car market by targeting clearly defined user
groups with specifically designed vehicles. Thus, the Japanese have
successfully targeted the markets for smaller cars, second cars, sports
cars, pick-ups, space cruisers and so on. In each case the definition
of the target market has greatly influenced the design of the car.
They have not attempted to break into the market for the traditional
'gas guzzler' American car, which many commentators feel is in any
case in long term decline. This is in contrast to the domestic manufacturers, GM and Ford, who have persevered with a diversified
range, trying to offer something to everybody. The outcome of these
contrasting strategies provides a clear illustration of the potential
value of market focus. Whereas the Japanese have progressively
built market share in a range of specialist segments, the domestic
manufacturers have staggered from one crisis to the next; finally, in
1992, GM declared a record breaking loss, the largest ever by any
commercial corporation.

It seems that even the largest corporations cannot be excellent at
everything, and in a competitive market, being merely good enough
is no longer adequate: companies need to be excellent compared to
their competitors in order to succeed. The starting point for this
pursuit of excellence is to recognize that it is impossible to be all
things to all people in a competitive world, and hence that companies
need to focus on the markets where they are best placed to succeed.
It is not that total quality, flexible manufacturing, and all the other
sophisticated techniques of modern management are unimportant
in the pursuit of competitive success, but rather that these things
will be less effective unless they are done within a framework of
market focus. Thus, at the most basic level, market focus is the
starting point for the achievement of competitive success.

The ultimate goal of most commercial organizations is sustained
profitability: they seek profits to survive in the present, to invest in
the future, and to pay dividends to their shareholders, and profits
will only accrue once sales have been made to customers. Of course,
not all organizations will define their goals purely in terms of financial
criteria. Hospitals, charities, educational institutions, and other
non-profit seeking organizations will each have their own distinctive
criteria. However, while they may not specifically seek a profit, even

these organizations need to generate revenue just to survive. What-ever their ultimate goals, all organizations need to generate revenues, and in the long term, customer satisfaction is the basis of the ability to do this. In other words, in order to be profitable, or otherwise achieve their goals, organizations need to create and keep customers. But in a competitive environment, they can only do this if they achieve superior competitive performance.

Market focus is the basis of competitive success, which in turn is the route to creating and keeping customers, which is itself the route to revenues and profits. Thus, there is a clear link between market focus and an organization's ability to achieve its ultimate goals. Of course there are hundreds of other variables which impact upon company profitability, and a gross error or problem in any one of them can undermine even the most profitable company. But the achievement of competitive success and customer satisfaction are absolute fundamentals in any commercial business. If market focus is the basis of competitive success, then surely it is also the basis of sustained profitability.

2 Customer orientation

Customer orientation is the starting point for market focus. The idea that organizations should focus on their customers has long been understood by economists: two hundred years ago, Adam Smith wrote about the 'sovereignty of the consumer', a quaint way of saying that the customer is king. In recent years, this simple notion has become the underlying principle behind a great deal of management activity. For example, total quality management is essentially about organizing to deliver customer satisfaction, rather than quality *per se*. Organizations from airlines to building societies and telephone companies spend vast sums on advertising, telling their customers how badly they want to satisfy them, with further expenditure on customer care training for staff and so on. This is hardly surprising: spurred on by books like *In Search of Excellence*, and inspirational examples like Disneyworld and McDonald's, satisfying the customer has become the new business creed.

Yet in many organizations, while acceptance of the principle of customer orientation is widespread, the reality is little more than skin deep. Examples of this paradox confront everybody in their daily lives; bank staff wear name badges and are trained to smile, yet few people would seriously claim that the large clearing banks are genuinely customer oriented organizations. Banks widely publicize the fact that they are open on Saturdays to provide the customer with a better service, but anyone who visits a bank on a Saturday to conduct a normal banking transaction will find the banking counters closed, and is likely to leave severely disappointed. Privately, even employees admit that the objective of Saturday opening is to make sales of insurance policies, mortgages and so on, rather than to provide a better banking service.

The contradiction between what organizations say about customer satisfaction and what they actually do is not confined to banks. Indeed, many managers who work for companies which claim in public to be dedicated to customer satisfaction have a fund of anecdotes which illustrate how their company seems perversely dedicated to doing the opposite. It is one of the most baffling aspects of modern business life that a creed which is accepted in principle by so many is followed with total commitment by so few. The exhortations of the business leaders and management gurus have certainly succeeded in gaining acceptance of the principle of customer satisfaction as the basis of business success, however many businesses seem to have failed fully to implement it in practice.

This chapter will examine why this paradox has arisen, why it is that companies find it so difficult to implement a management concept so deceptively simple as making profits through customer satisfaction. The era of simply persuading people that customer orientation is manifestly a good idea is coming to an end, we need to go beyond mere exhortation. The reasons why companies find it difficult to adopt the philosophy of customer satisfaction for real are rooted in the structure and systems of every organization, and until we understand these barriers we shall have no hope of overcoming them.

Structural barriers to customer orientation

Pursuit of functional objectives

Henry Ford was the first man to set up flow line assembly of motor cars; before him, all cars had been hand built, just like stagecoaches. This had a dramatic impact on the car market, since he could sell his cars considerably cheaper than his competitors and still make good profits, because his cars cost much less to make owing to his vastly superior production efficiency. Henry had a straightforward marketing philosophy: he made one model only and said 'the customer can have any colour he likes − so long as it's black!'. He was enormously successful because he realized the benefits of economies of scale in the motor car production process. His prices were so much lower than those of his competitors that customers did not mind the lack of any choice. However, as soon as Alfred Sloan set up his General Motors production line and offered red as well as black, Henry Ford's philosophy was in trouble. Sloan could compete on price, but he also offered the customer a choice. Immediately the balance started to swing away from economies of scale and towards customer choice.

Ford and Sloan knew that the greatest operating efficiency is achieved by having as little variation as possible in the production process: however, customers have different tastes and requirements which can only be met by diversity of product. This is the classic production manager's dilemma, outlined in Figure 2.1. The balance can either be moved to the right towards greater economies of scale and lower costs, or to the left, towards greater customer choice and more sales opportunities. This simple diagram helps to explain the constant battle which takes place between sales and production in

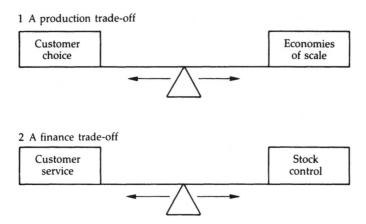

Figure 2.1 *Management trade-off decisions*

many companies: production's objective of operating efficiency and sales' objective of maximum customer choice are in complete conflict with each other. This answer involves a balanced management decision which weighs the relative benefits of moving to the left or the right, recognizing that there is always a fundamental trade-off between customer choice and operating efficiency.

Looking at other management functions, similar dilemmas arise. The finance executive naturally wishes to control stocks – in practice this means he wishes to reduce them, or at least prevent them from increasing. His justification for this is perfectly reasonable. Stocks tie up working capital, and every ten pounds saved in working capital is ten pounds off the firm's overdraft; every ten pounds off the overdraft is a pound saved in interest charges, and every pound saved in interest charges is a pound more on the company's profits. However, the sales manager does not see things in quite the same way. He knows that customers demand a service, and if stocks in the distribution depots are reduced, some items are going to go out of stock and be unavailable when wanted by a customer. Such a customer could easily turn to a competitor and be lost, not only for this sale, but for ever. Thus we have another classic management trade-off decision, also shown in Figure 2.1. The balance can be moved to the right reducing stocks and saving working capital, or to the left enhancing customer service. Hence the battle which rages between sales and finance!

Management is, of course, full of these trade-off decisions, but the curious thing is that many of them are a trade-off between something the customer wants, and something which is convenient, cost efficient or interesting for the firm's managers to do. Thus, production managers try to reduce variety and accountants try to reduce stock levels, whereas greater customer satisfaction may be achieved by doing the opposite. Equally, engineers may strive for technical excellence in the product, reaching new frontiers in its technical specification, whereas the customers may simply want something that is reliable, easy to operate and does the job they want done. Quality controllers may have their own professional statistical standards which determine the quality they wish to achieve, but surely the real determinant of quality objectives must be the quality the customer wants and is prepared to pay for.

Thus, the first barrier to customer orientation is quite simply that different managers have a different functional view of what the company needs to do to be successful. The production manager wants a smaller product range and a highly efficient factory; the finance manager wants lower stocks and hence lower interest charges; the R&D manager wants to develop the latest technology; while the sales manager wants as wide a product range as possible and higher stocks. All of these could be potentially winning formulae, the problem is choosing which to go for. In a functionally oriented business, it is difficult to resolve these trade-offs in a rational and consistent way. However, in a customer oriented business, each function uses its understanding of the needs of the target customer to resolve the trade-offs inherent in any funtional management role.

For example, if a car company determined that the two things its target customers wanted above all others was better rust prevention and better reliability, it would have a profound effect on all the company's operating functions. R&D might want to design a new high technology engine, but the primary focus would have to switch to improving reliability rather than performance. Production might want ideally to increase assembly track speed and reduce labour input, but their focus would have to be to improve the quality of body seals and other rust proofing measures. Speed of throughput, as well as labour input, might have to be sacrificed to a certain extent in order to achieve this. Purchasing would naturally want to get down the cost of bought-in components, but in the search for more reliable components, their traditional focus on achieving lower supplier prices would have to switch to supplier quality and reliability. Therefore, genuine customer orientation would have a very direct impact on each of these functional managers, in a sense, it would set the agenda for their function. All this is, of course, easy to say but to persuade managers to shift from their traditional functional orientation can be extremely difficult to do.

Customer visibility

The traditional model of company organization is like an inverted tree. The branches spread out into sub-branches and finally into a mass of twigs, the whole thing only finally coming together at the central trunk. In a traditional organization, the branches are the functions, each one having a line reporting system from the twigs at the sharp end to the main branch in the boardroom. Writers on organizational design have commented that while this type of organization works well for information flowing up and down the functional branches, it is less effective in encouraging an information flow across functions. In this sense, the traditional structure reinforces the functionally driven objectives referred to above.

Once it is accepted that the customer should be at the centre of the whole organization's thinking, the real problem with the traditional structure becomes all too apparent. The tree organization actually excludes the most important person of all, the customer; worse still, the only strong link between the organization and the customer is at the sharp end of the field sales force. Given the difficulty of communication between the branches of the tree, not to mention the fact that salesmen spend most of their time away from the company, it is hardly surprising that the customer is not terribly visible to the other members of the organization. Indeed, the members of most of the other functions could spend their entire corporate lives in blissful ignorance of the fact that customers even exist, let alone recognize that these invisible people are the ultimate reason why their business survives.

The ideal organizational model would look very different, each function would have direct links to a highly visible customer, and would only make decisions based on both customer and functional criteria. This type of approach is illustrated in the dartboard organization shown in Figure 2.2, in which the word 'marketing' is interposed between the functions and the customer. But marketing in this sense does not mean the marketing function, it does not mean a group of people, it means marketing as a business philosophy which is shared by all functions, a philosophy in which customer orientation is a task for every manager, regardless of function. Customer orientation for real involves all functions doing the things which suit the customer rather than the things which they find operationally efficient, convenient, or interesting. It means placing the customer at the centre of the business decision making process for every function; however, in order to do this, the customer needs to be highly visible to those functions.

Traditional systems of organizational structure emphasize func-

Figure 2.2 *Customer orientation in all functions*

tional reporting lines and functional values, as well as consigning the customer to a position of very low visibility. Genuine customer orientation requires a significant shift in functional attitudes as well as much higher customer visibility. However, even if the structural barriers could be overcome, the systems barriers would still remain. If customers really are so important one might believe that company systems would specifically be designed to highlight problems in the company to customer relationship. Such a belief would be naive in the extreme; indeed company systems, like the structure, seem geared up to exclude customers rather than satisfy them.

Systems barriers to customer orientation

Business efficiency

Most managing directors see their primary responsibility as making a profit, and if possible a steadily rising profit each year. Of course, the amount of profit must be related to the amount of capital employed. Measures of return on investment (profit divided by capital employed) tell investors how much the managers are making on each pound invested in the business. These measures come in various forms, a popular variant being return on shareholders' funds, which extracts borrowing from the capital employed figure, and shows what return is being made on that part of the company's capital owned by the shareholders.

What all these basic measures of company performance have in common is that they measure the efficiency with which the managers are using the funds at their disposal. They have spawned a whole range of ratios which are used both internally and externally to assess company performance; sales per employee, output per worker, output per machine hour, stock turnover, sales per square foot, profits per square foot, and so on. These and many more similar measures are meat and drink to managers and external company analysts alike. They are measures of efficiency, derived by comparing a given output with the input needed to generate it. The efficiency of an engine can be increased by either boosting the power output while holding the fuel input constant, or by using less fuel to achieve the same power. The same is true for business efficiency measures; either increase the output for the same input, or decrease the input required to produce a given output. Figure 2.3 shows examples of some well-known efficiency measures.

Return on capital employed	$= \dfrac{\text{Profits}}{\text{Capital employed}}$	$\dfrac{\text{Output}}{\text{Input}}$
Sales per employee	$= \dfrac{\text{Sales}}{\text{Number of employees}}$	$\dfrac{\text{Output}}{\text{Input}}$
Productivity	$= \dfrac{\text{Production}}{\text{Machine hours}}$	$\dfrac{\text{Output}}{\text{Input}}$
Stock turnover	$= \dfrac{\text{Sales}}{\text{Stocks}}$	$\dfrac{\text{Output}}{\text{Input}}$
Sales per square foot	$= \dfrac{\text{Sales}}{\text{Number of square feet}}$	$\dfrac{\text{Output}}{\text{Input}}$

Figure 2.3 *Measures of business efficiency*

The underlying concept common to these systems, that good management is basically about the pursuit of efficiency, has seeped into every pore of business life. The carrier of this pernicious virus is the ubiquitous management control system, which forms the basis of so many management discussions. Managers at all levels see various versions of the monthly figures, and use them to set priorities, redefine targets, set up special investigations, take decisions, and assess the performance of other managers. Over time, companies develop their own unique range of measures, specific to that business, and some have taken the art to a breathtaking level of sophistication.

For example, a major UK brewery includes in its monthly management accounts for each trading area a measure of the amount of tyre wear on delivery lorries compared to the amount of beer delivered, known internally as millimetres of tread wear per thousand barrels delivered. The justification for this is that tyres are expensive and costs have to be controlled, and that it enables the section responsible for purchasing tyres to forecast demand more accurately. It also provides an early warning system in case of pilferage of tyres by unscrupulous employees; all good reasons one might think. Of course, the company's directors do not actually discuss this kind of detail when they meet every month to review overall company performance figures, however, they like to keep their eye on it to assure themselves that it's 'right'. Ensuring that relatively minor things like tyre wear are right, means in practice a quick, almost subconscious check, to see that they are in line with established company norms. After all, a primary purpose of control systems is to highlight variations from the norm.

Given that the directors are looking for maintenance of norms, it is hardly surprising that managers down the line try to deliver just that. Thus, contracts are not sought with outlets which are a long way from the standard delivery route, as that would damage a whole series of the distribution function's operating norms. In the case of the brewery, a new outlet was acquired which had a badly surfaced car park, and the decision was made to resurface this to prevent potential damage to tyres, and thus help to keep the tyre wear ratio within the accepted company norms. The manager who took the decision explained that since the resurfacing work was paid for out of the capital budget there would be no impact on operating profits in any case! For that individual manager, the decision was a rational one; for the organization as a whole, it was a complete nonsense.

Business efficiency, the ability to generate more output from a given input, is such an intuitively appealing concept that few people stop to question its validity. Unfortunately however, the systems used to measure it encourage managers to take decisions which suit the system rather than decisions which make the best commercial sense, in other words, they lead to financially driven rather than customer driven decisions. Efficiency systems also involve norms, like sales calls per person for example, but these are only relevant in a given set of market circumstances. If the market changes, the old norms may soon become rapidly out of date, and companies working to more relevant norms will gain an advantage. While all businesses undeniably need to be efficient, the dilemma is that many of the measures of efficiency take no account of customer satisfaction.

Marketing effectiveness

Efficiency is widely accepted as a central tenet of good management practice: every manager is trained to be efficient, expected to be efficient, has systems imposed upon him to measure his efficiency, and is rewarded and promoted on results demonstrated by these systems. Taken overall, this forms a formidable package from a management motivation viewpoint. Given the strength of this package in the minds of managers, Peter Drucker defined business efficiency as 'doing things right'. But Drucker contrasted this with an alternative concept of management, effectiveness, which he defined as 'doing the right things'. Although the words used in the definitions are similar, the meanings are fundamentally different. Doing things right means doing the things which suit the system and hit the norms, whereas doing the right things means doing the things which will create and keep customers. A company which is effective will emphasize the ability to innovate with new ideas, adapt when the market changes, and invest to create a competitive advantage: this is an external management orientation.

By contrast, in a company which seeks success through efficiency, the managers will focus on the achievement of maximum output from minimum input by good management of their own internal affairs. Queueing theory was an important item on the management science agenda at business schools in the 1970s, and the application of this to a business decision illustrates neatly the contrast between efficiency and effectiveness. Applied to a company's telephone sales office, a queueing system can drastically reduce the number of sales clerks required to handle a given number of calls: this, of course, will greatly improve each clerk's efficiency. But unfortunately it means that potential customers will sometimes have to wait to have their calls answered; it is a policy of saving costs by making customers hang on. While this may sound bizarre in the 1990s, it was the subject of a great deal of time and investment in the 1970s.

A company taking decisions on the grounds of efficiency would make the ratio of sales clerks to calls answered a top priority, and invest in a call queueing system, the cost being justified on the grounds of the savings in manpower being offered. By contrast, a company interested primarily in effectiveness would set a goal that, say, 98% of calls should be answered within the first five rings, a very different management priority indeed. One well-known distribution service company actually aims to answer calls on the first ring, and this is a key criterion upon which the department manager's performance is judged. This is clearly not the way to achieve the highest levels of sales clerk utilization, but it may well be crucial in

	Ineffective	Effective
Inefficient	Die quickly	Survive
Efficient	Die slowly	Thrive

Figure 2.4 *The contrast between efficiency and effectiveness*

securing a valued order from a customer who is in a hurry, or in retaining a previous customer's loyalty. In other words, it might not be efficient, but in that business it might be highly effective at creating and keeping customers.

The contrast between internal efficiency and external effectiveness is shown in Figure 2.4, and more formal definitions of the two concepts are given in Figure 2.5. Companies which are both inefficient and ineffective will obviously die, whereas companies which can achieve both efficiency and effectiveness will thrive. However, the interesting aspect of this matrix is in considering the top right and the bottom left quadrants. Companies in the top right quadrant are externally effective, and thus can create and keep customers, so by definition they will be able to survive; nevertheless their relatively low level of internal efficiency will result in low profits. By contrast, companies in the bottom left quadrant are highly efficient and therefore profitable, but if the market changes they will find it difficult to adapt and find new customers, since they are externally ineffective. In the long run, the market will change and they will inevitably die, however, they will die slowly and relatively profitably. The matrix illustrates that a company must be able to create and keep customers even to survive, and certainly to thrive. If it cannot create and keep customers it will surely die, and improving efficiency will only slow the process down; efficiency improvements alone can never save a company when the market is changing.

The paradox is that calls for improved efficiency are always loudest when market problems have led to financial problems. The

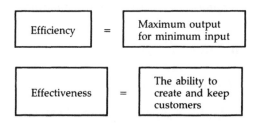

Figure 2.5 *Definitions of efficiency and effectiveness*

chairman announces that times are tough, and we have to become 'fitter and leaner' to survive. This, in effect, means retrenchment or cost cutting, and it is worthwhile considering the kinds of activities which suffer during these programmes. Risky new product innovations, capital investment, recruitment, R&D expenditure, training, and advertising are all examples of areas which are easily cut during a perceived crisis. It goes without saying that these are precisely the areas in which a company will need to invest to adapt to a changing market. Cutting them may only make the problem worse, thus inviting a further round of cuts. Without realizing it, a firm may slide into a vicious circle of decline followed by cuts followed by more decline. By emphasizing cost controls and short term profitability, the firm may have damaged irreparably its ability to be competitive in the marketplace. While it is undeniable that judicious cost reduction in non-critical areas is often a good idea, companies must beware the industrial anorexia syndrome, for this is the excessive desire to be fitter and leaner, which results in emaciation and eventual death.

It should not be imagined that all top businessmen are naively unaware of this critical issue. For example, it was addressed by the Chairman of United Biscuits, Sir Hector Laing, in an eight-page booklet sent out to his shareholders, warning of the dangers of an excessive preoccupation with the pursuit of short term profits.

> While earnings per share growth must be a very important criterion by which a company's performance is judged, at least as important is the underlying long term strength and competitiveness of the business on which those earnings depend. It is not difficult for a manufacturing business to maximize short term profitability and boost earnings per share for reasons of expedience by compromising standards of quality and service and by under-investing. The price, however, is inevitable decline.

Laing's is a dire warning of the consequences of becoming a victim of the anorexia syndrome, and is one which all business leaders should heed. However, they might reasonably ask how to do it in a climate which emphasizes steady growth in earnings per share.

Achieving customer focus

Tackling the systems barriers

It is clear that companies must create and keep customers in order to survive and thrive, in short they must achieve marketing effectiveness. The problem is that traditional management control systems emphasize efficiency in every minute corner of the business, and the excessive pursuit of efficiency may terminally damage effectiveness. Given that accepted business structures and systems seem dedicated to undermine customer orientation rather than enhance it, it is hardly surprising that companies find it difficult to do in practice. Exhortation by business leaders and management gurus to focus on customers is fine, but exhortation alone will never overcome these fundamental organizational barriers to customer orientation. Thus, while customer satisfaction is manifestly a good thing for a company to aim at, it is discouraged by both the structural and systems barriers inherent in many organizations. However, once these barriers have been recognized, steps can be taken to overcome them.

Firstly, the financial control system should be examined to differentiate between those few controls which are crucial to the management of the business, and the rest. Many of these will be doing more harm than good, since the damage they inflict on the company's ability to be customer oriented outweighs any additional control they offer. Clearly, the crucial controls should be retained, but the other, non-essential controls, should either be done away with, or at least reduced to the status of early warning systems for operating managers, rather than being used as performance yardsticks by senior managers. This inevitably means that relatively low level functional managers will need to be given the freedom to decide say, what level of tyre wear is appropriate, or how many calls each salesman should make. However, this will also give these operating managers the ability to make commercial, market oriented decisions, rather than being tied into the pursuit of outdated norms.

Another aspect of complex management control systems which is frequently overlooked is the enormous amount of bureaucracy involved in driving them, not to mention the endless meetings which result in order to review them. An energetic attempt to reduce the scope and complexity of a company's management control system will often enable surprisingly large savings to be made in the cost of data collection and processing, as well as giving operating managers the ability to become more customer oriented. It may thus offer the ability simultaneously to improve both effectiveness and efficiency. Bureaucracy is truly one of the curses of large organizations, and indeed may contain the seeds of their ultimate downfall. The reasons for this have been summed up by Jack Welch, President of General Electric (GE) one of America's largest corporations.

> Bureaucracy is evil, because it destroys productivity by distracting attention from useful work. It makes people look inward at the organization rather than outward to the customer and the competition.

While making an effort to give operating managers the freedom to make commercially oriented decisions, and simultaneously reduce bureaucracy may sound an eminently reasonable objective in theory, it is not so easy in practice. The problem is that no board of directors will want to give up the veneer of control, the feeling that they know what is going on. But they should bear in mind the damage that having numerous efficiency measures does to the company's effectiveness, not to mention the bureaucracy required to collect and process all the data. By ruthlessly cutting out super-fluous measures we can both create the potential to improve customer orientation and reduce bureaucracy. Less bureaucracy should mean lower costs, thus a truly fundamental review of the control system and all its supporting structures may well lead to improvements in efficiency as well as effectiveness.

At the same time as measures of efficiency are being reduced or re-designated, parallel measures of effectiveness should be introduced. These require analysis of the kind of market data which are probably already available somewhere within the company anyway, but in any case will need to be collected by any organization which is genuinely customer oriented. Marketing effectiveness can be measured by monitoring the level of customer satisfaction, the level of complaints, the proportion of repeat purchasers, the number of warranty claims, proportion of shipments received on time, perhaps even the number of customer calls answered before five rings, and similar readily measurable criteria. Market research can be used to track criteria like brand awareness, perceived product quality, per-ception of distribution and availability, and awareness of advertising, many of these being particularly useful when measured relative to leading competitors.

This is not a comprehensive list of potential marketing effectiveness criteria: each company needs to determine which measures of effec-tiveness are considered key to its particular business, in exactly the same way as it needs to draw up its own shortlist of critical efficiency criteria. The ideal control system should aim at a dozen or so key controls, half measuring efficiency and half effectiveness. These should be controlled tightly, the rest should be used as early warning systems and controlled loosely, or abandoned altogether. It is im-possible to be specific about what parameters should be controlled tightly, the list will be unique to each business. The board should draw up its own list, the starting point being a consideration of what it is crucial to control and what it is merely nice to know about.

The operation of this kind of 'tight/loose' control system is one of the essential steps towards achieving market focus. Without this, it is impossible to bring about the shift in emphasis which needs to take place, from the single minded pursuit of efficiency towards the pursuit of effectiveness. The point is not that efficiency should be abandoned, businesses have to be efficient, but that every manager must realize the importance of effectiveness and take decisions which enhance customer satisfaction rather than damage it. While it is acknowledged that the need to measure and analyse external criteria will lead to some increase in data collection and processing activity, without this information no company can hope to be market oriented. In any case, much of the information may already be available, and any increased costs should be offset by the savings made in abandoning elements of the efficiency based system.

Tackling the structural barriers

While the systems barriers to customer orientation are relatively tangible and permit at least some vision of possible solutions, the structural barriers may at first sight appear insuperable given that functional structures are a fact of life in most organizations. However, there are two major approaches to overcoming them, firstly improving customer visibility, and secondly improving cross-functional links on customer related issues. Customer visibility is dealt with in greater detail in Chapter 8, which outlines a programme designed to highlight important external market issues to all managers in the company, and ensure that managers are fully aware of the needs of the company's target customers. The idea is to try to get every functional manager to think about the impact his decisions will have upon the company's ability to meet the needs of its customers, and hence whether it is likely to enhance or damage the overall level of customer satisfaction.

Thus, improving customer visibility is partly a question of making information about the company's customers and markets more widely available. However, it is also necessary to raise awareness of the fact that it is basically customers who will ensure the success of the business, and ultimately the future careers of the employees themselves. This is an educational task whose purpose is to build positive attitudes towards customers and their role in the company. While this is covered more specifically in Chapter 9, an example of the kind of positive message which needs to be communicated is contained the following extract from a poster which is prominently displayed around the offices of L.L. Bean, a successful specialist mail order company in Maine USA. British readers may find this a little too American in style, but it does nevertheless communicate an essential message in a very direct way.

What is a customer? A customer is the most important person ever in
this office, in person or by mail. A customer is not dependent on us,
we are dependent on him. A customer is not an interruption of our
work, he is the purpose of it. We are not doing a favour by serving
him, he is doing us a favour by giving us the opportunity to do so.

Increasing customer visibility therefore requires education and the
provision of information, but it is essentially a long term task to
build customer awareness and responsiveness. The improvement of
cross functional links on the other hand is somewhat more tangible,
in that it aims to build a series of multi-functional, customer focused
teams made up of representatives of each major function, each team
specializing in a particular market area or customer type. While it is
acknowledged that in most companies the functional approach to
organization is likely to continue as the overall model, it should
nevertheless be possible to build cross-functional teams designed
along the lines of Figure 2.2, with each member responsible for
improving customer orientation within his particular function. Each
different target customer or target market segment would have its
own cross-functional team. Breaking down traditional functional
views of what is the best way to run the business will never be
easy, and the setting up of cross-functional customer segment focused
teams must be accompanied by an educational effort aimed at raising
awareness of the customer oriented approach to business management and determining functional objectives.

Understanding customer focus

As outlined above, several practical steps can be taken to break
down the internal barriers to customer orientation, but to fully
resolve the functional trade-offs it is necessary to understand the
real nature of customer focus. It is useful to start with a simple
definition of marketing. While there have been many definitions
suggested, all probably equally valid depending on your point of
view, one based on the definition of effectiveness (see Figure 2.5),
seems to communicate the basic idea of marketing very well. Effectiveness is the ability to create and keep customers, but this alone is
insufficient as a definition of marketing, since it does not discriminate
between different customers in the way that any company committed
to market focus needs to. Contrary to popular belief, marketing is
not the pursuit of any customer at any price. Such an approach
would be entirely unfocused, and a company which tries to be all
things to all men is in danger of ending up being nothing special to

```
┌─────────────────────────────────┐
│            Marketing             │
├─────────────────────────────────┤
│ 'The ability to create and keep  │
│ profitable customers'            │
└─────────────────────────────────┘
```

Figure 2.6 *Definition of marketing*

anybody. In order to turn the definition of effectiveness into a definition of marketing we need to add one word which implies a need to discriminate between different customers and markets, and that word is profitable (see Figure 2.6).

If marketing is the ability to create and keep profitable customers, it is worthwhile thinking through the implications of including the word profitable. The first is clearly that companies cannot completely abandon efficiency in the pursuit of effectiveness. Companies have to be efficient, otherwise they will not be as profitable as they should be. However, they should aim to achieve efficiency within the context of an effective marketing strategy, not as a goal in its own right. The second implication is a little more subtle, and is based on the notion that not every customer will be equally profitable for every company, some will be more profitable than others. Thus, it makes sense to focus on the most profitable markets and customers, or those which are likely to become the most profitable in the longer term, and accordingly be prepared to de-emphasize the others. Focusing on the customers we can serve most effectively must therefore form the basis of any effort to create and keep profitable customers. The markets and customers which are likely to be most profitable will be those where we have an advantage over the competition, an ability to provide the customer with something better. Thus, market focus does not mean merely customer orientation, it involves determining specifically which customers we shall focus upon, and in which market segments we can achieve competitive advantage.

Resolving the trade-offs

The invaluable corollary to this is that customer focus is also the route to resolving the trade-offs inherent in functional management decisions. If the customer needs can be specified clearly, it becomes much easier for the production manager to determine the right production policy, for the finance manager to determine optimum stock levels, and for the quality control manager to resolve quality trade-offs. If on the other hand customer targets are not clear, the production manager is expected to make low cost commodity items in vast quantities for one set of customers and simultaneously be equally good at making a wide range of specialist items for another set of customers. In other functions also, similarly impossible to achieve targets are likely to result from a lack of clear customer focus.

An example of the practical implications of such issues is the business of making polypropylene plastic film for packaging. The largest market for polypropylene film is the food industry, where it is used for wrappings and seal packaging of biscuits, potato crisps, confectionery and a host of other food products. Other major uses are for cigarette wrappings and adhesive tape base. In addition there is a range of specialized applications from electrical components to flower wrappers and gift wrapping paper. Customers are typically large companies such as United Biscuits and Nestlé, although they may be much smaller, particularly in speciality markets. Like most users, the food industry looks for many different kinds of film, involving variation in gauge, handling quality, sealability, appearance, printability, and so on.

Film is essentially a packaging material, and food manufacturers are frequently prepared to pay a higher price for films which can enhance the value of their products and achieve higher margins. One example is in snack foods, where everyday products such as crisps tend to be packaged in relatively low cost film, whereas more sophisticated, added value 'adult' snack foods tend to be packaged in more attractive and prestigious films. Food manufacturers also place a high priority on innovative new film products, which will enable their own products to stand out on crowded retail shelves, or to offer better keeping qualities than those of competitors. Examples include the use of polypropylene film for labelling and for yoghurt pot lids.

Despite this diversity, however, the 80/20 rule tends to operate, with a relatively high proportion of sales coming from a relatively small proportion of product types. Inevitably the higher volume, more standardized films exhibit commodity characteristics, and purchase decisions tend to be driven by price and delivery for a given specification. In speciality products, price and delivery are still important, but a whole range of other factors can assume equal or even greater significance. Given this market, manufacturers find that they have to meet a range of customer needs. The customer's manufacturing department may be looking for good service, ease of handling on packaging lines and trouble free sealability; the quality controllers may be looking for good food preservation characteristics; the marketing department may be looking for good appearance and printability; the stock controllers may be looking for short lead times, and a proven just-in-time delivery capability; and of course the purchasing department will be looking for the best prices.

The market for polypropylene film is similar to many others in that there is a wide range of customers with different needs. While they all want what is basically a similar product, they have a different emphasis on the importance of price, delivery, service, quality, appearance, innovation, technical properties like sealability and breathability, quantities purchased, width, thickness, product range, and a whole host of other variables. However, while different customers have needs in some or all of these areas, they are all inevitably prepared to make trade-offs; nobody expects highly innovative, high quality products purchased in small quantities to be provided at the lowest price. At the same time, customers buying standardized, high throughout products in large quantities, will expect to be quoted very competitive prices.

Users of standard films	Users of speciality films
Lowest price for given specification	Flexibility/adaptability
Consistent quality	Response to special requests
Excellent delivery/service	Competitive price (but not the lowest)
High volume	Low volume (but wide product range)
Very short lead times	Close-development liaison
	New ideas input

Figure 2.7 *Polypropylene film: customer needs*

Figure 2.7 presents an overview of the needs of two types of customer, one buying large quantities of standardized film for crisp packets, and one buying smaller quantities of specialized products for packaging a wide range of up-market adult snack foods. The question for the film manufacturer is how to organize the company to meet these needs, indeed whether it is possible to meet both sets of needs equally well. The areas in which the film supplier must excel in order to meet the needs of each customer are indicated in Figure 2.8, summed up as the 'key factors for success' (KFS) that the supplier needs to achieve in order to satisfy the customers in that particular market. Whereas to succeed in one market a company needs to emphasize the achievement of the lowest costs in the industry, to succeed in the other it needs to concentrate on flexibility, and the ability to differentiate its product. The problem is that the required company responses are to a great extent in conflict, indeed any company which intends to achieve the best performance in one

Standard films	Speciality films
Lowest cost production	*Flexibility*
• Low labour cost	• Fast changeover
• High volume	• Response to customer and R&D support
• Long runs	• Marketing skills
• Maximum plant utilization	• Quality control
• Minimize wastage	• Technical sales force
• Minimum range	• Ability to make small runs at reasonable cost
• Low stocks	• Fast response to innovations
• Close links with suppliers	• Adaptable machinery
• Round the clock operation	
• Unfailing reliability	

Figure 2.8   *Polypropylene film: key factors for success*

area will have to do things likely to undermine its ability to perform well in the other.

A whole range of practical management issues stands in the way of achieving excellent performance in both of these markets. For example, large, high throughput machines would be necessary to achieve the lowest possible cost, whereas a larger number of smaller specialist machines would be required to make a wider range of specialist products. In order to achieve the lowest costs labour and overheads would have to be cut to the minimum, whereas the provision of customer responsive technical support, and a high level of product innovation would inevitably increase overheads. Long runs of standardized products would be necessary for one approach, whereas short runs of specialized products would be necessary for the other.

Focus on the customer

The list of operating differences goes on endlessly, and this would have a knock-on effect in requiring different control systems highlighting different management variables, different staff training, and in short an entirely different philosophy from both management and workforce. It is inconsistent to argue that it would be possible to pursue both markets equally effectively simultaneously, neither could a firm pursue one option one week and the other the next. The firm which would be likely to win in each market would be the one which geared up its entire resources and philosophy to meet the specific needs of that group of customers, in other words the one which fully embraced the concept of customer focus.

In this way, customer focus leads to effective management decision-making in all functions. Once the management team has understood

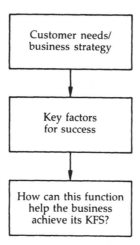

Figure 2.9 *Flow chart for functional decisions*

the needs of its target customers, it can establish the key factors for success which need to be achieved to meet those needs. Only then can each functional manager identify how his own function can be organized to help the company achieve its key factors for success. This simple flow chart for functional decision making is shown in Figure 2.9. The key point is that functional decisions start with customer focus, and this is true for all functions. To start with each function's own internal view of what its operating objectives should be can only result in conflict and lack of direction. Customer focus is the basis of functional decisions; therefore customer orientation is the essential starting point for building a market focused organization.

While it is evident that small companies may only have the depth of resource to focus on one tightly specified customer target, this is clearly not the case with larger companies. As the available resource base becomes larger, companies are able to address more customer groups and market areas. Thus, customer focus does not mean focusing on a single target, indeed there are sound reasons to maintain a number of targets, since this spreads the risk and increases opportunities. Of course there is a balance to be struck, too wide a range of targets and focus will be lost, too narrow a range and the risk of over commitment will increase. However, while having several market targets may be appropriate for larger organizations, this does not the subvert the logic of customer focus. For each target market, the company has to gear up a distinctive element of its operation to meet the needs of those customers effectively, otherwise it will lose out to competitors who can do it better.

This chapter has argued the logic and the concept of customer focus and shown how an assessment of the needs of the target customer is the starting point for all major operating decisions. The next question to be addressed is how to do this, how to identify a coherent customer target group and develop a competitive advantage so as to offer them something better than the competition. This leads us on to Chapter 3, and the task of market segmentation and positioning.

3 Market positioning

Marketing is not the pursuit of any customer at any price, but the pursuit of profitable customers. The most profitable will be those the firm can serve most effectively, those to whom it can make the most attractive offer compared to its competitors. Establishing the company's target customers is the first major step in achieving market focus; the second is to determine how we can offer them something better than our competitors. This is the concept of market positioning, and involves the two-way process of identifying a target market segment, then offering the customers in that segment a compelling reason to buy from us rather than our competitors, in other words finding a competitive advantage. This chapter examines in detail this crucial process, looking first at the identification of target customers through the technique of market segmentation.

Market segmentation

The concept of segmentation

Fundamental to any focused marketing plan is the ability to define groups of customers with distinctive needs at which coherent marketing offers can be aimed. All consumers are different people, each of us is the product of an infinite number of genetic and environmental variables, which ensure that each individual in society is truly unique. This individuality is expressed in our purchasing behaviour; for example, look around a roomful of people even from similar backgrounds and the chances are that you will be unable to find two people with identical clothes. The clothes we wear, the cars we drive, and the furniture we choose for our homes are all important ways in which we each express our own individuality.

Of course, we also judge products by physical criteria; a chair must be comfortable, a car must be reliable and reasonably economical, clothes must suit the purpose we have in mind, and all must offer acceptable value for money. There is no doubt that we choose things that will satisfy these physical and practical needs, but once people have sufficient wealth and the necessary choice, they will also seek to express their individuality in their purchases; even in

China, blue dungarees are no longer *de rigeur*. The concept of market segmentation is based on the fact that people choose between products to satisfy their individual needs, both physical and psychological.

However, although we are all individuals, it is nevertheless possible to classify people into groups with similar needs. This is the process of market segmentation, a market segment is a group of consumers with similar needs. Having identified the segments present in the market, we can then determine which segments the firm is best equipped to serve, which segments we can serve better than our competitors, and thus which segments we should focus our efforts upon. Market segmentation therefore is fundamental to the whole idea of customer targeting and market focus. A firm that does not carry out effective market segmentation can never be a genuinely market focused organization.

The art of segmentation is to identify which variables best explain the purchasing behaviour of a particular group of customers, and thus give us the opportunity to differentiate these from other groups of customers. In essence we are looking for the reasons why one set of people choose one product and another set choose something different. Each of the segmentation criteria discussed below is a variable which may help us to do this. Clearly, some variables are highly relevant to some products but completely irrelevant to others, and in most cases an accurate picture of market segments can only be built up using several of these variables. However, at its most basic level, a segmentation exercise should enable the manager to build up a mental 'snapshot' of the type of person being aimed at. The purpose is firstly to enable the whole marketing package to be focused on meeting a clearly differentiated set of customer needs, and secondly to ensure that the firm can stake out an area of the marketplace where it can compete effectively and concentrate its resources.

Geographic segmentation

This is the most primitive approach to market segmentation and is based on the proposition that people in different regions buy different things. Perhaps the best example is beer: in Yorkshire, drinkers favour light coloured beers with a tight creamy head, hand-pulled through the traditional 'sparkler' pump. Beers from the south of England are rather different, often darker and with a very modest head indeed. There are still fierce local loyalties to traditional regional brews: Tetleys is the leading brand in its West Yorkshire stronghold, whereas drinkers in Nottinghamshire would regard it as a foreign interloper!

That such regional differences exist in certain products is beyond doubt, yet with a few exceptions, geographic segmentation alone will never give us a sufficiently accurate snapshot of our target consumer. As mass communication grows ever faster and more all pervasive, people increasingly have a wider range of potential aspirations than traditional regional values. Geographic segmentation used alone ignores the fact that even in a well-defined coherent region, consumer tastes and aspirations will differ, and it is simply unrealistic to pretend that everyone from, say, central Scotland will behave the same way. Thus, while geographic segmentation may have relevance to some products, it should always be used in combination with other variables which more accurately describe customer needs.

Demographic segmentation

This approach is based on measurable demographic data, often obtainable from the official census. Many demographic criteria can potentially be used to segment markets, including disposable income, education, family size, marital status, religion, ethnic origin and occupation. One interesting approach is life stage, where consumers are segmented according to the stage their life has reached, such as independent young adult, family with children, couple with children now gone (this category sometimes being known as 'empty nesters'), and so on. While all these criteria can be used to segment various markets, examples are given below for two of the most commonly used demographic variables, age and sex.

The consumer's age is an obvious explanatory variable in purchasing behaviour for some products. A good example is package holidays, where one of the most successful companies in recent years has been Saga, an operation whose holidays are aimed specifically at older people. Equally, a range of specialist operators focus at the other end of the age scale. The proposition is simple – people of different ages want different holidays, and Saga has achieved success by targeting a specific age group with a specific package. Sex is another widely used demographic variable, clearly observable in magazine publishing, where many products are aimed exclusively at women or exclusively at men. Social class is also sometimes regarded as a demographic variable, although some academics argue that it should be classified along with the so-called psychographic criteria. The debate over academic classification systems need not concern us unduly here, since social class is in any case sufficiently significant to warrant separate treatment.

Social class segmentation

Social class is still perhaps the most widely used segmentation variable of all. The best known system of social class segmentation categorizes people into six classes according to the occupation of the head of the household as follows:

A Higher professional/managerial
B Lower professional/managerial
C1 White collar/clerical
C2 Skilled manual workers
D Unskilled manual workers
E Unemployed etc.

This classification is still used by many companies as the sole segmentation variable, indeed, it is often telescoped into just two categories, A/B/C1, and C2/D/E.

However, despite its popularity, there are a number of problems with this approach. It is well established that the system as a whole is losing its relevance as a barometer of society, owing to structural changes such as the growing economic significance of the C2 category, the decline of the D category, and the expansion of the numbers and aggregate economic wealth of retired people. In addition, people who are nominally members of, say, the C2 category, are increasingly likely to share the aspirations and attitudes traditionally associated with the C1s and Bs. However, most fundamentally of all, to pretend that the variable nature of our modern society, and the individuals who make it up, could ever be compressed into six simple job related categories, let alone just two, is blatantly simplistic. Why then, does loyalty to this out-moded system persist in the world of marketing?

The main reason is probably sheer tradition and inertia; a whole generation of marketing executives was reared on ABC1 and C2DE in the 1960s and have passed it on to their successors. But in addition, newspapers and television stations prefer to classify their audiences in social class terms, so it makes the task of selecting the right media seemingly far more straightforward. And, of course, the system is indisputably measurable: census data can be quoted as unassailable fact, to three places of decimals if required. This gives a veneer of science to the marketing department, and the warm glow of reassurance to senior executives in what is, in reality, a highly judgemental area of management decision making. Measuring something which is fundamentally flawed to three decimal places of accuracy, then using it to justify millions of pounds of expenditure may strike outside observers as odd, but many companies still do it.

Usage rate and application segmentation

In many product categories, a relatively small proportion of consumers accounts for a relatively large proportion of sales. This is the 'heavy user' segment that characterizes products as diverse as dog food, soft drinks and deodorant. While the heavy users are obviously important in terms of sheer volume, the light users should not be overlooked, for they may have specialist needs, and thus offer the opportunity to differentiate and add value. Heavy users of dog food are more likely to go for low price and bulk purchase, whereas light users with only one small dog to care for, are more likely to buy higher quality speciality foods. Basically, heavy and light users have different needs, and this calls for different products, packaging, advertising and pricing policies.

Some products may also be used for different purposes by different consumers. For example, orange juice may be used as a breakfast drink, as a mixer for alcoholic drinks, or as a general purpose soft drink. Different consumers use products in different ways, and this gives the opportunity to stake out a distinctive market position from competitors, by adapting the product formulation, pack design, advertising and promotion, pricing, and distribution. Usage rate and application are both examples of behavioural segmentation, which divides consumers into groups according to their use, attitude to, or knowledge of a product. The consumer's attitude to unfamiliar products, which is particularly relevant to innovative new products, is an important special category of behavioural segmentation which is discussed below.

Attitude to innovations

When a product is not only new, but completely different to anything previously encountered, consumers will approach it with different attitudes, which will be manifested in different purchasing behaviour. Some will be cautious, even suspicious of the new-fangled idea; others will be prepared to try it only after it has been endorsed by their peers; a few, however, will welcome it and actively seek to buy it, excited by its very newness. Accordingly, it makes sense to target innovations at the people who will most readily accept them – the innovators. This is a key segment for any company launching an innovation to target, since these are the people who are likely to be most receptive, and to recognize the product's benefits. Just like personality and lifestyle segmentation, it is sometimes difficult to quantify and specifically target the innovators, but as we shall see in the next chapter, they are of crucial importance to the success of any innovation.

Benefits segmentation

An obvious way to segment markets is according to the benefits sought by the customers, another of the so-called behavioural approaches to segmentation. For example, toothpaste buyers are driven by needs such as decay prevention, fear of bad breath, the desire for attractive white teeth, plaque removal, the protection of sensitive teeth, or simply a low price. Products can be targeted at consumers where one or perhaps two of these needs predominate: the product formulation can then be specified and appropriate advertising and packaging designed. Any product claiming to meet all these needs equally well would scarcely be credible with consumers. People who feel a specialist need are likely to believe a specialist product is best for them.

Another example is cars; all cars have to perform a basic function, but beyond that it is open to the manufacturer to stress a particular aspect of the design. Different people feel the needs for different levels of performance, safety, comfort, economy, load-carrying, versatility, off-road capability, and so on. Consumers and designers are faced with a set of compromises, and no one vehicle can do all these things equally well. Consumers can be segmented into benefit groups, and models can then be aimed at providing the best compromise for a given group.

Personality and lifestyle segmentation

Products can enable consumers to make statements about the type of people they perceive themselves to be: personality and lifestyle are the major so-called psychographic segmentation variables. This approach is undeniably very different to traditional demographic or social class segmentation; clearly, people within the same demographic group can exhibit very different psychographic profiles.

There are many examples of so-called 'image' products: our clothes can send important clues to the rest of society about our values, as can cars, drinks, cigarettes, newspapers, and a whole range of other things we use. The need of consumers to display such clues should not be derided as superficial, since they can serve a very practical social purpose in signalling and acknowledging peer group membership. Beer companies sometimes refer to 'badge drinking', the implication being that it is important to some consumers to be seen by their peer group to be drinking a particular brand. Lifestyle segmentation is similar; the growth in sales of off-road vehicles, many of which are never actually used in off-road conditions, is a result of people wanting to express their individuality and make a statement about how they perceive their lifestyle.

In examples like this, it is frequently difficult to separate lifestyle and personality, and it is often equally difficult to separate these from tangible customer benefits. People with a particular lifestyle and personality will tend to seek matching benefits, and the successful product will be the one that combines both the benefits sought with the image sought. The benefits offered by a Volvo such as safety, practicality and longevity, are totally consistent with its sober and responsible image. By contrast, a BMW offers the image of performance, high technology, and chic design, again totally consistent with the dynamic and go-ahead image of the brand. But in both cases it is impossible to say what came first, the benefits or the image, the two are totally interlocked. Nevertheless, both have established a distinctive and successful position in the luxury car market by appealing to both the physical and psychological needs of a clearly defined group of customers. Interestingly, the fact that some Volvos actually go faster than some BMWs does not seem to undermine the essential image of either.

Residence segmentation

A fundamental problem with personality, lifestyle and benefits segmentation is the difficulty of quantifying the segments, and the associated problem of drawing cut-off lines at segment boundaries in what clearly is a series of grey areas. Although sophisticated research techniques can be used to allocate respondents to particular psychological profiles, this is costly, and the results are inevitably 'soft', particularly when exposed to critical questioning by a hard-nosed finance director. A further difficulty is distinctively reaching those consumers which fit a particular psychological profile, in terms of both sales outlet and target media selection.

Residence segmentation is an attempt to overcome some of these difficulties, particularly the problem of measurability. The concept is based on the proposition that where people choose to live is a reflection of their personality and lifestyle. Thus, measurable criteria, house type and location, are used as a surrogate for less measurable psychological factors. The best known system is ACORN, an acronym for 'A Classification of Residential Neighbourhoods', and it has been a great commercial success in recent years. Housing is classified by observers into one of around fifty types, and companies can target consumers by selecting particular combinations of housing types. This system really comes into its own for direct mail, which can clearly be targeted very accurately, and it is of course highly quantifiable. However, the problems of accurate fitting of outlets and media remain.

Residence segmentation is extremely useful for certain product categories, for example it is widely used in insurance and financial services, and by home improvements companies. Where used in an appropriate market, residence segmentation does offer an apparently attractive combination of both demographic and psychographic variables. Its unique strength is that it encompasses 'hard' variables like disposable income, age, and life stage, together with a more quantifiable but less precisely descriptive surrogate for 'soft' psychographic criteria such as aspirations, personality and lifestyle.

Business to business markets

Where sales are made to other businesses rather than to individual consumers, some alternative segmentation criteria become relevant. It is just as important to segment business to business markets as it is consumer markets, since it is equally true that without effective segmentation there can be no hope of achieving market focus. The type of industry, type of production process and methods of handling materials are examples of obvious production related segmentation criteria. However, factors related to an organization's purchasing behaviour may be just as significant. For example, companies with committee type buying practices may have very different purchasing criteria to those where purchase decisions are made by individuals, while those where a product's actual users make the ultimate decision will have different criteria to those where professional purchasing managers are the key influence.

Average order size, and whether purchases from established suppliers are treated as routine re-orders or as one-off tasks are further purchase related criteria. Company size is another potential segmentation variable, and can sometimes be a useful predictor of the extent of purchase bureaucracy. More subtle is to segment by the target customer's own market positioning aspirations, since this will give an indication of the willingness to trade-off perceived technical excellence, quality, or overall supplier credibility, against price. The markets or customers served may similarly give an idea of what that customer looks for from suppliers.

Although the possible segmentation variables outlined above may seem prosaic compared to some of the psychologically oriented consumer segmentation criteria, it should be remembered that organizations are collections of individuals, who have psychological drives at work just as they do at home, and that organizations themselves can develop a distinctive character. Thus, some companies will take a risk and try something new, whereas others will not; some will constantly push the frontiers of technology, while others will be content to follow behind. Similarly, some managers will always go for the safe option whereas others will take more risks to obtain a potentially better solution. Equally, there is no doubt that brands can be important sales aids in business to business marketing, despite the fact that the benefits of a brand are as much in the area of psychological reassurance as in demonstrable superiority. Some companies even feel that being seen to be using equipment from well-known brand suppliers, be it German delivery vans or Swiss machine tools, enhances their own image and reputation in the eyes of their customers.

Like consumer markets, business to business markets may be segmented using a wide range of potential criteria, related both to tangible physical needs and to less definable psychological needs. Therefore, the search for the most appropriate criteria should not be limited solely to the strictly practical. The manager's task is the same, to try to select the criteria most relevant to that particular business, in the effort to identify a specific target segment and thus achieve market focus.

Segmentation in practice

Market segmentation, the ability to divide the total market into groups of customers with similar needs, is the basis of all practical marketing planning. After all, it is impossible to make rational choices about product specification, pricing, advertising, packaging, outlets used, or any of the other marketing variables without first specifying who you are aiming at. Like customer orientation, segmentation is easy to understand, and manifestly unchallengeable at a conceptual level. Unfortunately, it is once again not so easy in practice.

The first problem concerns segment sizes, and the difficulty of drawing clear segment boundaries. Since we are all individuals, the only totally accurate segment specification would be for just one person. This is clearly impractical for mass-produced and distributed goods, where sales volume is important. Hence, there is a difficult to resist tendency for segment definitions to grow broader and broader, until they grow into statements like 'ABC1 males aged between 18 and 55'. This is a reassuringly large segment, and it is precisely quantifiable, both features guaranteed to please the accountant, but unfortunately it is totally meaningless in terms of providing a snapshot of the target customer, and thus a focus for marketing activity. Companies who make customer target statements of this kind have no hope of achieving genuine market focus.

The ultimate driving force of consumer needs, and thus their purchasing behaviour, is their psychological make-up. The further we get away from that starting point by using surrogates such as social class, the less reliable any segmentation exercise becomes. The dilemma is that consumer groups based on psychological profiles are difficult to measure, target and even describe, and it rapidly becomes a highly judgemental exercise, which is in danger of being both inaccurate, and of being dismissed as 'typical marketing talk'. Therefore, while segmentation is a simple and unchallengeable concept, it is an art rather than a science, a question of backing one's judgement rather than relying on formulae. We shall never segment markets effectively if we demand totally accurate quantification.

In practice, market segments are usually best described using two or three segmentation criteria. These should be selected according to their relevance to the product concerned, and in the knowledge that some criteria are quantifiable whereas others are not. Usage rate may be highly applicable to one product, but inapplicable to the next, where personality and lifestyle may be more important. The best segment definitions are based on relevant criteria rather than indiscriminately applied standard formulae such as social class. The potential segmentation criteria outlined in the previous few pages should be seen as examples rather than a comprehensive list. Segmentation is a creative exercise, and thinking up new criteria, which no competitors have used before, can result in re-segmenting the market and creating a new market position.

It may sometimes be helpful to draw up a simple perceptual map to describe the market in which you are competing. In the market for domestic furniture polishes, a perceptual map helps to contrast the differences between consumer attitudes to home cleaning, and the types of furniture they prefer (see Figure 3.1). 'Shiners' are people who derive pleasure and satisfaction from cleaning, whereas 'recliners' want to get the job over with as quickly as possible. 'Traditionalists' furnish their homes predominantly with natural wood, whereas 'modernists' choose a variety of surfaces including synthetics. Products with a high wax content are harder work to use, but offer more satisfying results, whereas those with a higher water content are easier to use since they require less polishing. This simple example shows that different product formulations can be targeted at different segments of users, with appropriately different packaging and advertising.

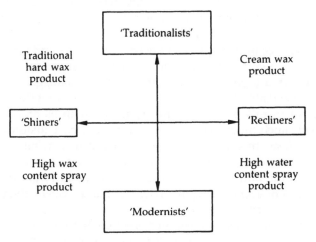

Figure 3.1 *Perceptual map for furniture polishes*

Perceptual maps are a useful way of conceptualizing new approaches to segmentation, or for examining whether all the potential positions in a market have been occupied. In a segment where many identical products are jockeying for a share, competition is likely to be fierce, and perceptual maps can aid the thought process in finding relatively uncontested areas, and thus establish perceptual space around a product in the customer's mind. Three segmentation criteria can be handled on a perceptual map by thinking of it as a cube, but further criteria can only be built in by using computer models. Fortunately, this is in most cases an unnecessary elaboration, since studies have shown that the three most important segmentation criteria for a given product are normally adequate in practice. The key to effective segmentation is choosing which criteria to use, and the selection of possible new criteria to re-segment the market, and create a new market position.

Competitive advantage

Seeing the customer's viewpoint

Once the segmentation process has indicated the range of possible
segments in a given market, the next issue is to determine in which
segments the firm can compete most effectively. In other words, in
which areas of the market have we got the most advantage over our
competitors and conversely, in which areas do they have the most
advantage over us? It is essential that managers try to see competitive
advantage from the customer's viewpoint rather than the company's.
A competitive advantage is something which is perceived by the
customer as something better, regardless of whether or not the
firm's employees think it is better.

The difference in perceptions between customers and managers is
seen most frequently, although not exclusively, in technology based
companies. In a high technology environment, managers can often
get very excited about a technically superior feature that the customer
may regard merely as 'nice to have', rather than as an advantage
which will clinch the purchase decision. If the target customer never
wishes to measure a tolerance below ten microns, what additional
value does he see in a product's capacity to measure down to one
micron? On the other hand, if aimed at a different target customer,
with a different application, this may become an over-riding source
of competitive advantage.

In order to encourage a customer oriented analysis of competitive
advantage, it is suggested that two key questions are addressed
when reviewing marketing plans. The first is 'what can we do for
the target customer that's better than our competitors' offerings?'
Addressing this question will help to ensure that the company's
offer has been looked at from the customer's viewpoint. The second
key question is 'what can the customer gain by buying our product
rather than those available from competitors, and how badly does
he need that benefit?' This explores the extent of added value being
offered to the customer. Raising questions like these will help to
expose projects where no significant competitive advantage exists:
companies should be wary of committing substantial resources to
such proposals.

Sources of competitive advantage

Possession of superior proprietary product technology is an obvious
source of advantage, and if this can be patented, so much the better.
Drug companies, for example, invest millions of pounds in R&D,

trying to discover new superior therapeutic compounds. Service is also a powerful form of advantage; IBM does not make the most technically advanced or the cheapest computers, but it does offer service to large computer users which is second to none. A sophisticated selling operation can be a decisive factor in some businesses. For example, selling civil aircraft is a highly complex business, involving intensive contact over an extended timescale with many different parties; Boeing has the largest sales force with the greatest cumulative experience, and this gives it a significant advantage over its competitors, even when product differences may be marginal. Possession of a well-known and trusted brand name is a considerable advantage in many industries: in consumer goods markets, names like Mars and Nestlé are probably the most valuable single assets their owners possess, although like many sources of competitive advantage are only grudgingly recognized as such by the accountants.

Building a defensible market position
- Superior proprietory technology
- Specialized skilled labour
- Sophisticated service systems
- Complex selling systems
- Established brand/company credibility
- Markets requiring critical mass
- Overwhelming cost advantage

Is your competitive advantage *sustainable* or can it easily be copied by competitors?

Figure 3.2 *Some sources of competitive advantage*

It should be apparent that potential sources of competitive advantage are many and various; in fact, an advantage can be built around any of the marketing variables which collectively make up the marketing mix. These range from product features, service response, sales methods and distribution, through to branding, packaging, different methods of promotion, types of outlet used and so on. Some of the more powerful sources of competitive advantage are shown in Figure 3.2, although it is emphasized that this is in no way a comprehensive list. A complete classification of all the major elements of the marketing mix is given in Chapter 7.

Building sources of advantage

Different sources of advantage are appropriate to different companies and industries, and it is impossible to lay down a formula approach to building potential sources of advantage in each case. Nevertheless, there are three broad avenues which may be explored. The most obvious is to examine the market leader's source of advantage, and try to do it better. As discussed at several points in this book, this can often be a risky approach, particularly if the leader has a highly defensible advantage, however, there are circumstances where it can work: these will be discussed in detail in Chapter 6 under 'challenger strategies'.

The most positive approach is to do something completely different, to innovate and find a new competitive advantage. Innovation is a potentially powerful weapon in the search for a sustainable advantage, and will be discussed at length in Chapter 4. A third possible avenue is to try to enhance and build on something which you are already doing which seems to work well. Jack Trout and Al Ries advocate this method in their book *Bottom Up Marketing*, and sum up their approach as finding a tactic which works, then building it into a strategy. They suggest working through all the marketing mix elements, trying to identify one which either already is an advantage or could be turned into one. This leads on to the formulation of an action programme to enhance this aspect of the company's marketing, and create a more powerful competitive advantage.

Sustainable advantage

It is axiomatic that any competitive advantage must be sustainable, after all, if it can easily be copied it will not remain an advantage for long. Unfortunately, however, relatively few sources of competitive advantage can safely be regarded as unbroachable in the long term. A firm which seeks to sustain its competitive advantage must accept that it will have to pursue a constantly moving target. Inevitably, if one company establishes a source of added value, its competitors will seek to catch up. If the leader does not invest to stay ahead, or create a new alternative advantage, its lead will be eroded. Thus, a company which has an advantage cannot be content to rest on its laurels, it must constantly strive both to stay ahead in its traditional area of superiority, and to find new ones.

The simple truth is that no advantage is sustainable for ever, although some clearly are more sustainable than others. For example, an advantage based on patented technology is sustainable until the patent runs out, or someone else finds a better technical solution. The most sustainable of all are advantages which require significant critical mass in order to be challenged effectively: to attack head-on a massive sales or service organization, or a major established brand name, without a large customer base to support the necessary investment is an extremely high risk strategy. The potential challenger would be better advised to seek a new, different advantage. On the other hand, some sources of advantage, like offering faster or more frequent delivery times, are inherently easier to copy and therefore relatively less sustainable. This is not to say that such advantages should not be sought; often a competitor's own systems or attitudes may slow down its ability to respond to a surprise move that may, on the face of it, be easy to match. However, the more transient the advantage, the less sustainable it is, and consequently the more the pressure constantly to find new sources of advantage.

Thus, in order to be considered a genuine competitive advantage in that particular business, it is important to consider the length of time over which the advantage can be and needs to be sustained; six months, two years, ten years, or more? The answer to this question depends firstly on how long it takes to change customer perceptions in the market concerned, and secondly on how defensible is the source of advantage. If customers can successfully be influenced quickly, and the source of advantage is relatively difficult to copy, then a newly conceived advantage is likely to be both sustainable and of real commercial value in a relatively short timescale. If on the other hand, the customers are slow to change their traditional way of doing things, and the advantage can be copied before the customers are even aware that it exists, then it is unlikely to become quickly established, and in any case, can scarcely be regarded as sustainable.

Unique selling proposition and competitive advantage

Managers often ask whether there is a conceptual difference between a unique selling proposition (USP) and a competitive advantage. A USP is by definition something unique or different, and clearly a competitive advantage must be something different to what competitors are doing, otherwise it would not be advantageous. But uniqueness alone is not sufficient, because although it may be physically unique, the real test is whether that unique feature is of value to the customer, and the level of potential added value which is created as a result. The phrase differential advantage is also encountered from time to time and similar comments apply; of course an advantage must be different, but this alone is not sufficient. If one were being pedantic, the right term to use would be sustainable differential competitive advantage. Perhaps, though, it is more practical to stick to competitive advantage as a shorthand version. Provided we all have a shared understanding of the concept, the terminology is of relatively minor importance.

Price as a source of advantage

Charging a lower price for a similar product is superficially a simple and attractive route to competitive advantage. After all, everybody wants value for money, so surely price must be an important motivating factor for the customer. Unfortunately, however, a competitive advantage of low price is normally an abject failure when subjected to the sustainability test; price is perhaps the least sustainable route to competitive advantage: anyone can cut the price, and they can do it tomorrow. A price-cut is eminently copyable, and the same applies to special discounts, selective discounts, dealer loaders, and all the other jargon expressions employed to disguise a price-cut by using different words.

Price can only be considered a source of sustainable competitive advantage when the company has significantly lower costs than its competitors; this makes lower prices sustainable, although not necessarily desirable. It could be argued that even if it does have lower costs, a company should still strive to create non-price forms of advantage, giving it the opportunity to add value to its product. In this way, the benefit of its lower costs may be retained as higher profits, rather than being passed on to the customer. An important exception to this arises in the case of a price cut intended to enlarge the total potential market significantly, by opening up a new market segment. This strategy will be discussed in detail in the next chapter.

The pursuit of cost leadership

In the light of the above discussion of prices and costs, it is worthwhile considering how, in practice, companies can achieve the lowest costs of any contestant in their business. This must be the single minded goal if cost leadership is to be pursued as a basis for competitive advantage; after all, having the second or third lowest costs can scarcely be considered an advantage. One obvious method is to develop new and far more cost-effective production technology, and in this case, production methods would be a real source of potential competitive advantage. However, even assuming that production methods are reasonably similar, it is nevertheless possible for significant cost differentials to arise according to the strategies pursued by competing firms.

Any production engineer will confirm that in a given factory the greater the variety of products manufactured, the higher the cost; work in progress and raw materials stocks are likely also to be higher, and economies of scale in purchasing will be less. Companies with large design departments, marketing departments and sales forces will have relatively higher costs than those without. In other words, there is a cost to variety, customer service, design, and marketing; of course, on the other hand, these activities should also permit the company to add value.

These are the fundamental trade-offs that were discussed in the last chapter, and are the same issues as those raised in the example of the polypropylene film business. It was established that companies in this business, and indeed in any other business, need to make a clear decision as to which kind of customers they intend to satisfy, before they can determine functional priorities. Firms making a conscious decision to focus on the low cost end of the trade-offs, are said to be pursuing a strategy of 'cost leadership', whereas those who focus on the flexibility and high added value end, are said to be pursuing a strategy of 'differentiation'. It will be apparent that unless they have overwhelmingly superior production technology, or access to very cheap labour and/or materials, companies who are pursuing a strategy of differentiation have no hope of making price a sustainable source of competitive advantage. Once a firm is committed to a strategy of differentiation, it has to mean it, and must seek to satisfy its customers by adding value, not by giving discounts.

The routes to competitive advantage discussed prior to this section all involve adding value by enhancing the package offered to the customer, through superior technology, better service, branding, or whatever. However, this is easier said than done; competitive advantages cannot be pulled out of thin air! Given the difficulty of rigorously pursuing an added value approach, a cost leadership strategy may appear an attractive option. However, pursuit of cost leadership requires an extraordinarily single minded 'no frills' approach to management, not one that managers accustomed to life in large organizations will find easy. In addition, it is a strategy which is extremely vulnerable to technological and market change, and is thus relatively more suited to mature industries with slow rates of change. Thirdly, cost leadership denies the company the ability to make profits by adding value, an approach which leaves many options open. By contrast, it seeks to make profits by squeezing costs, an avenue which leaves management with far fewer strategic options.

The strategies which must be pursued in order genuinely to achieve the lowest costs in a given industry mean, in effect, that we have a choice between cost leadership and added value as basic routes to competitive advantage. The danger lies in not doing one

or the other decisively, because an added value strategy will inherently be damaged by excessive cost cutting, whereas a cost
leadership strategy will inherently be damaged by costly attempts
to add value. This dilemma is far more prevalent than might be
imagined: many companies claim to be pursuing cost leadership
when they have no realistic hope of achieving it, while the cost
controls they adopt in the process undermine all attempts to add
value. Failure to pursue either route assiduously leads to the unenviable fate of being 'stuck in the middle', and unable to pursue a
coherent strategy, thus being rendered vulnerable to competitive
pressure at both ends.

However, it is important to remember that a cost leadership
strategy does not imply the indiscriminate cutting out of all customer
oriented expenditure; what it does imply is the ruthless removal of
all costly items of customer oriented expenditure. Equally, differentiation does not imply a company bereft of all controls where
money is no object, but it does imply a company where the controls
are looser, and the control system has a fundamentally different
character to that in a company pursuing cost leadership. Michael
Porter sums this up very succinctly.

> A firm should always aggressively pursue all cost reduction oppor-
> tunities that do not sacrifice differentiation. A firm should also pursue
> all differentiation strategies that are not costly. Beyond this point,
> however, a firm should be prepared to choose what the ultimate
> competitive advantage should be and resolve the trade-offs accordingly.

Porter also tells us that a third possible option exists, to specialize
in a single segment and to resolve the trade-offs specifically to

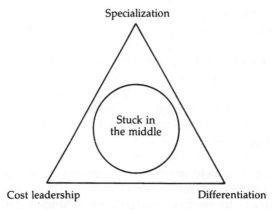

Figure 3.3 *Three routes to competitive advantage*

satisfy the needs of that one segment. This approach enables a company to become highly cost-effective at serving the needs of a single defined segment, by realizing the benefits of specialization and enhanced closeness to that particular market and customer. Porter calls this strategy 'focus', however, it may be clearer to refer to it as 'specialization' in the context of this book. The choice between the three basic approaches to competitive advantage is shown diagrammatically in Figure 3.3. Single segment specialization of course, does imply possible vulnerability to market changes. Nevertheless, the benefit it offers is the wider range of options inherent in an added value strategy combined with the ability to resolve the fundamental management trade-offs by reference to a single coherent set of customer needs.

Positioning

The three 'Cs

Marketing is the ability to create and keep profitable customers, and possession of a competitive advantage is the best way to ensure that customers are profitable. By contrast, attempting to compete without an advantage over the competition is always an uphill and un-rewarding activity, and usually at best of marginal profitability. Of course, a given competitive advantage is unlikely to be valued equally by all customers across an entire product market. It is likely to be valued more by a segment of customers whose needs are consistent with that advantage, and consequently who value it highly.

Thus, competitive advantage tends to be specific to a given market segment: this means that the concept needs to be combined with market segmentation in order to be fully meaningful, so that in practice, the two become almost inseparable. This combination of market segmentation and competitive advantage is known as positioning. Segmentation tells us who we are aiming at; competitive advantage tells us how we are going to beat the competition in satisfying their needs. A definition of positioning is given in Figure 3.5, but put in very simple terms, positioning equals target customer plus something better.

Positioning decisions revolve around an analysis of three elements beginning with 'C'; customer needs, competitors' offerings, and the company's capability to offer something better. Customer needs analysis leads us to market segmentation and a snapshot of our target customer and his needs. An understanding of the skills of

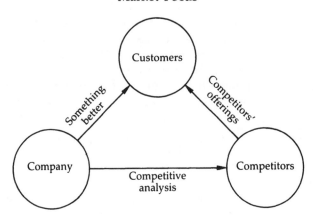

Figure 3.4 *The three 'C's of positioning*

competitors, and the products they are offering the target customer, will tell us what we are up against, what it is we have to offer something better than. Analysing our company's capabilities will tell us whether we have the ability to do this. If we cannot offer something better, the process should be repeated for a different target customer. The positioning analysis process involves an in-depth understanding of the three 'C's as illustrated in Figure 3.4. These are the basic information requirements which underpin the concept of positioning.

Role of positioning in market focus

Competitive advantage is the fundamental source of added value and therefore, in the long run, the reason why one firm succeeds and another does not. However, a given competitive advantage may be highly relevant to one customer but irrelevant to the next; this is why competitive advantage is rather a vague concept when looked at in isolation. But combined with market segmentation, it becomes the mainspring of the ability to create added value. This explains the crucial importance of positioning to any company which wants to achieve market focus; it helps us to focus scarce resources onto areas of the market where we can create added value better than the competition.

Concentration of resources is a principle well known to students of military strategy. Rather than spreading resources thinly across the entire range of the enemy's forces, they are far more effective if concentrated on specific targets. Equally in marketing, it makes sense to concentrate resources into areas of the market where competitive advantage can be gained, rather than spray them ineffectively at every apparent opportunity (see Figure 3.5). The 'spray and pray' approach to resource allocation is the antithesis of market focus, and positioning is a key element in getting the focus right.

---

1 **Market segmentation**
   A market segment is a group of consumers with similar needs
2 **Competitive advantage**
   What can we do for the customer that is better than our competitors' offerings. 'What's in it for the customer' − and how badly do they want that benefit?
3 **Positioning**
   A combination of 'market segmentation', defining *where* we shall compete, and 'competitive advantage' defining *how* we shall compete

---

Figure 3.5 *Definition of positioning*

Analysis of the three 'Cs will also indicate whether the company possesses the key skills required to compete effectively in the market under review. This will lead on to consideration of how these skills can be developed even further, or if one is deficient, whether there is a reasonable chance that it can be sufficiently improved. These are the key factors for success (KFS) referred to in the last chapter, the areas in which a company needs to achieve excellence in order to compete effectively in a given market. Identifying KFS is an important corollary to positioning analysis, since programmes to strengthen performance in KFS will form an essential element in subsequent management actions. Indeed, plans to strengthen KFS must be the primary focus for such actions.

Role of positioning in the marketing mix

In addition to resource concentration, positioning is also essential to ensuring a customer oriented operating plan. Without an accurate snapshot of the target customer, and a clear understanding of our competitive advantage, it will be impossible to put together a marketing package that will satisfy the customer's needs. Achieving this requires managers to take a set of related decisions collectively known as the marketing mix. Without an effective positioning strategy, it is impossible to devise a marketing mix which is focused on the target customer. The concept of the marketing mix is discussed in greater detail in Chapter 7; this section is intended as an overview of the major elements, to illustrate their linkage to the positioning decision.

The marketing mix is the range of variables which, added together, make up the overall package which a firm offers to its customers. Customers rarely buy on product features alone, they want it at the right time and in the right place as well. Everybody wants good value for money, but value means different things to different people – price is a key element in the purchase decision as well as product. And if they have been told of the product's benefits by persuasive and informative promotion, this too will influence the purchase decision. In short, the customer's buying decision is shaped by the 'total offer' made by the firm, not just by one element of it like price or product or advertising. Planning the marketing mix involves getting this total offer right for the target customer, bearing in mind the offers made by competitors.

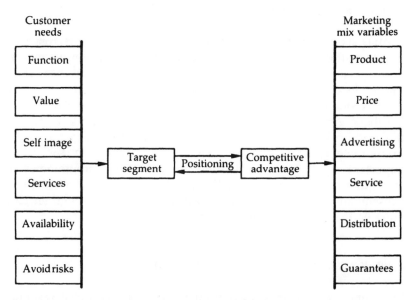

Figure 3.6 *Relationship between customer needs and the marketing mix*

The relationship between customer needs and the marketing mix is shown in Figure 3.6. The target segment is defined by a given combination of customer needs, while the competitive advantage is expressed through the elements of the marketing mix. Positioning is the crucial interface between the needs of the customers, and the way we plan to respond to them. Looked at in this way, the job of the mix is to support, enhance, and communicate your competitive advantage to the target customer. These, of course, are the two planks of positioning, and it follows that until the positioning strategy has been determined, no rational decisions can be taken about the marketing mix.

The same logic applies to setting the marketing budget: until decisions about the marketing mix have been made, no rational decisions can be made about budgets. For example, how can a sales budget be set until pricing decisions have been taken and numbers of target customers identified; how can an advertising budget be set until the appropriate message and media have been determined; how can a distribution budget be set until decisions about distribution methods and operations have been taken? Thus, it is impossible to take rational decisions about the marketing budget until decisions have been taken about the marketing mix, and it is impossible to take rational decisions about the marketing mix until positioning has been determined. A basic marketing decision flow chart, showing the relationship between these major building blocks is given in Figure 3.7.

It is worthwhile remembering that determining, managing and implementing marketing mix decisions comprises the vast majority

Figure 3.7 *Basic marketing planning flow chart*

of what most marketing managers actually do in practice. Marketing in a day-to-day sense is not concerned so much with ethereal strategic conceptualizing as with intensely practical activities such as selling, advertising, deliveries and price lists. Managing the marketing mix is the essential daily bread and butter of marketing management, and perhaps more importantly, in a market focused company it will have a decisive impact on what most of the firm's other employees do as well. Positioning is the only route to getting this crucial set of inter-related decisions right. An effective marketing mix is the practical outcome of the market focus process: everything in this book is aimed ultimately at achieving a marketing mix which is focused onto a clearly defined customer target and embodies a sustainable competitive advantage.

4 Innovation for competitive advantage

In the last chapter, various underlying principles of marketing were established. First, a company must have a competitive advantage in order to be able to compete effectively, and the advantage must be reasonably sustainable, otherwise it will be easy to copy and nullify. Second, the advantage must be of value to the customer, and given that different people have different needs, it makes sense to target a product at market segments where its competitive advantage is greatest. These principles underlie the concept of segmentation and positioning, without which it is impossible to draw up a focused marketing plan.

All this is easy enough to accept at the conceptual level, but it fails to address the key issue to how a company can gain a competitive advantage. Perhaps another company's advantage can be copied on the principle of do the same but do it better. This is certainly a potential route to competitive advantage, but its success depends to a large extent upon the competitor not responding, which clearly cannot be relied upon in all cases. The unfortunate fact is that the incumbent holder of a sustainable competitive advantage, for example established brand strength, is inherently better placed to hold onto it and improve it than a challenger. It is not that challenger strategies never work, but that they only work under certain circumstances, and these are discussed more fully in Chapter six. However, where it is difficult or impossible to emulate an existing advantage the dilemma remains, how can we build a new competitive advantage?

By definition, a competitive advantage must be something which differentiates a product from its competitors: if everybody's offer is the same we have a commodity market, where no effective differentiation exists, and the customer's purchase decision is driven mainly by price. It follows that in order to generate a new competitive advantage a company has to do something new, something different, and this is the essential nature of commercial innovation. The dictionary definition of innovation is 'something newly introduced... a novel practice, method etc... the alteration of what is established', and this neatly sums up why it is of such profound importance across the entire spectrum of strategic marketing management. Unless an existing advantage can be copied and improved upon, the only route to building competitive advantage is to do something new, something different, in short, to innovate. In addition, innovation has the power to create entirely new growth markets, and it is this combination of the ability to build competitive advantage together with the ability to open up growth markets which makes innovation the most important single concept in modern strategic thinking.

The process of innovation

Understanding commercial innovation

The dictionary definition quoted above refers to 'the alteration of what is established'; innovation may involve technical novelty but does not necessarily need to as long as it results in the alteration of existing practices. Equally, an innovation is more than just a new product, it needs to shift consumer perceptions in order to alter established practice. The test of an innovation in marketing terms is whether it has the potential to change a market, if it is merely a new product which is competing on the same basis as existing products it can scarcely be regarded as a commercial innovation. What differentiates commercial innovations from other new products is that innovations have the power to create entirely new markets or radically change existing ones in a way which creates new patterns of customer behaviour. If a new product does not satisfy these criteria, it cannot be seen as a genuine commercial innovation.

So far we have referred to products, however, the concept of innovation can be applied just as well to systems and processes as to physical products. There are many examples where large existing markets were completely changed on the basis of innovation in distribution systems or manufacturing processes rather than product features. Commercial innovation normally involves a new product, but it does not have to; equally it often involves new technology, but again does not need to be technically novel at all. The point in marketing terms is that the customer must perceive the product as novel; a commercial innovation may or may not be technically novel, the test is whether the customer sees it as being novel.

A well-known example is the Sony Walkman, which is basically a small cassette player with a pair of lightweight headphones, both perfectly well-known pieces of standard technology at the time the Walkman was introduced. But the customer perceived the concept of the Walkman, and the benefit of travelling music, as novel, and the fact that no new technology was involved was irrelevant. It turned out to be a classic innovation which created an entirely new market, and gave Sony the competitive advantage of brand leadership; indeed its brand name has become the generic name for the product. Similarly, mineral water was nothing new when Perrier was launched on the UK market. Malvern had been available for decades. However, the customer perceived the product as novel, and it was able to take early leadership in what subsequently proved to be a rapidly growing and profitable market. These examples underline the critical importance of innovation in marketing: the only way to create a new market is to do something new, the only way to create a differential advantage is to do something different, in short, to innovate.

If we are to build a more innovative organization, the first basic step is to ensure that every manager understands the nature of commercial innovation. Unfortunately, in reality innovation tends to get confused with inventing new technologies and launching new products. While it may involve both of these it does not necessarily require either, because the real test of commercial innovation is whether it produces a change in customer perceptions, for it is this which underlies its power to create competitive advantages and new growth markets. New products, processes and systems which do not meet these market related criteria should be seen as incremental improvements rather than marketing innovations. While not seeking to denigrate the value to businesses of such improvements, this chapter is concerned with innovations which have the potential to change things in the market place. The ability to take up a clearly defined market position, and the need to achieve competitive advantage are two closely linked ideas which are fundamental to strategic thinking. The power of innovation to create new markets and competitive advantages underlies its significance in strategic marketing management.

Thus, an understanding of the nature of commercial innovations is essential to an understanding of the market focus process as a whole. Without innovation there will be no growth businesses to absorb the investment resources generated by the mature businesses; there will be no chance to develop the new market leaders which will generate the cash in five years time; and in mature markets, there will be no alternative to the expensive and usually unrewarding process of competing with established market leaders. By contrast, a commitment to innovation offers companies the opportunity to introduce a genuinely strategic approach to running the business, based on the effective exploitation of high growth markets and the development of sustainable competitive advantage.

The diffusion of innovations

Understanding how to manage innovations is best approached by first understanding how they grow and spread within society. Innovation is essentially a social phenomenon, ideas about new products are spread among people who learn from each other, particularly in the social groups with which they identify. However, some people learn quicker than others, some are more resistant to change, clinging on to old values, while others are happy to reject them in favour of something new. In short, individuals vary in the speed at which they adopt new products and ideas. In a pioneering piece of academic work, Everett Rogers showed that while the speed of adoption varies between individuals, it conforms to a normal distribution within a given social group. Rogers divided the distribution up into slices to form the five adopter categories shown in Figure 4.1. The proportion of the group allocated to each slice is simply expressed in terms of standard deviations from the mean, but it is the characteristics of members of each adopter category which is important, see Figure 4.2.

Rogers called the first category the innovators; they are numerically very small but of great significance for companies trying to market an innovation. Innovators are essentially risk takers; they love to experiment with new products and actively search for new ideas. They tend to be indiscriminate about which new ideas they adopt, their basic concern is whether it is novel. Most of us know an innovator; their houses are filled with gadgets, many of which do not work or are never used, and were purchased with relatively

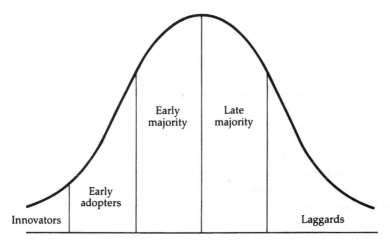

Figure 4.1 *The diffusion of innovations*

little thought then cast aside when something new came along. The majority of people do not take innovators or their opinions on new products particularly seriously, since they are so manifestly indiscriminate. The first people to use a Sony Walkman in public were regarded as somewhat peculiar for walking around wearing headphones, since most people were completely unaccustomed to such behaviour, and thus reacted with shock or surprise. Nevertheless, the innovators are a key group for any marketer, as they will always by definition be the first people to try something new.

Innovators Venturesome	willing to accept risks. Sometimes regarded as 'oddballs'
Early adopters Respectable	regarded by others in social system as opinion formers or 'role model'
Early majority Deliberate	willing to consider adoption only after peers have adopted
Late majority Sceptical	overwhelming pressure from peers needed before adoption occurs
Laggards Traditional	oriented to the past

Figure 4.2 *Characteristics of adopter categories*

Rogers called the next category the early adopters, and they are regarded very differently by the other members of their peer group. Whereas the innovators are regarded as oddballs, the early adopters by contrast are respectable; they are seen as social role models, and their opinions on new products are much respected by the majority of peer group members. The early adopters are rational decision makers, and only adopt a new product once they have a reasonable certainty that it is likely to work. They observe new products being used by the innovators and evaluate them, adopting those which work while rejecting those which do not. In other words they are unlikely to buy something merely because it is new, rather they tend to pick up successful ideas from the innovators.

The majority of each social group was divided by Rogers into the early and late majority. The early majority is defined as deliberate, only adopting something new after it has received the endorsement of the peer group leaders, whereas members of the late majority group are sceptical, requiring considerable pressure before they adopt. In practice, the differences between the two groups are marginal, the important point is that two-thirds of the members of a social group will only adopt a new product after it has been tried and endorsed by respected peer group members. Clearly, any company which wants to sell to the mass market must take on board the fact that the majority of their potential customers will take a considerable time to change their minds, abandon their old practices, and try something new.

The slowest of all to change their existing practices are the laggards, who are essentially traditional; they are oriented to the past, and unwilling to adopt something new until their tried and trusted traditional product becomes unavailable. While this may at first sight appear to be a rather uninteresting adopter category, this is not the case at all, since laggards can be a very profitable customer group. They prefer old products, little advertising is required to sustain their loyalty, and the fact that the market is declining may encourage competitors to exit the market and discourage new entrants. All this adds up to excellent profit potential for the company which is prepared to recognize it has a laggard oriented product and is prepared to manage it accordingly.

The essential point of Rogers' work is that innovation is driven by a gradual process of learning among the members of social groups, and that individuals learn at different speeds. In addition, some individuals have a higher propensity to try new products than others. In order to sell an innovation to the majority of consumers, companies have to recognize that their attitudes will be driven primarily by endorsement from respected peer group leaders, who themselves will only adopt once they are reasonably sure that the product's apparent benefits will in fact be delivered. Thus, innovation takes place as a result of the diffusion of new ideas within society, it is a social learning process.

The diffusion process in practice

The diffusion of innovations takes place essentially within social groups, in other words among people with similar interests, background, type of employment, and so on. Thus, any one person may be a member of several social groups in his various work and leisure activities. For example, golfers form a social group, spending considerable time together, much of which is spent in discussion of golfing and golf equipment. Yachtsmen, marathon runners, rock climbers, caravanners and regular participants in any number of sporting and leisure activities are similarly likely to be members of a social group linked by a common interest. Each group would have its oddball innovators, its respected early adopters, its majority, and its diehard laggards.

The long-handled putter is a special golf club with a shaft the length of a broomstick, which many golfers have found to improve their putting accuracy. However, the first golfer to use such a putter would have been regarded by his fellow golfers as eccentric to say the least when he produced this unusual looking implement. If it had resulted in no improvement in performance it would have been consigned to the scrap-heap of discarded golfing gadgets, but if the ball suddenly started to go into the hole with greater frequency people would certainly take notice. The early adopters would then take up the innovation, and as their putting performance improved, and as they told their peers of the virtues of the putter, so the majority would overcome their natural scepticism of yet another gadget and try it themselves. Of course, in any golf club there are a few laggards, who resolutely refuse to have any truck with new-fangled equipment, and they would doggedly carry on using their trusty set of traditional clubs. Anyone who is a member of a golf club or any other interest related peer group can see the adoption process at work: one does not have to be an experimental psychologist to know that members of peer groups influence each other to adopt new ideas, and that some people adopt these ideas quicker than others.

Customer targets for innovation

Peer group processes also operate in the work environment, for example, studies by pharmaceutical companies have shown that doctors fit the diffusion of innovations model very well. The majority of general practitioners (GPs) are rather conservative when it comes to prescribing new drugs, and in practice tend to prescribe from a very limited repertoire of drugs which they trust and have been shown to work reasonably well with few unpleasant side effects. Since the majority of GPs have a limited repertoire, it follows that to get a best selling drug, a pharmaceutical company needs to get onto the average GPs prescribing repertoire, and in so doing may need to displace some other trusted product, since the length of the repertoire is restricted by the doctor's memory. A further problem is that doctors are somewhat sceptical of the claims advanced in phar-maceutical company advertising and by salesmen: it is not that they disbelieve the claims of reputable organizations, it is just that they have seen it all before and feel that somebody trying to sell something will inevitably present a rather one-sided message.

To displace a trusted product from the doctor's prescribing reper-toire and substitute it with something with no track record is far from easy, especially when the doctor is in any case sceptical of company promotion, but that is the challenge facing pharmaceutical companies. However, the more aware companies have realized that doctors conform to the diffusion model, and the way to sell to the majority is to influence the peer group leaders, those people in the medical community who are looked up to by average GPs. Obvious examples would be the acknowledged leaders in particular areas of therapy, although these people are normally based in large hospitals, and are thus somewhat remote from the average GP. One pharmaceutical company has found that in group practices where several GPs work, there is normally one doctor to whom the others defer, and from whom they take their professional lead. It is far better to concentrate efforts to get a new drug established onto these peer group leaders than to spread the effort thinly across every doctor. The company which accurately identifies the early adopters can thus focus on these people, in the knowledge that they will drive the adoption process once successfully convinced. On the other hand, the majority will remain unconvinced until the peer group leaders adopt the product, so targeting the average doctor too early is a waste of time.

Promotional messages for innovation

Identification of the right target group within the diffusion and adoption process will influence the style and content of promotional material. An example is farmers, another social group which has been shown to fit the normal distribution well. Once again, the majority will only buy a new chemical or piece of equipment once it has received endorsement by the early adopters. Equally, farming has its oddball innovators who will try anything new and of course its laggards who doggedly stick to 'the way father did it'. The early adopters tend to be the large successful go-ahead farmers, known by agricultural companies in the UK as 'parish leaders', and in the USA as 'bell cows'. They observe the innovators to see what works, and make decisions based on a reasoned analysis of the evidence put before them, as opposed to the innovator who acts on impulse.

In other words, early adopter farmers go through a rational decision making process, and it follows that in order to influence them, rational arguments need to be presented. They tend to be better educated than their peers and can understand technical messages. In the first year they will do a trial of a new product on a single field rather than commit the entire farm, and will seek help from the skilled professional agronomist. The agricultural company seeking to influence early adopters needs to recognize these characteristics and focus on technical data, field trials, and rational arguments, rather than up-weight advertising, which could even antagonize the rationally minded early adopters.

However, when the emphasis switches to the majority farmer, the technical aspects should be toned down, because these customers are less technically literate, and in any case it is the peer group leaders who have convinced them of the product's efficacy, not the company's messages. For the majority, more simple but memorable advertising is more appropriate, since it provides reassurance and reinforcement for a decision which, in effect, has already been made. Thus, accurate focusing on the early adopter or the majority can have a significant impact on the style and content of advertising, the target customers to be called on by the sales force, and the balance of expenditure between technical applications work and commercial promotion.

Planning the launch strategy

Speed of the diffusion process

It is important to try to understand from the outset the likely speed at which the market for an innovation will develop, as this will have a significant impact on the launch budget and strategy. The speed at which the market develops is dependent upon the speed at which the diffusion process takes place, in other words, how fast people learn from each other about the innovation and how soon they decide to purchase it themselves. This is represented schematically in Figure 4.3 which contrasts a fast diffusion process above with a slow diffusion process below. Fast diffusion leads to a fast growth market which reaches saturation very quickly, whereas slow diffusion leads to a slow growth market which takes many years to reach saturation.

In order to predict the speed of diffusion of an innovation, five main factors need to be considered (see Figure 4.4). The first is relative advantage, or how much better the innovation is than the product it is substituting. Products with a high level of relative advantage will clearly take off more quickly. However, when an innovation has an entirely new function, and is not a direct replacement for anything currently available this may limit its speed of adoption since there is nothing for the customer to compare it with. Clearly, price is a factor here, because their is always a trade-off between relative price and relative efficacy.

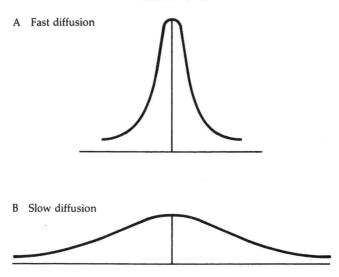

Figure 4.3 *Differences in speed of diffusion*

The second factor is compatibility, or how closely the innovation fits with the customer's existing attitudes, values, practices and equipment. If an innovation is compatible with current custom and practice it will be adopted more quickly, but if it requires a change in systems and thinking, the process will take much longer. For example, a new and revolutionary type of sail would be more likely to be adopted quickly by yachtsmen if it fitted existing boat rigging and methods of sailing, rather than one which also required the purchase of new masts and the learning of new skills.

The third factor influencing the speed of diffusion is complexity, or how easy it is to understand and use the innovation. Clearly if a consumer finds an innovation difficult to understand, and the instructions for its use are complex and hard to follow, the likelihood of peer group recommendation and subsequent adoption is lower. One of the primary initial selling points of the Apple Macintosh personal computer was that it was far easier to use than its rivals in the same product class. Apple had identified that many potential users were not computer literate, and rather afraid of being unable to use a personal computer. The Macintosh was designed specifically to enable such people to use it without an in-depth understanding of computer jargon.

The fourth factor is communicability, or how easy it is to demonstrate the benefits of the innovation. A paint company invented a new type of wood varnish that would last for ten years, even in a salt-laden marine environment. Previous varnishes needed to be renewed at least every five years. The company carried out extensive accelerated weathering trials under simulated conditions to prove to their own satisfaction that the new product would last twice as long as the existing one. Unfortunately, the target customers were not impressed by the trials, they wanted to see the varnish in service on a real boat for ten years before they would pay a higher price than for the traditional product. Consequently, the adoption process was painfully slow.

The final factor is trialability, or the capacity to try the product on a low cost or experimental basis. Consumer goods manufacturers launching new products frequently offer very small trial packs to enable the consumer to make a low cost trial without the expense of purchasing a standard size package. In agriculture, products which can be tested on a few acres are more likely to be adopted quickly than major new items of capital equipment where a substantial long term commitment needs to be made.

1	**Relative advantage**	how superior it is to existing alternatives
2	**Compatibility**	with existing equipment, attitudes and experiences
3	**Simplicity**	ease of understanding and using the innovation
4	**Observability**	ease of observation by/communication to target customers
5	**Trialability**	can small scale/low risk trial purchase be made

Figure 4.4 *Factors affecting speed of diffusion*

Seeing the customer's viewpoint

Before launching an innovation, it is advisable to look down the factors outlined in Figure 4.4 and try to make an assessment of the speed at which it is likely to take off. However, it is essential that this is done from the customer's perspective rather than the company's. The compact disc (CD) player is a case in point. An audio engineer would pronounce the CD's relative advantage over a standard record player as very high indeed. In technical terms he would be absolutely correct, the CD has measurably better performance on all the leading technical criteria such as rumble, wow and flutter, dropouts, hiss, stereo separation and so on. Furthermore, all these parameters can be indisputably measured with sensitive and accurate instruments, this serving to prove scientifically the engineer's opinion. However, from the customer's point of view the argument is less clear cut. While most people would concede that the CD sounds somewhat better than a record player, they lack the instruments or the understanding to measure this scientifically, and few of them will be able to replay the CD through the kind of amplification equipment available to the audio engineer. In any case, people's hearing starts to become increasingly inefficient past the age of 30. The argument is not whether it sounds better, but whether it sounds sufficiently better to justify a purchase, and whereas the engineer would say unequivocally yes, the customer might not be so sure.

On the issue of compatibility, the CD to an audio engineer is totally compatible with existing practice, after all it was specially designed to be plugged straight into the standard sockets on domestic sound equipment. Unfortunately, the customer does not see it this way, as he has an existing record collection which he is unable to play on a CD player, indeed, the new equipment is totally incompatible with his existing practice. The fact that it is compatible with his existing equipment is scarcely a compensation. The audio engineer would be unlikely to see the CD as complex, again the customer might not agree. Furthermore, it is not easy to demonstrate the benefits of the CD in the average retail environment, and finally a CD player is not trialable or low cost, a purchase is a major decision. The five factors taken together show why CD took ten years to become fully established, which was far longer than the manufacturers initially expected given its technical merits.

Overestimating the speed at which a diffusion process is likely to take place can lead to severe consequences for a company. First, internal expectations are raised to an unrealistic level, and once it becomes clear that initial hopes will not be realized it is easy for a climate of failure to set in, leading to a denial of further resources for what may still be a potentially promising product. High initial sales forecasts are also often accompanied by a high launch expenditure, and when this fails to generate sales, personal recriminations against those responsible may result, and this may add to the general loss of confidence in the product itself. Trying to evaluate the speed of the diffusion process in advance, by examining the five factors from the customer's viewpoint prior to the launch, can save a lot of premature wasted expenditure, and a potential loss of confidence in both product and management. More importantly it may lead to a more sensible plan, where launch expenditure is phased over the period of predicted growth rather than blown on a short intensive launch campaign. Such launches are appropriate only when the speed of diffusion can be predicted to be fast.

Role of advertising in launching innovations

This begs the question of whether advertising and promotion can be used to speed up the rate of adoption of an innovation; in other words, what capacity is there for a company to drive the diffusion process? While it must be acknowledged that effective advertising can lead to greater awareness, and that must help the diffusion process, one should nevertheless be aware of overestimating its impact. The reasons for this caution lie firstly in the nature of the other sources of information consumers are subject to, and secondly in the operation of the consumer learning process itself.

We are all as consumers subjected to a constant barrage of information about new products from a bewildering array of sources. Advertising and salesmen are obvious examples, along with mailshots, brochures, point of sale merchandising, and other forms of sales promotion. Then there is editorial, whether in general magazines or newspapers, on television, or in professional publications, along with seeing things in retail outlets or simply in the street. We also have a variety of personal contacts such as work colleagues, social peers, neighbours, spouses, children and other family members, and professional advisers and consultants. This enormous variety of sources of information is not always consulted purposefully, in order specifically to find out about a new product, mostly the information is just dripping in on a regular but often subconscious level.

These sources of information are viewed by consumers with varying degrees of belief; some are seen as highly credible, others less so. The majority of people find advertising and salesmen, together with promotional material, the least credible sources of information, whereas peers and colleagues are the most credible. This should not be surprising; we trust sources which we see as unbiased more than we trust those which are seen to be specifically designed to plug a particular product. Clearly, the source of information seen as most credible varies according to the individual and the product category. For example, some consumers hold consumer magazine reports in very high regard when purchasing durable products such as washing machines. Equally, some commercial buyers are highly influenced by the advice of professional consultants whom they regard as unbiased experts in their field. Engineers and scientists often set great store by technical brochures and data sheets, despite the fact that they are issued by the product's manufacturers, provided they are seen as scientifically valid. However, the fact is that overall, customers trust unbiased sources more than sources which are seen to be playing the supplier's tune. When the subject is a relatively unfamiliar innovation, this effect is magnified.

Thus, although advertising and promotion can stimulate awareness, it needs more than this to encourage customers to adopt an innovation. For this to happen they need to be given time to change their attitudes and values, and this is something which only a social learning process can accomplish. Supplier advertising accordingly has a limited capacity to drive the diffusion process, and managers should recognize these limitations, rather than trying to pretend they do not exist. Of course, every company which believes it has an innovation wants to get it out into the market quickly and achieve rapid sales growth to stay ahead of the competitors. Unfortunately, doing this is not as simple as merely spending a large sum of money on an up-weight launch campaign. The adoption of an innovation is a social learning process, and if the factors are against a rapid diffusion process taking place, then it is simply beyond the capacity of even excessive amounts of advertising to overcome these limitations.

Indeed, high budget launches can often have a negative effect, since they may well alienate the early adopters, who see themselves as rational decision makers and do not like being bombarded with advertising. Worse still, a high profile launch will attract the attention of competitors, and may well convince them that they need to jump on the bandwagon before it is too late. Far from its original purpose of keeping ahead of competition, a high profile launch may have exactly the opposite effect, whereas low profile technical work among the key early adopters may lead competitors to think they can afford to wait and see.

Four management guidelines

Innovation is one of the most controversial and least understood aspects of strategic marketing thinking. However, this review of the innovation process has established four basic guidelines for the management of this critical area. Beyond this starting point, further complications arise, which are discussed in the remaining sections of this chapter.

1 We need to recognize the confusion between commercial innovation and technical invention. Here we are using the word innovation to signify something that has the power to create an entirely new market or radically change an existing one, and this may or may not involve new technology.
2 Innovation is driven by a learning process within social peer groups, and different people learn at different speeds. The majority are rather conservative about new ideas and they take their lead

from the early adopters. Companies should focus their efforts initially on the early adopters with messages appropriate to their rational decision making style.

3 The speed at which an innovation is adopted depends on relative advantage, compatibility, complexity, communicability and trialability. Companies need to assess carefully whether these factors are likely to lead to a fast or a slow adoption process, and adjust their product launch plans accordingly.

4 Consumers learn about innovations from a wide variety of sources, and generally speaking those which suppliers are seen to control are least credible. Innovation depends on a social learning process taking place, and supplier advertising has only a limited capacity to drive this.

Managing growth markets

The product life cycle

The 'product life cycle' (PLC) is one of the best known concepts in the whole field of marketing planning; it is also one of the most controversial. It is appropriate to discuss it in this chapter, because an insight into the process of innovation is fundamental to an understanding of the implications and limitations of the PLC. The launch strategy, discussed in the previous section, is just the beginning; a successful product still has to be managed effectively through its growth phase, and indeed through the rest of its life. Managing a growth product still requires an understanding of the innovation process. The need for a commitment to commercial innovation does not cease with a product's launch, it lasts throughout its period of growth.

The basic proposition of the PLC concept is that products grow relatively slowly when first introduced, then if successful, move into fast growth which continues until saturation is approached, when growth slows until it plateaus into maturity. The maturity phase continues until changing consumer tastes or superior technology lead to a decline in sales which continues until the product finally dies. A stylized model of the PLC is shown in Figure 4.5, but the single smooth curve shown here is far from realistic. Indeed, some marketing books show alternative shapes, a tall PLC for a fashion product, a peaked one for a fad, even a scalloped PLC for products that fall in and out of favour. There is little doubt that these stylized shapes never occur in practice; studies have shown very strange looking life-cycle curves for real products. Real life PLCs are far more complex than the theoretical model.

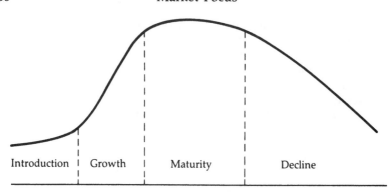

Figure 4.5 *Stylized model of the product life cycle*

This contrast between the model and the real world has led to the PLC concept causing endless debate among academics, and opinions vary from those who believe it is the fountainhead of all strategic thinking, to those who believe it is little more than a theoretical irrelevance. It is sometimes difficult to understand the passion of the proponents, because both points of view are to a certain extent true, and equally both are to a certain extent false. For reasons which will be discussed later, PLCs in real life are a conglomeration of mini-PLCs and sub-PLCs, so that to see them in terms of the stylized models is indeed unrealistic. Nevertheless, it cannot be denied that all products grow, all mature at saturation, and all, eventually decline. This process happens more quickly in some markets than in others but the cycle of birth, growth, maturity, decline, and death happens just as surely in marketing as it does in the natural world. For example, Figure 4.6 shows the life-cycle patterns for various domestic electrical products in Japan, and demonstrates that while the stylized models are not reproduced, the stages of growth, maturity and decline are nevertheless still a reality for the manufacturers concerned.

The important point from a perspective of strategic thinking is thus to determine whether a product is growing, maturing or declining, because that will drive crucial strategic decisions: to that extent the PLC concept is indeed a fundamental building block. It is, of course, superficial to try and assess whether a product is in growth, maturity or decline by looking merely at sales figures. These reveal only the historical picture, they say nothing about whether the past trends are likely to continue. This is where an understanding of the diffusion of innovations becomes so relevant, because it is this very process which drives market growth. Rogers depicted his diffusion model as a normal distribution, or bell curve. If, however, we re-draft this in cumulative form it becomes an 'S' curve (see Figure 4.7). Comparing this with Figure 4.1 it can be seen that the innovation diffusion process drives the growth phase of the product life-cycle. If a product can be shown to be, say, at the early adopter stage, there is a reasonable chance that it will continue to grow. If, however, it has already reached the late majority, then we know that growth is likely shortly to slow down.

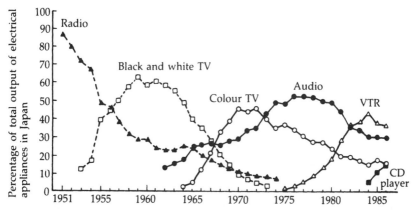

Figure 4.6 *Actual product life cycles: the Japanese electronics industry (Denta Shimbun)*

The drivers of growth, maturity and decline

Market growth is driven essentially by the behaviour of the consumer population. If the consumer base is expanding year by year through the operation of the diffusion process, we have a growth market, but if no new customers are adopting the product, and the consumer base and usage rate are stable, the market is mature. Of course, if it can be shown that the consumer base is shrinking as previous customers switch to alternative new products, then the market for the product is declining. In addition to shifts in the consumer base, changes in the usage rate will also drive growth, and innovative growth products frequently exhibit increasing usage rates as consumers gain familiarity. The factors driving growth, maturity and decline are shown in Figure 4.8: these are characteristics of the consumer population, which can be measured and assessed using market research techniques. It is an understanding of what is happening in the consumer population which should lead to subsequent

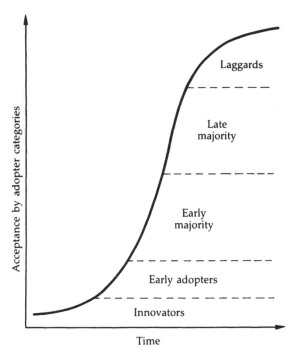

Figure 4.7 *How innovation drives the product life-cycle*

strategic decisions; reliance on historic sales figures is a totally inadequate substitute.

The market for mineral water in the UK provides an excellent example of what drives a growth market. Ever since the introduction of Perrier, the consumption of bottled water has been a steadily increasing social habit driven on by the diffusion process, as the use of mineral water has passed from the innovators to the early adopters and so on up the growth curve shown in Figure 4.7. Thus the consumer base has grown progressively, and, at the same time, consumers have been increasing their rate of consumption as they have become more familiar with the product. The contrast with the market for, say, beer in Germany could not be more clear: everybody in Germany who is likely to drink beer already drinks it, thus the consumer base is not expanding, and furthermore, Germany is near the top of the international league table in terms of consumption per head, so it is unlikely that the usage rate will increase either. The consumer processes driving the growth market for mineral water, and on the other hand, the mature market for beer, are summarized in Figure 4.8.

The implications for marketing strategy are straightforward. In a growth market, companies have the opportunity to grow by educating new customers and trying to get existing customers to consume more; indeed, competitors can grow together. By contrast, in a mature market, the only way to grow is by winning customers away from competitors. In other words, a company can only gain at the expense of a competitor, the only way to win is to force someone else to lose. This makes a significant difference to the nature and intensity of competition. The fact that a market is mature does not mean that there are no growth opportunities at all, because even in mature markets there are shifts of emphasis which flexible companies can take advantage of. However, in a growth market, the opportunities to grow are much clear cut and do not necessarily involve displacing competitors. These differences lead to very different strategic approaches which will be discussed in more detail in the next chapter. Suffice it to say at present that it is essential first to determine whether the market for a product is in growth, maturity, or decline, and this can only be done with any accuracy by understanding the diffusion process.

> *Drivers of growth markets*
> Constant flow of new users accepting and using product
> Increase in usage rate among existing users
>
> *Drivers of mature markets*
> No increase in consumer population using product
> Existing consumers cannot reasonably consume more
>
> *Drivers of declining markets*
> Shrinkage in consumer population using product
> Decline in usage rate (sometimes)

Figure 4.8 *Drivers of growth, maturity and decline*

Development of growth markets by segments

One of the major reasons why product life-cycles in practice fail to conform with the theoretical model, is that product markets are normally made up of a composite set of separate market segments, rather than being formed by only one segment. While there are clearly some very specialist products which are relevant to only one segment, most product markets grow through several distinctive groups of customers. Each group will have its own adoption process, some will adopt quickly and some slowly, some will be large and some small. The result is that the overall product life-cycle is in fact a conglomeration of smaller life-cycles, each one driven by the adoption process in a series of distinctive consumer groups.

Consider for example, the development of the market for pocket calculators during the 1970s. The first purchasers were engineers and scientists, because they had extensive and complex calculations to perform and existing technology, the slide rule and the log table, was slower and less accurate. Thus, engineers and scientists could justify the high purchase price of the early calculators owing to the fact that, for them, the product had a high utility value. Of course, the acceptance of calculators into the scientific and engineering community did not happen overnight. The majority would have been influenced by their peer group leaders, and no doubt there would have been some laggards who doggedly carried on using slide rules and log tables, determined to ignore the march of progress. In other words, a diffusion process would have taken place among engineers and scientists. One might designate these users as segment one (S1).

As the early manufacturers of calculators started to benefit both from technical advances and from economies of experience and scale, so prices began to fall. Calculators then began to become attractive to accountants and other commercial users. Their calculations were less complex, and existing technology, the adding machine, was quite adequate, so they could not justify the very high prices of the early calculators. Compared to engineers and scientists, accountants and commercial users had a lower utility value, and could only justify purchase when the price came down. However, the commercial user segment (S2) is potentially a much larger one than S1, although at a lower price owing to the lower utility value.

As calculator prices fell still further, so they began to become attractive to the wider general public (S3). Of course the utility value to these users was lower than to commercial users, but again the potential market was larger. The final segment to develop was schoolchildren (S4), the lowest utility value segment, but probably potentially the largest numerically. Again, as in all the previous segments, there would have been a diffusion process, the innovator children adopting first, and the majority waiting until successfully influenced by the peer group leader children.

The growth phase of the PLC for pocket calculators can thus be seen to be made up of a series of overlapping segments, each one with its own diffusion and adoption process (see Figure 4.9). In other words, the market did not grow as one smooth continuous curve, indeed the growth pattern was discontinuous, and it was the emergence of new customer segments which caused the discontinuities. Most major innovations seem to grow in this way, the market developing as a series of increasingly larger segments with a progressively declining utility value to the users. The example of nylon is often quoted: what started life as a high value fibre used for parachute fabric was subsequently used for ladies lingerie and finally for carpets. Again, progressively larger segments with progressively declining utility values.

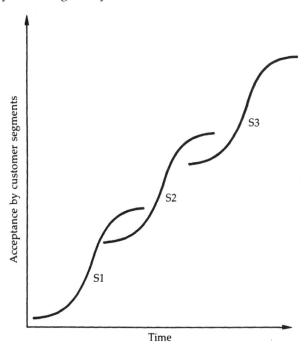

Figure 4.9 *Development of growth markets by segments*

The realization that markets develop through a series of discontinuities has a substantial impact upon strategic decision making for the would-be innovator company. Firstly, it is quite clear that if a company wishes to become or remain market leader, it has no option but to move with the development of the market. In doing so, it must accept that this will involve a change of target customer, and thus concomitant adjustments may have to be made to product, price, promotion, and distribution. Although a company may feel more comfortable, more at home, serving the early segment (S1) customer, there is no hope of maintaining its growth if it remains in this segment. While it may be possible to retain specialist leadership in the segment, it may also become vulnerable to attack at the margins as the overall market leader gains more and more volume in larger segments. It is extremely unlikely for example, that any specialist manufacturers of nylon fibre for parachute fabric still survive.

Competitive strategy in growth markets

While it is easy in theory to advocate that leaders have to be prepared to switch customer targets or risk losing the lead it is often difficult to do so in practice. For example, Hewlett Packard (HP) was the early leader in the market for scientific and engineering calculators, designated S1 in Figure 4.9, but it would have needed to change its entire approach to appeal successfully to the commercial user segment (S2). Accountants do not do the same calculations as engineers, they would want a calculator that would perform simple arithmetic tasks reliably, rather than the complex scientific functions required by engineers. This would have necessitated a change in HP's product development philosophy, and possibly its manufacturing methods. A calculator has an inherently lower utility value to accountants, and this would mean that HP would have to be prepared to substantially lower its prices to sell effectively to this segment. However, while this may have made sense in the marketplace, it could have been difficult to implement in the organization, since erosion of the level of margins traditionally enjoyed is rarely welcomed in any business. Selling to accountants would also have necessitated changing distribution channels, an extremely difficult thing to do when a firm's sales and distribution system is geared up, trained, and experienced in serving a different channel.

Marketing mix element	Engineers (S1)	Accountants (S2)
Product	Complex-many functions	Simple-basic functions
Price	High	Medium
Promotion	Scientific journals	Financial press
Place of sale	Specialist instrument distributors	Office equipment suppliers and stationers shops

Figure 4.10 *Calculators: shifting from S1 to S2*

Thus, adapting to the needs of a new customer segment at a discontinuity in the development of a market, often demands that substantial changes be made. It is apparent that a shift in customer target from S1 to S2 would, in fact, have necessitated the adoption of an entirely new marketing plan. The enormous contrast between the traditional approach and the new one which would have been required is shown in Figure 4.10. Given the difficulty of shifting into a new market segment at a discontinuity, it is hardly surprising that many companies choose not to do it. However, while this is understandable, it may well have the effect of surrendering leadership to the company which is prepared to develop the new segment. This happened on no less than two occasions during the development of the calculator market, and it is therefore most instructive to trace competitive developments in this market against the multi-segment model shown in Figure 4.9.

HP's early leadership in S1 was based on selling complex and expensive products to engineers and scientists, its traditional customers. HP proved less effective at selling to S2, the commercial users, and Texas Instruments (TI) rapidly took over volume leadership by successfully selling to this segment and subsequently to S3, the wider general public. TI had taken advantage of HP's inability or unwillingness to move into a new segment, a discontinuity in the market had allowed the leadership to change hands. However, TI itself subsequently proved unwilling to develop S4, schoolchildren, which would have necessitated selling the product at very low prices. This left the door open for Casio, which rapidly gained volume leadership, and was subsequently able to displace TI from S2 and S3. Again, a discontinuity had enabled the leadership to change hands. While all this was going on, HP had retained its specialist segment leadership of S1, protected by its technical competitive advantage. But even this advantage was to turn out to be unsustainable when Casio launched its own range of multi-function graphic display scientific calculators at prices HP was unable to match. HP retained leadership only in the esoteric field of reverse polish logic models.

This is a salutary tale for all high technology, innovative organizations. HP pioneered the market with its undoubted technological and entrepreneurial skills, but it was unable to translate this pioneering drive into long term market leadership. Commercial innovation is about far more than launching exciting innovative new products, it is also about managing them for sustained competitive success. Inability or failure to manage market discontinuities is one of the main reasons why pioneers often fail to achieve ultimate leadership. Success in innovation is not solely a matter of pioneering, of being 'the first with the most', this may need to be repeated through several very different segments before the market finally matures, and the leadership may be lost at any of the discontinuities on the way.

Targeting the best launch segment

On the other hand, expensive mistakes may be made by companies which try to get too big too quickly. Going for S3 in an emerging market before S1 and S2 have had time to develop is a classic strategic error. One example is the launch of Prestel, an interactive information system marketed by the British Post Office. The financial community must have a very high utility value for continuously updated interactive electronic information: in the world of stock and money broking, time and information are key success factors. Although this is a relatively small market numerically, the potentially high unit price would be invaluable in the process of initial cost reduction and system establishment; it is a typical S1, low volume but high utility value. The next potential users for an interactive information system would be the wider world of commerce and industry, for example travel agents, company information depart- ments and retailers. This is a potential S2, much larger unit volume but users with a lower utility value for the system. The largest segment of all is the general public, where the utility value would be relatively low, but of course unit volumes would potentially be very high; this would form S3.

The Post Office aimed its Prestel system directly at the general public at launch, at a price, presumably influenced by the initially small production volumes, well above the utility value of the system to these customers. In going straight for the big volume S3 segment, the Post Office had overlooked both the learning process and the fact that emerging markets nearly always start in small, specialist, high value segments. The intended customers neither understood Prestel, nor did they see any value in it for them, and the result was an embarrassing failure. Subsequently, Reuters successfully launched an interactive electronic information system aimed directly at the financial community at a high price. Despite being the first system on the market, Prestel threw away its lead by trying to go for the largest segment too early.

It should not be imagined that the development of growth markets through a series of segments is restricted to high technology products, since it happens equally in consumer markets. The growth of the margarine brand Flora to market leadership in what is a relatively low technology environment provides an example. Flora was the first low cholesterol margarine, and at the time of its introduction it was suspected that there was a linkage between heart disease and the intake of dietary cholesterol, a linkage which was being increasingly accepted by the medical community at the time. Accordingly, Flora was not aimed at the general grocery market but at victims of heart disease and those with a high risk of developing it. This was done by introducing doctors to the concept of a low cholesterol spread, and hoping they would recommend it to their patients. This is a classic S1, small in number but with a high utility value. Gradually, awareness of the alleged dangers of dietary cholesterol began to spread among the general public and Flora was then targeted at people who were fit, but who wanted to avoid the risk of developing heart disease by lowering their intake of dietary cholesterol. An advertising campaign was designed to target the product at people who were sufficiently concerned about preserving their health to switch to a new product. This was S2, larger in size than S1, but with a lower utility value.

Finally, several years after its initial introduction, the product was targeted at the general grocery buying public with a substantial media advertising campaign. This was S3, a very large segment, but with a relatively low utility value. What made Flora successful however, was not fundamentally the advertising campaign, despite the fact that it was widely acclaimed at the time: rather it was the way the product had been quietly and unspectacularly built through successive segments, which put it in the position to benefit from the final campaign. Another interesting aspect of the Flora story is that competitors were very slow to respond by developing their own low cholesterol product. Perhaps they thought it was just a small market and of no interest to them, unfortunately, by the time they realized its significance it was too late, Flora had become too well established to be overtaken. There is little doubt that the low profile adopted by Flora in its early days contributed to the complacency of its competitors.

Flora and Prestel provide a fascinating contrast between effective and ineffective management of the innovation process. The lesson for all of us is that innovations tend to start in small segments of customers who need the product badly, and this is the type of segment into which they should be launched. Launching into a small high value segment is in any case the lowest risk option, since initial start up and distribution costs will be lower than for the mass market. In addition, customers with a high utility value will be prepared to pay more, and will thus enable high prices to offset the initially high costs. By contrast, going for the largest segment first means trying to sell the product to people who do not really need it that badly, having to accept low prices owing to their low utility value, and making an immediate commitment to mass manufacture, promotion and distribution from the outset. In addition, a high profile launch is more likely to attract a response from competitors, whereas taking a lower profile may induce them to wait and see. The message is simple; focus an innovation on the people who need it most, and even within that group, target the innovators and early adopters first. As in many other areas of marketing, focus is the key to the successful launch of innovations.

Managing technological innovation

Finding applications for new technology

Our primary concern in this chapter is commercial innovation, rather than technical invention; however, when the two are combined there is no doubt that they are a powerful source of potential market change. Indeed, new technology is often responsible for the growth of entirely new markets, which nobody had any idea existed until the technology came along. This is to a certain extent at variance with classical marketing theory, which portrays marketing as the process of encouraging an organization to respond to customer requirements and market trends, rather than actually initiating and creating them. In harmony with this classical interpretation of the subject, marketing literature has traditionally portrayed new product development as essentially a market and customer led process, where new products are developed in response to known customer needs. Paradoxically, however, many major market innovations appear in practice to be technologically driven, to arise from a technology seeking a market application, rather than from a market opportunity seeking a technology to fulfil it.

Technology driven innovation is the antithesis of the classical marketing concept, which is to start with the customer then design something to meet his needs. The marketing concept is certainly intuitively a reasonable proposition, indeed, it was established in Chapter 2 that to be successful in a competitive marketplace, businesses have to focus on their customers. Unfortunately things do not seem to be as simple as this in the field of technological innovation: while market led product development may be appropriate in a market where changes are slow and can to some extent be anticipated, it may be less appropriate in faster changing markets with a higher technology content. In these cases there is no doubting the evidence of history; many of the most important innovations have been technology driven, the market for them has developed later. The real challenge from a commercial viewpoint is recognizing the potential of technical breakthroughs, and understanding how to manage them for long term business potential.

Thus, for successful technology driven market development, in addition to a technological discovery, there needs to be an element of insight as to how it should be applied. The X-ray scanner, now standard medical diagnostic equipment, works on a system known as computed tomography (CT), which uses two beams of X-rays at right angles to display a transverse 'slice' through the body or brain. CT was originally conceived as a means of examining metal bars for cracks and flaws, but it was the insight which led to its application in medical diagnosis which revolutionized the market for medical diagnostic equipment. In other words, major innovations frequently come about through finding and pioneering new applications for technology which may have been developed for a completely separate purpose.

This paradox is well known in pharmaceutical research, where scientists may be given a brief to investigate one area of therapy, and end up almost by accident, discovering a compound with applications in a completely different field. This creates significant problems for large organizations, because the scientist responsible for the invention is normally working on a specific project, and it is difficult releasing people to work on a completely separate and unauthorized programme which may lead nowhere. This problem will be exacerbated if his company has no expertise or track record in the new application, because senior managers may be totally unable to see its potential or nurture its growth. It is hardly surprising that revolutionary breakthroughs based on the application of a particular technology to a new market area can be rejected by the very organization which developed them.

A related problem is that companies set goals and criteria for their research scientists which may be highly appropriate to existing markets and applications, but totally irrelevant to new applications. The ubiquitous and highly profitable Post-It note, manufactured by 3M, only works because it uses a special kind of adhesive which sticks tight to paper, but peels very easily when required without any danger of damaging the paper. While this adhesive was under development in the laboratory, there was some concern because it failed many of the tests traditionally applied as goals for adhesive development programmes, such as shear adhesion and peel adhesion. Indeed, it was in many respects a very poor adhesive in technical terms, but rather than reject it, 3M sought an application for it. In the words of 3M's president Louis Lehr 'it was an adhesive which didn't stick, and the whole history of 3M has been to develop adhesives which stick better'.

There is no doubt that a technology which broke so many of the established rules and criteria would have been rejected in many large organizations. However, when a truly innovative company develops something with unique characteristics it does not abandon it, but instead looks for an application. Thus, technological innovations often require both technical invention and commercial insight, which may take the invention into areas of application undreamed of by the inventor and by the potential customers.

Recognizing technology limits

Technologies have inherent performance limits, and the limits of newer technologies often easily surpass those of traditional technologies: this is particularly true if the new technology comes from a totally unexpected direction, through the process discussed in the previous section. For example, the CT scanner, although it utilizes X-rays, is based on a completely different technical concept to traditional X-ray diagnostic procedures, and has a much higher potential diagnostic performance. A manufacturer of traditional X-ray machinery could have invested vast sums in research and development in its existing technology, and still failed to match the performance of even a rudimentary brain scanner. The traditional technology simply had inherently lower performance limits, and no amount of investment could overcome that fundamental problem.

In his book *Innovation: The Attacker's Advantage*, Richard Foster postulates that new technologies develop slowly in their early stages, performance improvements being made at relatively high cost in time and money. But when the technology reaches a critical stage, performance improves rapidly with further expenditure, until the technology approaches its inherent limits, after which even massive expenditures will effect only marginal improvements. A plot of relative performance improvement against cumulative R&D expenditure results in another 'S' curve (see Figure 4.11). Foster argues that all technologies have their limits, and management needs to recognize when these limits are being approached, since at this point, continued R&D investment produces progressively less reward.

Figure 4.11 shows that the best R&D return comes from investment in developing technologies, in other words those already past their initial high cost/low reward stage. By contrast, emerging and mature

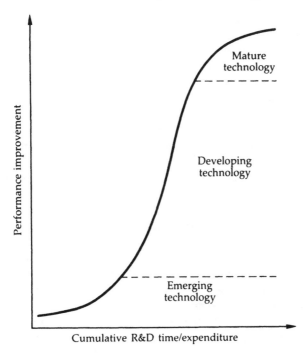

Figure 4.11 *The technology 'S' curve*

technologies have an inherently lower rate of return on R&D investment. However, the companies best placed to exploit a high return
developing technology are those which have already acquired experience through research done at the emerging technology stage.
Therefore, although it may appear appealing to wait until the developing technology stage, when the best R&D returns are gained,
to delay too long will almost inevitably result in losing the initiative
to those who have previously invested during the emerging stage.
Perhaps this may cause those senior executives who believe that
'blue sky' research is for research institutes rather than industry, to
pause for thought.

Equally, there seems little point in investing large sums in mature
technology, particularly if competitors are already working on competing emerging and developing technology. The problem is that
companies have a tendency to stick with technology they know, and
continue to invest R&D expenditure in it, rather than risk expenditure
on unknown newer technology. A given industry may experience
several of these technology 'S' curve cycles, each one overlapping
the next. Each time a new technology cycle starts it produces a

technological discontinuity which, just like a market segment dis-continuity, may enable a competitor to gain an advantage. Foster quotes the example of the market for tyre cords, the fabric casings which form the inner carcass of a tyre (see Figure 4.12).

The first pneumatic tyres were built upon a carcass of cotton, however when Rayon, one of the earliest synthetic fibres, was in-vented, it was found to have a much better performance than cotton. Regardless of how much a cotton tyre cord manufacturer invested in R&D, it would have been impossible to match the performance of Rayon. This discontinuity enabled the Rayon manufacturer American Viscose to take leadership of the market for tyre cords, rapidly displacing the previous manufacturers of cotton cords. Subsequently, the invention of nylon enabled Du Pont to take leadership: again it would not have mattered how much American Viscose had invested trying to improve its Rayon cords, nylon simply had higher perform-ance limits, and the only real option open to American Viscose to retain leadership would be to start its own nylon programme. Sub-sequently, Celanese took the lead from Du Pont with the invention of Polyester. Du Pont finally found the answer with the invention of Kevlar, a very high performance fibre. Although polyester is still used in many tyres on cost grounds, no amount of R&D investment will ever produce a polyester tyre cord with equal performance to Kevlar.

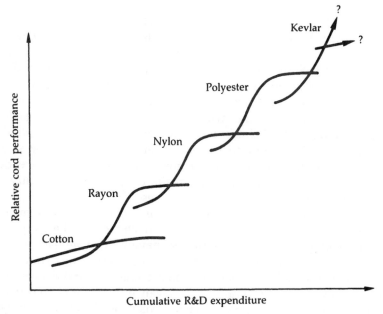

Figure 4.12 *Limits of technology: tyre cords*

But even Du Pont has no real idea where tyre technology is going, and the next discontinuity could destroy the technical superiority enjoyed by Kevlar. Du Pont would then face the same dilemma as before, whether to continue investment in Kevlar, or switch it into a new technology of which it may have little knowledge. It is here that the large organization has the greatest difficulty. In a survey of large American companies, the management consultants McKinsey found that 80% of R&D investment went into mature technology which was already close to its inherent performance limits. By contrast, R&D productivity was found to be five times greater in developing than in mature technology. The explanation of this paradox is simple; companies invest in the technology they know, even when they recognize that it is mature. The implications for management are equally clear: managers should try to make a realistic assessment of whether a particular technology is mature, and shift the balance of their company's R&D investment to areas where better long term rewards can be gained.

The challenge of technological innovation

Thus, new technology can play a highly significant role in the process of commercial innovation, particularly the creation of entirely new markets which could never have been foreseen. Nobody could possibly have forecast the development of the enormous market for CT scanners before the technique had been invented, and nobody in the traditional diagnostic X-ray equipment business could possibly have foreseen the potential threat. The ability of technological innovation to produce such massive discontinuities is a powerful source of competitive advantage, but large organizations are not well equipped to manage it effectively. Managing technological innovation effectively may mean backing unauthorized programmes in areas of no apparent interest to the company; it may mean changing traditional R&D goals and criteria, or permitting staff to abandon current programmes in order to pursue avenues of original thought. In addition, companies tend to invest in making marginal improvements in the mature technologies which have served them well in the past, rather than investing in emerging and developing technologies which may have far higher performance limits.

However, technical innovation is not only concerned with new and growing markets, it can also be a powerful route to competitive advantage in mature markets. Innovations which cause technological discontinuity can in Foster's graphic phrase 'turn leaders into losers'.

Market leaders tend to pursue the technology which put them in that position, sometimes regardless of the fact that newer technology has far higher inherent performance limits. The Swiss watch manufacturers chose to ignore the electronic watch until it was too late, despite the fact that they knew quite early the accuracy improvements available with electronic technology, and could have foreseen that costs would fall as volume increased. The organizational and financial cost of radical internal change clearly discourages companies from adapting to external change, however, the cost of not adapting may be much higher in the long run, to the benefit of the innovator.

While it is apparent that technological discontinuity can totally change the competitive balance in mature markets, it should also be recognized that marketing innovations can have the same effect even without any substantial technological breakthrough. The fledgling Japanese motor cycle industry, initially using standard technology, met a need for cheap reliable personal transport which was not being met adequately by the existing market leaders. The traditional manufacturers did not see these small machines as a threat to their market and allowed the Japanese gradually to build customer awareness, distribution and market share, and thus build a solid base for the launch of their own larger machines – the rest is history. Innovation is essentially a market phenomenon; technical breakthroughs are often involved, but are by no means essential.

Building a more innovative organization

The risk dimension in innovation

This chapter has established that commercial innovation is fundamental to the long term success of competitive businesses, but also that for a variety of reasons it is potentially an extremely risky activity. It involves companies in being prepared to pioneer new markets and technologies, when perhaps a more secure short term return would be obtained from focusing on the company's traditional business. It also demands a high level of organizational flexibility if successful shifts are to be made into new segments and new technologies, as growing products are managed through the discontinuities in the market and technology 'S' curves. Given the inherent risks of innovation, managers might reasonably ask whether these could be reduced by accurate market research and forecasting. After all, market research is the best method of reducing uncertainty about whether a product is likely to succeed in the marketplace, and thus reduce the risk element in any subsequent decision to invest or not.

Traditional approaches to new product development certainly do involve heavy reliance upon market research techniques. The best known is the one developed by Booz, Allen and Hamilton, a sequential process from idea generation through to product launch (see Figure 4.13). The process starts with the generation of a great many new product ideas through the use of brainstorming or similar creative techniques. These ideas are then screened, reducing the numbers to those which appear, *prima facie*, to be good business propositions. The ideas which pass the screening process are then subjected to an intensive business analysis process, involving market research to determine whether an adequate market exists, and concept testing to ensure that consumers will be likely to buy what the company is proposing to offer. It follows that at this stage, the system eliminates any product for which a market cannot be shown to exist, and also any product concept which consumers say they would be unlikely to buy.

Products which pass the business analysis stage are then developed by R&D, and obviously a few more ideas will drop out at this stage

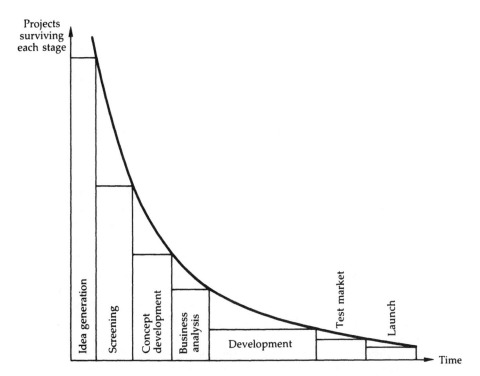

Figure 4.13 *Booz, Allen and Hamilton's new product development model*

because they are being not technically feasible. Products which make it through development are then test marketed, and again anything which fails to do well in its test market is likely to be dropped. Finally, any product passing successfully through every stage is launched nationally. This is the classic market responsive approach to new product development, and it is the epitome of the marketing concept. There is constant market testing and constant reference to measured customer needs; anything which the market does not want is ruthlessly rejected. Like so many classical marketing theories, all this sounds eminently reasonable, after all, businesses can only prosper by satisfying their customers. Regrettably, however, life is just not that simple when it comes to innovation. While the research based approach seems conceptually irrefutable, the problem is that if, as in the case of many innovations, no market exists, and if potential customers are unable adequately to understand the product, then market research can only provide negative answers.

Can we forecast innovation?

Research specialists would no doubt argue that this could be overcome by investigating the prospective customers' attitudes to the product's benefits, rather than the product itself. However, the problem here is that the benefits may not clearly be understood, or even perceived as a benefit by respondents. Even at innovation oriented 3M, the celebrated Post—It note did not initially get the excitement of the marketing department, possibly because they felt it offered the user no tangible benefits over existing practice. In the late 1970s, market research available to the major brewers indicated that there was no worthwhile market for mineral water, because the British would never pay for water. Only Bulmers Cider Company was prepared to take a risk by distributing the pioneering Perrier. No type of benefits research could have exposed its eventual potential, because the majority of consumers simply did not perceive its features as benefits at that time; it took years of gradual social change in attitudes and values for any significant number of consumers to perceive these as benefits. Research would have indicated only a small number of potential customers. Equally, a test market would have produced a very disappointing result: established research methods would thus have totally failed to recognize the scale of the real opportunity.

In addition, the perception of the nature of a product's benefits can change as the product becomes more familiar: it was initially thought that CDs would appeal to consumers primarily because of superior sound quality, whereas more recent research indicates that the mainstream customer (as opposed to the hi-fi 'buff') is more interested in convenience factors. Silk Cut was launched as a mild cigarette targeted at women, but the benefit which propelled the product from nowhere to market leadership in just a few years was its low tar content. Any consumer participating in pre-launch benefit research would not even have been asked about the benefit of low tar because this was not seen as a potential benefit even by the managers who launched the product, let alone the consumers at whom it was aimed.

Stephen King, former research director of a major advertising agency, sums up the research dilemma neatly. Consumer research 'can tell you what people did and thought at one point in time: it can't tell you directly what they might do in a new set of circumstances'. This is particularly true if those circumstances relate to something entirely new, and hitherto unknown to the respondent. It would be difficult to argue conclusively that market research stifles innovations by indicating that no market exists. While there are many anecdotes which indicate this, and while it may intuitively be plausible, it is unfortunately impossible to prove it, since nobody can tell whether a stifled innovation would or would not have been successful. However, traditional market-driven new product development, based on market research and concept testing, is inevitably based on knowledge of the world existing and past, whereas innovation is concerned with the world as it may be in the future, and that is something which managers, consumers and even market researchers find difficult to predict.

Learning from Sony

The Sony Walkman is an excellent example of the way market research could potentially have stifled innovation. Initial research indicated that the majority of potential customers would feel rather foolish walking around wearing a pair of headphones, and that they certainly did not see the Walkman's ability to provide music on the move as a benefit. Once it was launched, the Walkman sold slowly at first, no doubt vindicating the market researchers who predicted its failure. In a company following the market driven approach to new product development, the Walkman would have been unlikely to have survived the business analysis phase, and even if it did, would have been pronounced a failure after test marketing. Professional market researchers should be made to learn by heart the following quote from Sony's celebrated president Akio Morita.

> Our plan is to lead the public with new products rather than ask them
> what they want. The public does not know what is possible, but we
> do. We refine our thinking on a product and its use and try to create a
> market for it by educating and communicating with the public.

Morita's words stand the market driven approach to new product
development on its head; what he advocates is indeed a far cry from
any notion of finding out what the market wants then making it.
While it may be that this fundamental challenge to the marketing
concept creates considerable ambiguity, every manager should
nevertheless take notice of the man who built Sony from a small
domestic electrical company into a world class industry leader. His
view seems to be that an important element of marketing at Sony is
to seek applications and pioneer markets for innovative new products and technologies, regardless of whether consumers say they
want them. There is considerable evidence that a technology driven
approach to new product development has indeed resulted in
spectacular breakthroughs: penicillin, the transistor, the X-ray scanner, the jet engine, the digital watch, none of these were conceived
by a marketing man who then gave a specification to R&D and told
them to invent it. We all know that mankind's major advances have
come about through the discovery of something previously inconceivable – why should marketing be different? Morita is telling us
that marketing innovation is about finding applications for dis-
coveries, not throwing them away because there is no market.

While there can be little doubt that major innovations tend to be
a result of technology push rather than market pull, this is no
reason completely to reject the role of market research in new product
development. Of course it is incumbent on managers constantly to
improve and update products to keep them in line with changing
and known customer needs. Nobody would dispute, that for this
essential task, market driven product development is a wholly valid
and necessary activity. But managers need to recognize that market
driven new product development will tend to result in incremental
improvements to current products in current markets rather than
major breakthroughs in entirely new markets.

It is unfortunate that innovation gets confused with new product
development in so many marketing books and also in companies,
because our interpretation of the new product development task is
normally the market driven approach. However, this is a fundamentally different activity to the creation of entirely new markets,
which is essentially a social process. Innovations start very small
and get bigger, and consumers who adopt an innovation later,
frequently reject it in its early days. Few respondents have the
capacity to conceptualize what they might feel once they have had

the opportunity to re-evaluate and change their existing attitudes and values. It is marketing folklore that the first ever market forecast for computers predicted world-wide sales of ten units, and that the disastrous Ford Edsel was the product of extensive market research. Unfortunately, for every anecdote which supports the argument there is another which refutes it, everyone can think of examples of technology push disasters and market pull successes.

Therefore, any proposition that innovation can be made safer, that the risks inherent in the innovation process can be reduced, by the use of market research, appears to be highly suspect. Research will be able reliably to indicate the true eventual potential of an innovation only very rarely, indeed it may actually stifle an innovation by indicating that no market exists. Under these circumstances, companies are forced to rely on the judgement of their managers rather than hoping for irrefutable data from the marketplace. All this of course merely serves even more to emphasize that innovation is a risk business, and organizations can only innovate effectively if they are prepared to make risk investments.

Organizational barriers to innovation

It is apparent that innovation is not merely a matter of inventing things, nor can we afford to rely totally on concept testing and other market research techniques: innovation is perhaps the most complex aspect of the whole field of marketing decision-making. It involves an element of insight to find market applications for new products and technology, as well as the willingness to take risks on the basis of little or no hard market data. As such, it is a concept which fits somewhat uneasily into large organizations, which sometimes appear so beset with seemingly insuperable barriers to innovation, that one might expect many corporations to be the graveyard rather than the birthplace of potential innovations. Some of the more common organizational barriers to innovation are outlined below; senior managers may recognize one of more of these barriers within their own company.

- Pressure for quick volume sales from new product launches. This encourages managers to aim innovations at the largest potential segment, rather than the segment with the highest utility value, a potentially disastrous strategic error.
- A heavy reliance on market research to minimize risk when drawing up and approving plans for new products. Market driven approaches to new product development are fine for incremental improvements in existing products and markets, but can stifle major innovations that have the potential to create new markets.

- The use of financial techniques based on risk minimization to assess projects which are inherently risky. Innovations should be seen as long term strategic investments, rather than normal participants in the competitive bidding for corporate resources. They will inevitably be squeezed out by the application of standard financial criteria.
- Failure to recognize the limits of technology. This leads to an emphasis on investment in mature technology rather than developing technology, and a tendency to invest in what has served the company well in the past, rather than what may serve it better in the future.
- Systems of rewards and promotion which encourage a custodial approach to management. Exhortations to managers to take risks will be totally ineffective if they feel their careers will suffer when the risks go wrong.
- Inflexible organization structures and financial systems. An organization which is built around existing product and functional boundaries will inhibit the fast response flexibility necessary to manage innovations effectively.

The challenge for top management

Correcting such ills will never be an easy task, but given the crucial strategic importance of innovation, it is a challenge which top management must take up. In order to build a more innovative organization, senior managers should understand and take action to implement the seven steps outlined below.

Back the judgement of your managers

Market-driven new product development systems should be used only where appropriate, that is for products where respondents can reasonably be expected to understand the benefits. Investment in products where this is not the case can only be justified on the judgement of the managers responsible.

Do not expect or permit unrealistic sales forecasts

Expectations of big sales volume early from innovative new products must be curtailed, since such products are likely to appeal initially to only small numbers of innovative customers. Acceptance of this offers a measure of risk containment, since smaller numbers of customers should involve lower initial promotional, distribution and start-up costs.

Insist on tight customer target statements

Managers need to develop an understanding of the diffusion process, and the notion that innovation is a social learning process which supplier advertising has only a limited capacity to drive. An innovative product should be targeted at the segment which needs it most, and at the innovators and early adopters within that segment, rather than the mass market.

Establish an innovation fund

Financial techniques based on risk minimization are inappropriate for the evaluation of new ideas where it is impossible to assess risk and reward adequately. These must be seen as strategic risk investments financed by a specific, designated fund, which is free of the conservative financial systems applied to more established operations.

Reduce the career implications of failure, and increase the rewards for success

Perhaps the most challenging area of all for a large bureaucratic corporation is to introduce reward systems which encourage risk taking rather than a custodial approach to managing the commercialization of new ideas. Exhortations to line managers to take risks will have little impact unless the company encourages this with the promise of real rewards for success, and reduces the career implications of failure.

Set up a system to encourage and nurture innovation

People should be encouraged to come forward with new ideas, and R&D time and funds should be made available for research initiatives which do not fit into any specific current programme. Progress of these ideas and initiatives should be monitored by a small senior group which takes a personal, regular and formal interest. Clear top level support for new ideas is needed to encourage, nurture and promote them within the company.

Promote the need for change

Every manager needs to be educated about the character of environmental change, the impact it may have on an organization, and the need for the company to adapt its strategy and structure accordingly.

Building positive attitudes to change underpins the flexibility to manage discontinuities, which is essential to effective innovation.

A perspective on innovation and marketing

The nature of innovation serves to underline the ambiguity inherent in marketing as a whole. The discussion of the role of market research in innovation seems to stand on its head the very starting point of marketing itself, customer orientation. Indeed, the second chapter of this book argues that customer orientation should be the basis for the management of the entire business, and so it should be. Unfortunately, innovation does not fit this neat model at all well, and yet surely innovation and change, and the pursuit of competitive advantage are the very essence of marketing. There is no satisfactory way to resolve this dilemma, marketing involves doing both these things, while accepting that they appear to be inherently in conflict, and based on two diametrically opposed philosophies of marketing. Regrettably this is bad news for people who like things packaged into a neat consistent paradigm against which all marketing issues can be tested and resolved. Marketing is neither solely customer orientation nor is it solely innovation, it is both of these things; managers who find it difficult to live with such ambiguity would be best advised to find a job in a company where it is believed that innovation does not matter.

Of course, the two philosophies are not really in conflict. Customer orientation is indivisible from competitive advantage, and innovation of some kind is invariably critical to building long term differential advantage: the only way to create a new market is to do something new; the only way to create a differential advantage is to do something different. Innovations have the ability to create entirely new markets, or bring about substantial shifts in the balance of power in existing ones. The adjustments which need to be made in order to encourage innovation in large companies may break some of the established rules of corporate life. They will require changes both to corporate systems and structures and to the psychological approach of many managers to R&D, financial control, and product launches. However, without such changes, potential innovations will continue to be squeezed out by the system, which will thus deny the company the most effective means of survival and growth in a changing environment.

5   Focusing company resources

When asked what they understand by the term business strategy, managers often respond with statements like 'a company's strategy is its overall top-level business plan', or 'objectives are what you want to achieve, strategy is how you achieve it'. While both of these may be true, they do not give much insight into the real challenges of strategic thinking. For example, a military commander's objective is to win the war, his strategy is his overall battle plan to achieve this; that is undeniable, but it misses the point of how the battle plan is drawn up. The essence of the challenge for a professional commander is to decide how he deploys the men and equipment at his disposal. The factors that will influence this decision are the capability of his own forces, the capability and disposition of the enemy's forces, and the terrain of the battlefield. Using all this information, the commander's task is to deploy his resources in the most effective manner.

This analogy illustrates that the essence of strategy is the effective deployment of resources. All businesses, whatever their size, have finite levels of resource, in other words there are resource limitations in every business. Since resources are scarce, it makes sense to allocate them to the projects where they can be used most effectively, rather than spread them thinly, a little everywhere. The principle of concentrating resources onto the best opportunities was discussed in Chapter 3, and is a key underlying principle in the concept of market focus. Concentration of resources is perhaps the most difficult aspect of the market focus process to implement, because allocating resources disproportionately to one project implies denying them to another, something which quickly tends to become personal to the managers involved. Thus, resource allocation has a human dimension as well as the strategic planning aspect. These twin strands were well summed up by GE president Jack Welch:

> It takes courage and tough-mindedness to pick the best, put the resources behind them, articulate the vision to the employees, and explain why you said yes to this one and no to that one.

Jack Welch's words encapsulate what this chapter is all about. Strategic thinking involves identifying the best investment opportunities, focusing the company's resources behind them, shaping the long term vision, and securing the full-hearted commitment of the managers involved. During the last twenty years many concepts and techniques have been advanced to help managers carry out these tasks more effectively, and the more important of these will be reviewed here. However, it should be borne in mind throughout, that the fundamental purpose of all strategic models is to assist strategic thinking, and thus help managers make more rational decisions about the allocation of scarce resources. Unless they do this, then strategic concepts, however academically elegant, are useless to practical managers.

Foundations of strategic thinking

Benefits of a high market share

Many companies rightly feel that market share is important, and the reasons for this are not difficult to see. The market leader has higher volume than its competitors, and all other things being equal, should be able to achieve the lowest costs through greater economies of scale and superior bargaining power with suppliers. In addition, market leaders, because of their perceived credibility in the eyes of the customer, can often achieve higher prices. This combination of low costs and high prices tends to give the leader the highest margins in the industry, which, combined with the highest sales inherent in a leadership position, produces the highest profits. Thus, according to the theory, it is intuitively reasonable to conclude that market leadership produces the highest industry profits.

This does indeed seem to be true in many cases, indeed, it was demonstrated empirically by the famous Profit Impact of Market Strategy (PIMS) research project in the USA. This showed that there is a statistically significant positive correlation between return on investment and market share (see Figure 5.1). Of course, the diagram shows only a statistically fitted trend line; very few data points would have fallen exactly on the line, indeed some would have been well away from it. This means that although the relationship between market share and profitability generally holds true, it is perfectly possible for companies with a high share to make low profits or for companies with a low share to make high profits. Nevertheless, most will follow the statistical trend.

More recent research indicates that in many industries, the more important factor is high segment share, rather than high share of an overall generic market. This is becoming increasingly true as what

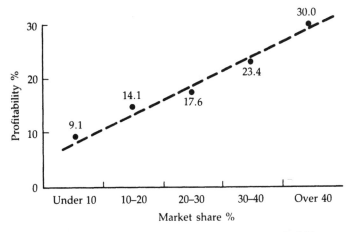

Figure 5.1 *Relationship between market share and profitability*

were once mass markets become fragmented and segmented under the impact of new technology and diverging customer needs. Indeed, generic market leaders in such fragmenting markets can become vulnerable to specialist segment leaders gradually nibbling away at the market, increasing their own segment size at the expense of the mass market. One commentator described General Motors (GM) in the 1980s as being 'nibbled to death' by the specialists of the motor industry such as BMW and Toyota, as they chipped one segment after another away from the industry leader's market. Holding a dominant share leadership of the US car market seems to have done nothing for GM's profitability: in 1993, GM announced the biggest ever annual loss by any commercial corporation. This incident alone does not invalidate the theoretical profit/share relationship, but it does mean that it requires some sophisticated interpretation; it is certainly not a matter of assuming a simple linear correlation. Increasingly it will become necessary for companies to have a view about clearly defined market segment sizes and shares rather than the more vague product related criteria that used to suffice; market definitions need to be customer rather than product oriented in order to form a useful basis for strategic thinking.

Having said that, there is still room in many industries for a large scale overall market leader as well as a range of more specialist segment leaders, either approach can lead to competitive success. However, the companies which get squeezed are those which are

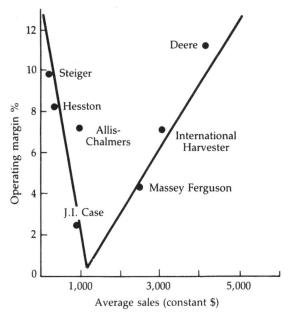

Figure 5.2 *The farm equipment industry*

not large enough to gain sufficient economies of scale to compete effectively across the board, but are too large to be able to be sufficiently focused to achieve specialist segment leadership. A study of the US farm equipment industry in the late 1970s, shown in Figure 5.2, illustrates this point. John Deere is the world's largest farm equipment manufacturer, and as overall market leader is in a strong and profitable position. International Harvester is in a less good but still tenable position. Steiger and Hesston, while very much smaller, are nevertheless making high margins owing to their leadership of specialist segments. The vulnerable players are Massey Ferguson and Case, who are too large to be able to rely on specialization, and too small to be effective in the mass market. Subsequent events in the industry have vindicated the findings of the study, with a wave of mergers and failures among the medium-sized manufacturers during the 1980s.

Challenging the market leader

Thus, market share is a key element in strategic thinking, because a high share is, both intuitively and empirically, good for profits. This applies particularly to segment leadership, but also applies to overall leadership, unless it is a market which is rapidly fragmenting and a generic leadership position is becoming increasingly untenable. While all this seems eminently reasonable, the real question is how does a firm achieve a high market share in practice?

The most obvious way to achieve a high share is to attack the existing leader. Unfortunately, this is rarely likely to lead to success, since leaders have high profits with which to defend themselves, and are far more likely to survive a war of attrition than an attacker with fewer resources. The military historian Von Clausewitz studied a number of battles where one side had a very well-defended position under attack by their opponents. He found that in the vast majority of cases, the attackers needed overwhelming numerical superiority in order to achieve victory. This led to one of his principles of warfare, 'superiority of defence'. He advised commanders not to attack well-defended 'citadels' unless they possessed enormously superior resources, and were prepared to sacrifice significant numbers of them in the attack. Another of his principles was 'concentration of force', the underlying basis of the whole idea of resource allocation.

Nevertheless, there are some circumstances when it can make sense to attack the market leader. Clearly, if the leader is weak, passive, or slow to respond, it will improve the chances of success. Perhaps the leader can be attacked in a specialist segment, like the 'nibble' strategy referred to above. As we saw in the last chapter, the most effective way to attack an incumbent leader is through innovation, since technological discontinuity can turn leaders into losers. All of these potential competitive strategies, and others, will be discussed in greater depth in the next chapter, but suffice it to say here, that unless there are special circumstances, a head-on attack on an established market leader is likely to be at best unrewarding, and at worst suicidal. The moral is that if you are faced with a citadel, think twice before attacking it.

Pioneering for market leadership

It seems apparent that a head-on attack on the incumbent market leader is rarely a sensible route to leadership. The alternative to challenging in existing markets is of course to seek leadership in new markets, and sustain this as they grow. In order to understand the implications of this as a strategy to achieve long term leadership, it is worthwhile spending some time considering the economic position of various companies entering a given new market at different times. The cost position of each contestant in a developing market is in part due to the cumulative experience they have gained since entering that market: as a company gains experience in a particular business, its costs should fall. This effect is called the experience curve, and is analogous to the learning curve familiar to production engineers, which is based on the principle that for a given product, up to a certain point manufacturing costs will fall as manufacturing experience increases, owing to the cumulative benefits of learning from experience.

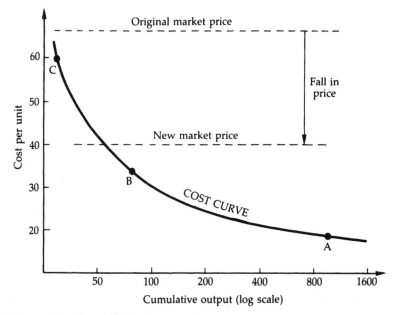

Figure 5.3 *The experience curve*

Figure 5.3 shows the relative cost positions of contestants at different points on the experience curve in a hypothetical developing market. Company A entered the market first, and hence has the most experience and the lowest costs; companies B and C entered later, and thus have less experience and higher costs. While the market price is at a high level, all contestants can survive, but if the market price falls, B and C will be squeezed, while A will still be able to operate profitably. This means that late entrants to a market are under constant cost pressures compared to early entrants, particularly if prices fall as the market expands.

The experience curve is a controversial theory, for while it does seem to apply in certain high technology manufacturing industries, the application of research studies based on these industries to all companies, regardless of the industry they are in, is not valid. As far as the detractors are concerned this is enough to undermine the whole idea. However, there is a second curve in operation as well, which could be referred to as the 'market franchise' curve (see Figure 5.4). The company with the most experience will have had a longer time to build up its brand reputation among customers and improve its access to distribution channels, as well as gaining more insight into product applications and problems in the marketplace. This company would thus be in the strongest position to secure customer trust and loyalty. In addition, and crucially, the first entrant has the best opportunity to take a clear-cut market position, to take up territory in the market which is then easier to deny to the followers. Thus, company A potentially has both the lowest costs and the highest market franchise, and this puts it in a very powerful competitive position.

As a growing market takes off, many entrants will be attracted by the prospect of fast growth. However, as the market starts to approach

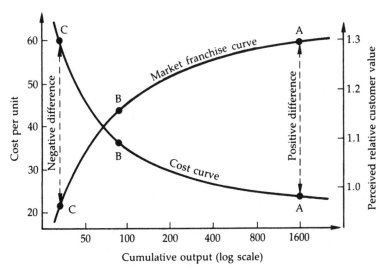

Figure 5.4 *The market franchise curve*

maturity, and growth slows down, the leader will seek to continue its own growth, and with the market's own growth rate slowing, the only way to achieve this is by increasing market share at the expense of the followers. This will put pressure on the weaker followers, and eventually drive them into unprofitability. This process is known as the 'shakeout', and has been observed in industry after industry as the early growth market enters maturity, and companies lacking a defensible market position get squeezed. The operation of the shakeout is the reason why mature markets tend to be dominated by a few well-entrenched large companies, their weaker brethren having been squeezed out long ago. By contrast, growth markets can often sustain large numbers of contestants, all of whom can survive in the buoyant market environment.

Surviving the shakeout is thus key to attaining a large share of the subsequent market, and those who do survive it tend to be those which were strongest before it began. The strongest of all has the best chance of becoming market leader, and enjoying the profitability that leadership often brings. A pioneering early entry is often critical to being strongest at the shakeout. The reason lies partly in the potential cost benefits of the experience curve, but probably more significant is the fact that early entrants have the best opportunity to develop customer awareness and access to distribution, and thus establish a defensible position in the market. It is this combination of the cost and market position effects of experience that give early entrants their advantage.

Of course, this does not mean that it is impossible for late entrants to catch up, or for early entrants to squander their lead, but all things being equal, the early entrant is best placed to stay ahead. Indeed, aficionados of strategic games such as chess or go, will confirm that given players of equal ability, these games are often won or lost in the first few moves: so it is in an emerging market. Thus, the theory says, market leadership is achieved by pioneering new growth markets, aggressively staying ahead while the market grows, then surviving the shakeout to emerge ultimately as leader.

Do pioneers win leadership?

All this may sound eminently reasonable in theory but it overlooks a number of important problems. Firstly, the pioneer is most likely to hit unanticipated problems or make mistakes, always a risk of pioneering. It overlooks the fact that followers may be able to catch up by acquiring, buying or licensing experience from elsewhere, or merely by hiring key personnel from the pioneer. It may be particu-

larly easy for followers to catch up where they have relevant experience in different products which allows them to short-circuit the
pioneer's experience gathering process. Followers can also bypass
the leader by a leapfrog into a new segment, while the leader is still
concentrating on the original segment. Even in high technology
markets, the experience curve does not always work: it is well
known that IBM entered the market for personal computers very
late, but by taking advantage of several of the catch up routes
outlined above, was able to establish market leadership in a very
short time.

Given the number of processes whereby later entrants can overhaul
the original pioneer, and the fact that even in high technology
businesses, the whole concept can be stood on its head, one might
think it extraordinary that the experience curve could ever have
been thought to play such a key role in strategic marketing thinking.
In spite of its theoretical attractiveness, surely there are just too
many exceptions to the rule for it to work reliably in practice. The
major implication of the experience curve concept is that early entry
into new growth markets is essential to achieving leadership when
the market matures. However, if the concept itself is suspect, then
so is the conclusion. We need to test just how valid is the simplistic
assertion that early entry into growth markets is essential to achieving
market leadership.

Average market shares at maturity	Consumer products	Industrial products
Pioneers	29%	29%
Early followers	17%	21%
Late entrants	13%	15%

Figure 5.5 *Market shares achieved by pioneers and followers*

Fortunately, research into this issue has recently been published,
and it shows us that, for all its warts, the experience curve may have
some validity, or at least that the value of an early market entry has
validity. Robinson and Fornell have shown that in both industrial
and consumer goods markets, pioneers ended up with, on average,
double the share at maturity of late entrants (see Figure 5.5). Even
this work is scarcely conclusive, because it shows us the pioneers
which succeeded, and thus obscures the high failure rate of those
which did not. It overlooks the fact that to make a late entry may be
a lower risk venture, and to end up with a small share obtained on a
low risk basis may be preferable to a high share obtained on a high
risk basis. But the central finding is clear: pioneers, on average, end

up with the highest shares of mature markets. From a practical decision-making viewpoint, this is highly significant, although managers should remember that being the first into a marketplace does not guarantee an easy path to ultimate leadership, equally, being a follower does not deny the chance of ultimate leadership. The experience curve and the market franchise curve work better in some markets than others, and followers always have the opportunity to catch up, particularly if they are large well-resourced organizations in analogous businesses.

It is clear that pioneering innovators do not always necessarily become industry leaders. However, companies whose style is to wait and see should be aware that it may not be sufficient to sit on the sidelines until a clear growth market is emerging and then hope to jump on board. Of course, early entrants have to be prepared to take risks, to enter markets whose potential is unproven and whose parameters are unknown. But the risk takers are those who stand the best chance of establishing that crucial early lead; by then, it may be too late for the others to catch up. This sums up the challenge of innovation to the large corporation: the new opportunity in an unknown market may seem a low priority now, but it may be the only way to get in a position to be a major market leader in five or ten years time. By contrast, if management is too cautious and waits for a sight of a clear market before moving, it may pass up that opportunity for ever.

Impact of growth on cash flow

So far we have established two key principles of strategic thinking. The first is that a high segment share lays the foundation for high profitability. The second is that the most positive route to achieving a high share is to make an early entry when the market is in its embryonic stage, then aggressively maintain a dominant lead as the market grows, so as to be the strongest player at the shakeout. This is why the two key parameters in classic strategic business thinking are the rate of market growth and relative market share. However, before examining how these two parameters are modelled to provide a framework for decision-making, it is necessary to understand the implications of differing business growth rates for cash flow.

Accountants have succeeded in surrounding cash flow with a mystique and complexity that it does not deserve. Consequently, some non-financial managers seem to have little real understanding of this fundamental area of management knowledge which, when stripped of the mystique is relatively easy to understand. What makes formal cash flow calculations seem so complex is the non-operating items such as depreciation and deferred tax, but if we think of cash flow in terms of 'real money', it becomes much simpler. Companies can get money from a variety of sources, for example they can sell equity (shares) to new or existing shareholders, or they can borrow. These are both obvious sources of cash which can be used to invest in the business. For each there will be a balancing cash outflow, dividends paid to shareholders and interest paid to lenders is cash flowing out of the company.

Money flowing in from, or flowing out to, external parties is easy enough to visualize as cash flow. However, it is the operational cash flows which are particularly significant from a strategic perspective. Buying assets such as plant and equipment is an obvious way of using cash, equally, selling such assets is a potential source of cash. Increasing working capital (stocks and debtors) obviously absorbs cash, whereas cutting working capital releases it. When a company makes sales revenues, what is left over after deducting costs is profit, and this is a further source of cash. Of course, if costs are higher than revenues a loss results, and this absorbs cash from the company's resources if the business is to be sustained. These positive and negative sources of cash are summarized in Figure 5.6, however, the strategic significance of cash flow becomes clear when one examines the impact of whether a business is growing, mature or declining upon its cash flow position.

Sources of cash	Uses of Cash
Profits	Losses
Decrease in working capital	Increase in working capital
Sell assets	Buy assets
Mature and declining businesses	*Growing businesses*

Figure 5.6   *Cash generators and cash consumers*

Growing businesses frequently have relatively high discretionary costs such as advertising, promotion and selling expenses, particularly in their early days, as well as high R&D expenditure. This means that costs often outstrip sales revenues in new businesses, resulting in losses. In addition, growth businesses are by definition expanding, and expansion requires a steady increase in stocks and debtors as the scale of the business increases; similarly, growing businesses normally need to invest heavily in new assets. For all these reasons, growth absorbs cash. By contrast, mature businesses should be profitable, because discretionary expenditure and R&D costs should be relatively lower, compared to sales revenue. In addition, a mature business is by definition not expanding; hence there will be no need to increase stocks and debtors, while asset purchases will be restricted to replacements. Therefore, mature businesses should generate cash from their profits, without requiring excessive amounts of cash to finance expansion, and should thus be cash positive.

In the case of a declining business, stock and debtor levels can gradually be reduced as part of a managed decline, and perhaps assets can gradually be sold as well, these two effects generating cash. Understanding the innovation process tells us that declining businesses will be selling mainly to laggards. Such customers tend to be extremely loyal to the traditional product they know and trust, and can thus be retained by the supplier, albeit in declining numbers, with relatively low levels of discretionary expenditure. Depending on the level of their loyalty, it may even be possible to increase prices to such customers. These two effects serve to make declining businesses potentially relatively profitable, and this, added to the cash liberated by the decline in working capital and fixed assets, means that declining businesses are capable of generating significant cash flows. Of course, the business has to be managed purposively to generate cash, it is entirely possible for declining businesses to spend all the cash they generate, indeed, this frequently happens in companies which lack strategic vision. These effects are summarized at the foot of Figure 5.6.

Establishing strategic priorities

Clear strategic priorities emerge from an understanding of the impact of growth upon cash flow. Managers of growing businesses should manage for growth, and this requires cash to be invested. If cash inflows are restricted, it will limit the ability of the business to grow, and may leave the door open for a follower. This does not mean that growth businesses can never generate cash, they can, particularly further up the growth cycle, when sales and profits are higher. However, this does not subvert the logic that the primary objective should be growth in volume, and that to set onerous profit or cash flow targets will restrict the ability of the business to grow and may endanger its market position. Managers of mature businesses should manage for profit, because profit is the primary source of cash flow in mature businesses. However, a mature business may be expected to continue for some time into the future, and it makes sense to invest moderately to defend its competitive position. Therefore, profit should only be pursued consistent with maintaining the product's position in the market. Managers of declining businesses should manage purposively for cash flow, generated partly from profits and partly from a managed decline in the scale of operations.

The implications for senior managers responsible for a group of products or businesses are clear. Assuming that some products are growing, some mature and some declining, the strategically minded manager should organize a steady shift of both cash and human resources out of the mature and declining products, into the growing products. This resource allocation task is shown diagrammatically in Figure 5.7, in simple product life-cycle terms, although more structured models to help do this in practice are discussed in the next section. Of course, these overall strategic priorities are still open to interpretation when they come to be implemented, and this all important question is the subject of the next chapter. But no effective plan for implementation can be drawn up until what we are trying to achieve in terms of resource flows has been determined. What we are concerned with in this chapter is establishing strategic priorities about the allocation of company resources. Failure to do this will restrict the potential of the growth products, and may mean excessive amounts of resource being allocated to mature and declining products. However, it is not easy to achieve, since it means denying resources to one manager or project, in order to allocate them to another. The strategic marketing planning models which follow have been evolved to help managers come to more rational decisions about this critical process.

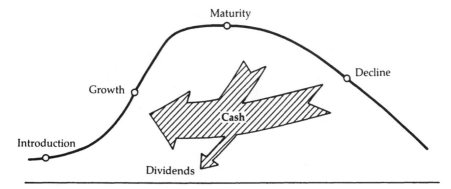

Figure 5.7 *Managing cash flows in the product life-cycle*

Product portfolio analysis

The Boston Consulting Group product portfolio matrix

The last section established that in theory, the two most important factors in strategic decision making are the rate of market growth and a company's relative market share. The original, and still the best known system of portfolio analysis was devised by the Boston Consulting· Group (BCG), and utilizes just these two parameters (see Figure 5.8). This model is sometimes known as the growth/ share matrix, the Boston matrix, or more correctly as the BCG product portfolio matrix. It shows in a very appealing and easily understood way, the strategies that should be pursued, and the ensuing implications for cash flow, for products and businesses with different

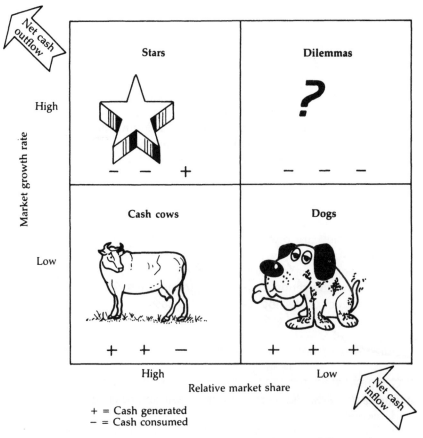

+ = Cash generated
− = Cash consumed

Figure 5.8   *The Boston Consulting Group product portfolio matrix*

market positions. The fact that it was all based on impeccable economic logic, and the memorable names which BCG allocated to each quadrant added to its appeal in its early days, and the system became widely publicized during the 1970s.

In Figure 5.8, plus and minus signs are used to indicate in simple terms the cash flow implications of having a product in each of the four quadrants of the matrix. The leading product in a high growth market (top left quadrant), is indeed in an enviable position, and BCG called these products 'rising stars', now normally abbreviated to 'stars'. These should be given the cash they need to continue growth and sustain their leadership, thus a star will predominantly be a cash user. However, its leading market position should also enable it to generate some cash, indeed, stars can become net cash generators when higher up their growh curve. By contrast, a product with a low share of a high growth market (top right quadrant) is in a weaker follower position, albeit in an attractive growth market. These are quite literally 'dilemmas', since considerable amounts of cash will be required to catch up with the leader, and in addition, the low sales and weak market position will yield lower profits. It should be noted that dilemmas have also been variously referred to as 'question marks', 'problem children' and 'wildcats'.

The leading product in a mature market (bottom left quadrant), should generate a strong positive cash flow, owing to the high profits which should result from its leadership position. However, if that position is to be maintained, a certain amount of resource will need to be re-invested to defend the product from the inevitable attacks of challengers. The BCG matrix implies that a follower in a mature market (bottom right quadrant) is strategically in an unenviable position, since it offers neither growth nor market share. These were designated as 'dogs', although contrary to this somewhat unfair title, they are often capable of generating considerable cash flow. This is particularly true if they are managed purposively for cash by adopting a strategy of managed decline, owing to the relatively low discretionary expenses required to do this, and the fact that the act of decline itself releases cash.

Applications of portfolio analysis

BCG argued that just two parameters, share and growth, were all that was necessary to carry out the basic analysis of a product's fundamental strategic position. Once products or businesses had been allocated to a quadrant of the matrix, major strategic decisions could easily be reached. The first of these is how each product or business is to be managed, in overall terms, in other words what strategic priority should be set. The three basic strategic objectives (i.e. resource allocation objectives) are set out in Figure 5.9. A strategy of 'build' is suitable for a star, and implies investing cash to expand the business. A strategy of 'maintain' is suitable for a cash cow and implies managing for profit to generate cash flow, but only so far as this is consistent with maintaining one's market position. A strategy of 'harvest' means a managed decline aimed at generating cash, and is suitable for a dog. Any one of the three strategies may be suitable for a dilemma, depending on the circumstances.

> 1 *Resource allocation to each product/business unit*
>
> **Build**
> Manage for growth
>
> **Maintain**
> Manage for profit consistent with maintaining market position
>
> **Harvest**
> Manage for cash flow
>
> 2 *Build a balanced portfolio*
>
> **Too many stars**
> Run out of cash
>
> **Too many cash cows**
> Low growth and long term decline

Figure 5.9 *Applications of portfolio techniques*

Build, maintain and harvest are the three basic strategic objectives which can be set for any product, and they are mutually exclusive. Without knowing which of them to pursue, a manager is forced into making impossible compromises. To try simultaneously to maximize market share, cash flow, profits, and sales, while trying to minimize working capital and selling expenses is clearly utterly impossible. Expecting operating managers simultaneously to achieve several objectives which are completely in conflict with each other could scarcely be called an effective management style, but that is the nature of the task which managers are frequently set in real life. The way to avoid such conflicting objectives is to ensure that one of the three strategic objectives is explicitly nominated as the priority. Therefore, the first application of portfolio analysis to enable us to determine clear strategic priorities, from which all other business management decisions flow.

The second application is that it enables us to build a balanced portfolio. After all, while stars are highly desirable, if a company has too many stars it will be unable to finance them and either run out of cash, or be unable to support any of them properly. And while cash cows are desirable in that they generate cash, unless a company has some high growth products it will have no long term future. Inevitably, every company is likely to have some dog products and arguably will need some as a source of strong positive cash flow; equally every innovative organization will also have a few high risk dilemmas. Thus, the ideal portfolio is one which is balanced, with products in all four quadrants, rather than being weighted towards any one of them.

The need for a balanced portfolio indicates that product portfolio techniques offer a mechanism with which to achieve a balanced cash budget. Cash inflows and outflows must by definition balance, and the product portfolio is a means of achieving an equalization of cash positive and cash negative projects at a key point in a company's planning cycle. The fact that the product portfolio is essentially a cash flow management tool is emphasized on Figure 5.8 by the two arrows indicating 'net cash inflow' and 'net cash outflow'. These imply that if net cash is flowing out of the system in the form of dividends to the shareholders or remittances to corporate head office for example, then the matrix itself must carry more minus signs. By contrast, if net cash is flowing in, either from existing investors or new borrowing, then the matrix can carry more plus signs. The ability to use the product portfolio as the company's basic cash management tool is highly significant, because it unites the financial and strategic management of the business in a common framework. The contrast between the traditional approach to cash budgeting and the strategic approach outlined here will be discussed in detail in Chapter 7.

Problems with the BCG matrix

It seems almost too good to be true that two parameters alone encompass everything that needs to be taken into account in resolving the complex issues underlying resource allocation. Indeed, it is inconceivable that in the real world, other factors do not need to be taken into account. Despite the fact that the underlying theory of market share and the experience curve is intuitively highly appealing, the BCG matrix takes no account of key parameters like the level of competition, or a company's technical strength. The simple two dimensional analysis involved in the BCG matrix is its major strength, because it is both easy to understand and relatively measurable. Unfortunately, this simplicity is also its undoing, because despite the attractiveness of the logic, it is just too simplistic to be an accurate reflection of a complex real world. This was recognized early on as a major defect of the BCG matrix, and other approaches to product portfolio analysis were subsequently evolved which tried to overcome this objection by adopting a multi-factor analysis technique.

Nevertheless, some problems are common to all forms of product portfolio analysis, including the multi-factor approaches. For example, it is frequently difficult to define market boundaries precisely in any portfolio system. Should, say, a brand of whisky be treated as a contender in the market for all alcoholic drinks, all spirits, all whisky, all Scotch whisky, or some particular specialist area of the market such as malt whisky? Depending on the definitions adopted, the same product can appear as a star if its market is defined very narrowly, or a dog if it is defined very widely. The only impartial way to define a market is by examining the customers or potential customers who make up the target segment. This fits well with the notion that segment market share is strategically highly significant. Thus, the target segment should be clearly specified before market boundaries are defined and performance compared with competitors. In general, finely drawn definitions are preferable to widely drawn ones as the basic unit of analysis. A coherent set of these product/segment units may then be grouped together to form a larger unit of analysis. In this way, portfolio analysis may be carried out at two or three levels in the company, ending up with the principal operating business units.

Another problem common to all portfolio systems is that of shared overheads and facilities. Frequently, particularly within sets of grouped product/segment units, products are so interdependent that even if it makes theoretical sense to harvest and terminate a particular product, it makes no practical sense if there is nothing else to put in its place, resulting in factory capacity lying idle, and overhead staff such as the sales force being under-utilized. This is made even worse if the accountants then re-allocate the under-recovered overheads to the remaining products which are then all made to appear less profitable. We have to accept that in practice, sometimes things have to be kept going until a better replacement can be found or capacity can be scaled down. This does not subvert the logic of carrying out the analysis process, because it is still necessary to indicate where new investment resources should be focused, and identify the areas of the business where it should be desirable to find replacement activities.

One of the most significant potential problems is that a portfolio analysis exercise inevitably results in apparently logical yet superficially simplistic conclusions for product strategy. While it is undeniable that the three strategic options are build, maintain or harvest, nominating an option is of limited value unless there is also a clear understanding of how it is to be implemented in practice. A portfolio matrix gives no clue about this, it can only indicate the most appropriate broad option. It is also worth remembering that no product portfolio analysis technique should be seen as a closed system in terms of resource flows. Resources can flow into the system from investors as well as out of the system back to investors, and the cash budget has to balance after taking these external inflows and outflows into account, the portfolio does not necessarily have to balance itself as an entity.

It is essential to understand these issues, and to use product portfolio analysis in an informed way, being aware of its limitations, rather than seeing it as a mechanistic way of reaching cast iron decisions. However, to abandon any attempt to use product portfolio ideas because of these difficulties, as some prominent academics have suggested, is surely to throw the baby out with the bath water. Strategy is essentially about the allocation of scarce resources, and without any guidelines and tools, it is far less likely that considered and rational judgements will be reached in this key management task. While it may be possible to allocate resources without the formal use of portfolio matrices, the basic underlying ideas and concepts must not be abandoned. To do this would be to act like a general telling his army to advance on all fronts simultaneously.

The directional policy matrix

The most well-known alternative portfolio management technique is the approach which has been ascribed variously to the US GE corporation, to Shell, and to McKinsey management consultants. The basis of the directional policy matrix (DPM) is that while growth and share are strategically highly important, they are not the only factors, and others must be taken into account. The additional factors to share and growth add up to an assessment of, on the one hand the overall attractiveness of the market, and on the other, the company's ability to compete effectively in that market, relative to its competitors. Market attractiveness incorporates, as well as growth rate, such variables as market size, customer trends, and intensity of competitive activity. Relative competitive capability includes, as well as market share, such parameters as manufacturing and technical capability, and access to distribution.

It is of course unrealistic to assume that one set of criteria will be

A Background

1 Definition of product/market area under review

2 Description of target customers and their key needs

3 Leading market contestants (with market shares)

1 _____

2 _____

3 _____

4 _____

5 _____

B The external environment

1 Rate of market growth – last 3 years historical
– next 3 years projected

2 Size of market (current year)

3 Intensity of competition (score H/M/L and comment)

4 Nature of competitive challenges

• Product characteristics) Identify most
) important single
• Price) focus for
) competitive
• Promotion/advertising) activity and
) comment
• Distribution methods)
)
• Other (please specify))

5 Opportunity to add value (score H/M/L and comment)

6 Impact of market/customer trends (rate favourable/neutral/unfavourable and comment)

7 Impact of legal/environmental trends (rate favourable/neutral/unfavourable and comment)

C Our competitive capability

1 Market share
• as % of total
• relative to leader or relative to no 2 if we are leader
• share relative to desirable critical mass (above/adequate/below and comment)

2 Manufacturing capability relative to competitors (score each 1–5 and comment)

3 Technical capability relative to competitors (score 1–5 and comment)

4 Management's closeness to market relative to competitors (score 1–5 and comment)

5 Cost competitiveness relative to competitors (score 1–5 and comment)

6 Distribution muscle relative to competitors (score 1–5 and comment)

Note   Rating scale for Part C, where required, is as follows:

poor	fair	good, but behind leader	equal to leader	clear leader
1	2	3	4	5

Figure 5.10 *Information requirements for strategic marketing analysis*

appropriate for all businesses, and it is first necessary to determine which are the key criteria that form the strategic parameters for the specific business being analysed. Figure 5.10 sets out the basic information requirements for strategic analysis; this is of necessity a generalized list, factors will need to be added or subtracted depending on the business being reviewed. Also, some criteria are clearly more important than others: technically, each should be allocated a weighting, the whole set adding up to a maximum potential score on each parameter out of, say, 30. Again, the weightings can be adjusted according to the priorities in the business. Finally, the results of this analysis are modelled on the nine-cell matrix shown in Figure 5.11. In the original version of the DPM, each of the cells was allocated an indication as to the appropriate strategy to be pursued.

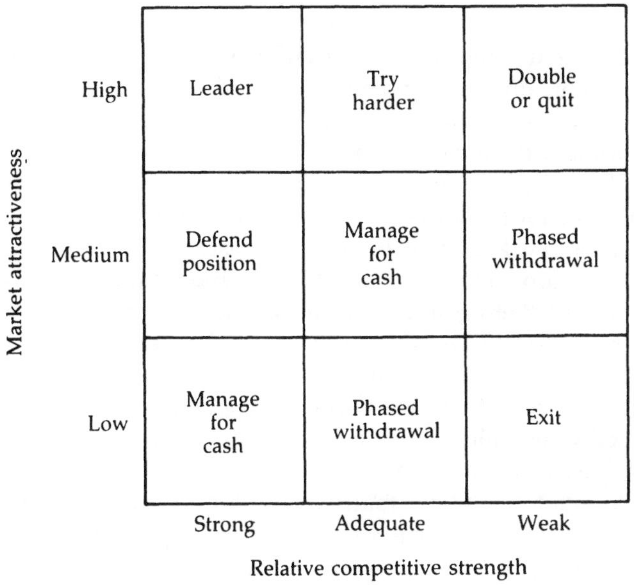

		Strong	Adequate	Weak
Market attractiveness	High	Leader	Try harder	Double or quit
	Medium	Defend position	Manage for cash	Phased withdrawal
	Low	Manage for cash	Phased withdrawal	Exit

Relative competitive strength

Figure 5.11 *The directional policy matrix*

One obvious drawback of the DPM is that it requires a great deal more data input and analysis than the simple BCG matrix. Detractors have described it as capable of inducing a 'paralysis of analysis' in its users, a process whereby the analysis itself consumes so much time and energy that little is left to implement any strategies. This is a clear danger, and it is always necessary to tread the fine line between carrying out too much detailed analysis and descending into over simplification. It can also be seen that the system as a whole is a lot more flexible than the BCG matrix, in that users can, in effect, choose their own parameters. While this is a good thing in many ways, it does mean that the DPM can be moulded to reinforce existing prejudices. Clearly also, much of the information required can never be precisely measured and quantified, it is highly judgemental. All this means that while the DPM is certainly comprehensive, it is far from a scientific management tool. Nevertheless, it does provide a focus for the management judgements that must in any event be made; it provides a common framework for management discussion; it also helps to promote a shared approach to information requirements and strategic priorities. However, it remains essentially a method of modelling a series of judgements, and its results should always be seen in that context.

The market evolution matrix

One significant objection to the DPM is that it compromises, to a certain extent, the clear link between product strategy and cash flow that is one of the major attributes of the BCG matrix. In carrying out an assessment of market attractiveness, the appeal of a multi-factor approach is that it takes a broader and more realistic view of the market's overall business potential by including a range of issues, rather than being a one-dimensional assessment based on market growth rate alone. However, whether a market is growing or declining has a very direct effect upon cash flow potential, and the introduction of other factors dilutes this linkage, to the extent that any multi-factor assessment will result in a potentially less robust cash flow management tool than the BCG matrix. The fact that strategy is concerned essentially with the allocation of resources makes this a very serious weakness indeed.

The 'market evolution matrix' (see Figure 5.12), is an attempt to overcome this criticism by comparing a product's position on its life-cycle with the company's relative competitive capability. This enables it to be used directly as a cash flow management tool as well as a basis for setting strategic objectives. However, the implication of this is that important external marketplace factors such as the intensity of competition, the impact of social and economic trends, and the size of the market do not matter in strategic decision making. As with the BCG matrix, this seems to be too unrealistic a basis on which to analyse the real world which businesses face. Therefore, while it results in unambiguous strategic objectives, and a direct link with cash flow planning, the decision to use this approach in preference to a system which involves multi-factor analysis on both axes involves accepting a significant lack of realism.

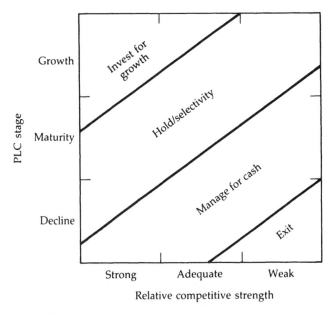

Figure 5.12 *The market evolution matrix*

The five-zone business screen

Of the portfolio analysis models reviewed so far, it is clear that the DPM is the most comprehensive. However, its very comprehensiveness undermines the direct link with cash flow and thus with resource allocation. This in turn leads to a further serious drawback, which is that the nine cell matrix does not lead directly to the ability to set strategic objectives of build, maintain or harvest. To do this is clearly desirable, as they give managers a clear and unequivocal indication of whether resources are to be consumed or generated, and thus form a basis for all subsequent management decisions. A variant of the DPM devised by this author, seeks to overcome this problem by dividing the matrix into five zones (see Figure 5.13). The 'five-zone business screen' is, like the DPM, based on an assessment of overall market attractiveness and relative competitive capability. These are determined using the list of factors for strategic analysis shown in Figure 5.10, suitably adapted to take account of any additional factors specific to the business being reviewed. Strategic objectives are then specified according to the five diagonal zones.

The Five-Zone Business Screen is a hybrid of the three systems outlined above. From the DPM it incorporates the multi factor approach to strategic analysis, while like the BCG matrix, it focuses

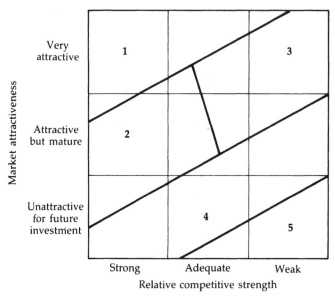

Figure 5.13 *The five-zone business screen*

on identifying clear strategic objectives. The diagonal zones in the style of the market evolution matrix are intended to make clearer the link with cash flow which the DPM obscures. This will always be difficult with any multi-factor technique, although the problem can be minimized to a certain extent by ensuring that rate of market growth accounts for at least 30% of the weighting, making it difficult for any market which is not growing to appear in zone 1. Similarly, in a declining market, there must come a time when it makes sense to start harvesting, regardless of the level of competitive strength. This is the reason why the zone lines are drawn somewhat asymmetrically. While the Five-Zone Business Screen has been found to work satisfactorily in practice, it is of course essentially a compromise. No perfect solution to the problems of portfolio analysis could ever be found.

Strategic analysis in practice

Approaches to strategic analysis

Having reviewed a selection of product portfolio analysis systems, it may be useful to step back and examine the essential similarities between these models. All approaches to strategic analysis seek to compare two basic sets of variables, internal company factors and external environmental factors. The idea of strategic analysis is to obtain the best 'fit' between these variables; in other words to identify good environmental investment opportunities, and match these to areas where the company has some special competence which will enable it to be more successful than its competitors. This will also indicate other areas where the environment is attractive but the organization needs to improve its skills in order to compete more effectively.

Figure 5.14 shows how each of the various models deals with these internal and external factors. The simplest and most traditional approach is SWOT analysis, where a list of opportunities and threats measure external environmental factors, while a list of strengths and weaknesses measure internal company factors. In the BCG matrix, market growth is used as a surrogate for all the external factors,

	Internal Factors	*External Factors*
SWOT analysis	Strengths Weaknesses	Opportunities Threats
BCG product portfolio matrix	Relative market share	Rate of market growth
Market evolution matrix	Relative competitive strength	Stage in product life cycle
Directional policy matrix and five zone business screen	Relative competitive strength	Overall market attractiveness

Figure 5.14 *Approaches to strategic analysis*

while market share is used as a surrogate for the various internal factors. In the DPM, and the Five-Zone Business Screen, the two parameters are overall market attractiveness and relative competitive capability. However, although the definitions of the two axes are different, all systems of strategic analysis have the same basic purpose, to achieve strategic fit between the company and its environment.

It is necessary to appreciate the fundamental similarity of these systems, and understand what they are all trying to achieve, in order to be in a better informed position to select the most suitable approach for a particular organization. SWOT analysis is certainly simple to carry out, but while there is nothing wrong with it conceptually, in practice it often results in long SWOT lists with no clear action oriented outcome. The genius of the product portfolio concept is that SWOT type issues are modelled onto a matrix framework, and this gives easily understood visual comparisons between the relative positions of rival investment opportunities, and thus provides a clear focus for management discussion and decision making. However, there is no reason why SWOT analysis should not be used as a basic input to building a portfolio if a management team feels particularly comfortable with this approach, after all, the issues are essentially the same.

Benefits of portfolio analysis

Strategic analysis is a very time consuming activity for any management team to undertake in a responsible manner. In the light of this, it is worthwhile summarizing the benefits which should accrue. Most fundamental of all, is that a strategic analysis exercise should enable the company to determine clear and unambiguous priorities to guide the subsequent management of each product in its range. It is impossible simultaneously to maximize growth, market share, profits, and cash flow, and unless operating managers know clearly what they are trying to achieve, they can never devise a focused marketing plan. Thus, to be of serious practical use, a strategic analysis system must lead to the definition of clear product line strategic objectives. However, it can also be used to communicate a vision of the future. A plan of the product portfolio three years hence can be superimposed on the current picture to indicate planned movements across the screen for various products. The use of circles proportional to sales volume shows which products are projected to grow or decline, and further adds to the visual impact.

A portfolio planning exercise should also assist the financial management of the company, as well as its product strategy. The company's cash budget must balance, and the product portfolio is the most logical place in the planning cycle to carry out this exercise. The only alternative is to make arbitrary adjustments to individual operating budgets, a process which is sure to undermine any attempt to devise customer oriented, focused marketing plans. In addition, a strategic analysis exercise should highlight the company's best areas of investment opportunity: the highest return on each incremental unit of investment should come from areas where the organization's capabilities most closely match the opportunities offered by the environment. In examining these potential investment areas, it is important to evaluate whether the company has sufficient resource to create leverage, or whether, given the scale of the investment required, it would always struggle to achieve critical mass. If this is the case, then an alternative strategy should be sought in an area where it is possible to create leverage.

The human resources aspect of strategic analysis and portfolio planning tends to be little discussed in text books, but paradoxically, is highly significant. Product portfolio analysis encourages, indeed demands, an information exchange between managers responsible for different areas of the business. This promotes understanding about otherwise remote functions and markets, which can only enhance the cohesiveness of the organization as a whole, as well as providing a forum for the exchange of information and ideas. In addition, it ensures that strategic assessments are made on the basis of at least some structured information rather than guesswork and hunch. The need to justify and explain this information to others creates an incentive to be as accurate and consistent as possible. Most importantly, the construction of a product portfolio by a team of managers promotes mutual understanding of why resources need to be allocated to one area and correspondingly denied to another. While this alone will never overcome the basic motivation of self-interest, it does promote a realization of the importance of teamwork to the achievement of market focus, rather than a culture where individuals seek to maximize the amount of corporate resource they can grab for their own product, regardless of its strategic role.

Finally, it is clear that different managers have different personal strengths and operating preferences. Some people are stimulated by the challenge of a project which requires entrepreneurial skills, whereas others will perform better where the business requires a more cautious custodial role. Indeed, an entrepreneurial manager could easily become frustrated with a custodial role, and compromise the business by taking unwarranted risks. Thus, an additional benefit of determining clear product line strategic objectives, is that managers can be assigned to products on the basis of their individual abilities as either entrepreneurial or custodial managers. The benefits which can accrue for the management of human resources from a continuing commitment to strategic marketing planning are often overlooked. However, not only does a structured approach to strategic analysis assist the company's financial and strategic decision making, it can also have a positive and constructive human dimension.

Selection of a portfolio system

Given that all product portfolio systems are addressing the same essential issue, the 'fit' between external and internal factors, selection of one particular system over the others becomes a matter of weighing the pros and cons. The benefits and drawbacks of the various models of portfolio analysis discussed in previous sections may leave managers a little confused in an attempt to decide which system is the best to use in their own organization. Each portfolio model has positive and negative aspects, is stronger on some points than others, and each is something of a compromise; thus, it is impossible to nominate a single 'best-buy'. The framework for strategic marketing planning outlined in the next two chapters is based on the Five-Zone Business Screen, although this does not imply that the other models could not be substituted. Indeed, one is bound to say that whichever system is used in practice, the conclusions tend to come out looking rather similar.

It must also be acknowledged that the outcome of a portfolio planning exercise can be achieved without using a formal portfolio model at all, provided a structured collective thought process leads to the determination of strategic objectives, and a balance between cash consumers and cash generators. A portfolio system is a useful focus for the exercise, but it is by no means indispensable. Even good old fashioned SWOT analysis is a perfectly sound approach, provided it results in clear strategic objectives and resource allocation guidelines through a process of management discussion. It is important to avoid getting sidetracked by the models themselves; it is the quality of the outcome which matters, not the technique itself. Strategic thinking is not fundamentally about models, it is about the allocation of scarce resources, and the concentration of sufficient resources into the best investment opportunities to create effective leverage, rather than spreading them thinly. Any organization which wishes to achieve market focus must accept that strategic allocation of resources and market focus are indivisible, regardless of the techniques used to reach the decision.

6 Competitive marketing strategies

Strategic analysis is all about comparing a company's ability to compete effectively in a given market, with the inherent level of attractiveness offered by that market. The outcome is an insight into the best marketing investment opportunities facing the business, enabling prioritization to take place and resources to be focused on the opportunities offering the best chance of reward. Various analytical techniques to assist this were discussed in the last chapter, but while the techniques may seem somewhat complex, the conclusions appear disarmingly simple. Regardless of which approach is used, the fundamental outcome of a strategic analysis exercise is to allocate product/market units to one of three basic categories. These will shape all future management decisions about that unit, as follows:

- *Build*: Manage for growth
- *Maintain*: Manage for profit, consistent with maintaining market position
- *Harvest*: Manage for cash flow

For some product/market units the decision is very clear, a leader in a growth market should be built; a leader in a mature market whose share has reached its optimum level should be maintained; for most declining products, harvesting is appropriate. However, there will always be a number of units in any business for which the decision is not clear, those where the market is relatively attractive but the company's competitive position is relatively weak. The terminology applied to this situation by strategic theorists underlines the uncertainty: 'dilemmas', 'problem children', 'double or quit' and 'the question zone' are hardly terms which indicate clear and unequivocal decision-making. Indeed, it may be appropriate either to build, maintain or harvest in this category, strategic analysis techniques alone cannot give a clear direction. A major part of this chapter will address the resolution of the dilemmas of the question zone.

A second major problem with strategic analysis arises precisely because the outcomes appear to be disarmingly simple. The three categories above undoubtedly set a clear strategic objective for each product and a framework for subsequent management actions.

However, on their own they are somewhat empty statements of intent; while they may be easy to comprehend, they do not constitute an actionable marketing plan. One of the primary criticisms levelled against strategic theorists is that while their models may be interesting and elegant, they rarely tell managers what actually to do in practice. A strategic analysis exercise will therefore be something of a waste of time unless it can be built forward into an actionable plan, and this chapter is about how to do just that. Setting a strategic objective is fine as far as it goes, but the next stage is to define a means of implementing the chosen strategy, and doing this within the context of the strategies being pursued, and likely to be pursued, by competitors. Deciding how to build, maintain or harvest, in the context of competitive circumstances, involves identifying an appropriate competitive marketing strategy.

Strategies for growth

The nature of growth strategies

The most clear cut case for adopting growth strategies is for a leader in a growth market, in other words, a BCG 'star', or a product in Zone 1 of the Five-Zone Business Screen. However, growth strategies may also be appropriate for a leader in a mature market whose share has not yet reached its optimum level, or for a follower looking to challenge the leader. The latter is a special case which is dealt with later in this chapter; the current section applies essentially to leaders in growth markets and the early stages of mature markets. Everything else being equal, they would have been allocated an objective of build during the strategic analysis process, indicating that the management emphasis should be to increase sales volume in order to retain a strong competitive position in a market which is highly attractive.

Since growth markets are likely to be characterized by rapid development and competitive activity, they require relatively high expenditures on research and development, sales and promotion, and expansion of distribution. Short term profit potential will be adversely affected by the need to spend relatively highly on such activities. This will in turn impact on cash flow, which will be further compromised by the need for working capital to finance expansion and fixed assets to expand the infrastructure. However, since increasing sales volume is the priority for Zone 1 products, profit and cash flow are of secondary importance. There are two basic approaches to increasing volume; expand the size of the market, or gain market share (see Figure 6.1).

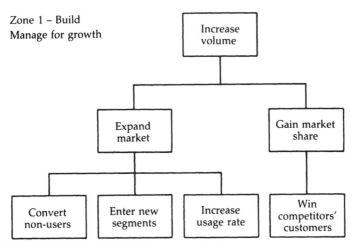

Figure 6.1   *Competitive strategies for Zone 1*

Expanding the market

In the very early stages of a new market, the pioneer's most important task is to convert non-users in the first segment to using the product. To follow up the example of pocket calculators from Chapter 4, the pioneer would have to target the innovators in the engineering and scientific community (S1), and try to get them to switch from slide rules to calculators. This is an example of a focused strategy, it converts the rather general objective of build into the basis of a plan clearly focused on communicating a specific message to specific users. The plan can then be adapted as the innovators start to purchase, and the message targeted at the early adopters and the majority as the product is managed through the innovation cycle for S1.

Once a high level of uptake was being achieved among engineers and scientists, the strategic priority would shift to entering a new segment, in the case of calculators the commercial users, or S2, this being the next route to continuing market expansion. This shift in emphasis would thus bring about a shift in the customer to be targeted, and this in turn would result in changing the message, the product and the distribution channel. In any given segment, there may also be an opportunity to increase the usage rate and thus continue expanding the market. But again, this will entail a change in the marketing plan, perhaps a smaller portable version of the product or a new promotional message. Thus the same strategic objective – build – can be implemented through completely different operating plans, it all depends upon which growth strategy is chosen for market implementation.

Going for market share

Once a growth market has reached all the available segments, and once all increases in usage rate have been secured, its characteristics change. It starts to be driven by the forces of maturity already discussed in Chapter 4: the population of consumers starts to stabilize as sources of new users begin to dry up, and saturation is approached once consumers reach the stage where they cannot reasonably consume more. While reaching maturity often takes longer than is commonly believed, it is undeniable that eventually it happens in every market. As a market approaches maturity, the leaders seek to continue their historic growth rates, and since this cannot come from market growth, the leaders put pressure on the followers in a bid to increase their market share, and a shakeout results. Companies which survive the shakeout are rewarded with a strong position in a mature market, and the potential for a healthy future profit stream. Companies which are squeezed in the shakeout either exit, or at best continue as specialist niche operators.

This brings us to the second major route to growth, gaining market share as against expanding the market. In a maturing market, it is essential for a leader to bolster its position by aggressively taking share from weaker competitors. This shift in competitive strategy will again result in changes to the marketing plan, perhaps in the form of more advertising, expanded distribution, a wider product range or aggressive quantity discounts. It can easily be seen that this kind of approach will continue to compromise short term profits, but this is an inherent aspect of a growth strategy. Of course, ultimately one reaches the point where increases in market share can only be achieved at expenditure levels disproportionate to the gain in share. When this optimum point is reached it is no longer rational to continue with a strategic objective of build; it then becomes appropriate to maintain.

Shifting the emphasis

In planning a shift of emphasis from expanding the market to gaining share, timing is of the utmost importance. Not only is it natural for a shakeout to occur as a market matures, it is a sensible strategy for a leader in a growth market to go for share at this stage rather than while it is in rapid growth. The most important task for the leader in a growth market is to stay in the lead, and the most positive way of doing that is to keep expanding the market, to keep innovating, to keep seeking new applications and new customers. It is inevitable that other contestants will be attracted into a growth market, and a leader may divert a great deal of energy into fighting off new entrants only to see others come in. By contrast if that energy is dedicated to staying ahead regardless of new entrants coming in, leadership will be retained in a very positive way. In any case, the weaker followers will be squeezed out at the shakeout. The key to managing a leader in a growth market is to stay ahead by continually growing the market, so as to be in the strongest possible position to survive the shakeout.

Perhaps the most important point to understand about competitive marketing strategies is that they need to change as the market develops. Periodic changes of emphasis of course bring in their wake all the problems associated with shifting the strategy outlined in Chapter 4; however, the danger of not doing it is leaving the door open for a competitor. It is also apparent that the options detailed on Figure 6.1 are not mutually exclusive. For example, it may be totally appropriate to continue a programme with S1 customers while at the same time managing a separate programme for S2, or to seek to increase the usage rate among early adopters while at the same time continuing to convert non-users among the late majority. However, every sales call spent trying to increase the usage rate with an enthusiastic early adopter is a sales call which cannot be devoted to winning over a cautious non-user; every pound spent advertising to engineers is a pound which cannot be spent advertising to accountants. Thus, while the options may not technically be mutually exclusive they nevertheless still involve making strategic choices: a company which tried to do them all at the same time would be in danger of doing none of them well. Achieving a focused competitive strategy in practice still means making choices about the allocation of resources.

Strategies for defence

Strategic choice in defensive strategies

Once the market has matured, and the leader has achieved a position where further growth in market share could only be gained at a disproportionately high cost, it becomes appropriate to adopt a strategic objective of maintain. The market share point at which the optimum share position is reached will vary with the circumstances, although it is certain that at some time the optimum will be reached, since it is clearly unrealistic for any leader in a genuinely competitive market to seek to secure and sustain a 100% share. Thus, the classical subject for an objective of maintain is an established leader in a mature market, in other words, a BCG cash cow, or a product in Zone 2 of the Five-Zone Business Screen. However, maintaining share may also be appropriate in some circumstances for followers as well as leaders, and this will be discussed more fully later in this chapter.

Managing a Zone 2 product is essentially a defensive operation, and requires a totally different approach to that required to implement a growth strategy. Nevertheless, both can involve aggressive actions against competitors, the difference is in the objectives being pursued. A strategic objective of maintain implies defending market share, but simultaneously improving profits in order to generate cash flow. There is clearly a contradiction here, as profit improvements where sales are not growing normally accrue from squeezing costs, whereas defending share will inevitably involve spending money. Immediately, the manager responsible for a Zone 2 product faces a strategic choice, to spend money on the defence of share, or to increase cash flow by reducing costs (see Figure 6.2).

It is important to recognize that primarily we are concerned with discretionary costs here, in other words money which the firm is

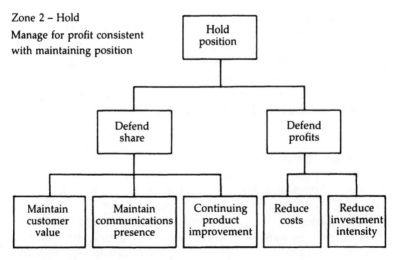

Figure 6.2 *Competitive strategies for Zone 2*

not forced to spend, or resources which can be allocated to alternative product lines. Examples include advertising expenditure, sales force costs, investment in research and development, giving increased discounts, and so on. These are the precisely the cost categories which would be likely to be compromised by the defence of share. This argument does not normally apply to manufacturing costs, since these are not discretionary, and reducing them would be unlikely to weaken a company's competitive position, indeed it may very well strengthen it. Hence, they do not present a strategic choice, and in general should be reduced wherever feasible. The possible exception to this is where perhaps to offer an improved product, it may be necessary to increase manufacturing costs. However, the essential nature of the strategic decision in Zone 2 is making a choice between diverting potential profits into the defence of share, or retaining them in order to maximize cash flow.

Defending market share

The key to resolving these strategic choices is monitoring and understanding the activities of competitors. If an aggressive competitor is attacking, and threatening to erode the leader's market share, and the leader's strategic objective is to maintain share, then the emphasis must be on the defence of share, and this will involve spending money on defensive actions. The competitor should be analysed to determine the basis on which the attack is being made. Is it discounts, sales force, or product features or something else? The defensive strategy should be aimed at nullifying the competitive advantage being offered to customers by the competitor. This does not necessarily mean replying in like manner, although this will often be the case. For example, the preferable way to fight a competitor's superior product is to match or exceed its performance with your own. Giving extra discounts is unlikely to be effective in the long term.

Whatever means of defence is chosen, it will almost certainly involve additional expenditure, and will also impact on the marketing plan. Referring to Figure 6.2, maintaining or improving price competitiveness will obviously influence pricing, maintaining or improving communications will impact on the advertising or sales force plan, continuing product improvement will impact upon research and development time. While all these actions could theoretically be undertaken simultaneously, there is again an implicit element of strategic choice, since expenditure on one form of defence will compromise the amount which can be allocated to the others. Thus, in order to create a focused marketing plan, it is essential to be specific about the competitive strategy to be pursued, in order to implement the strategic objective of maintain.

Improving profits

Of course, if the leader is not being aggressively attacked by competitors, if the attacks are ineffective, or if the follower seems content to remain number two, then the leader has no need to resort to expensive defensive measures and can turn its attention to improving profits. This can be achieved by cutting discretionary costs, in other words reducing advertising expenditure and sales force time, tightening up discount structures, and reducing research and development time. In addition, investment intensity can be squeezed, perhaps by not replacing equipment as quickly as might otherwise be the case. Similarly, working capital can be reduced by squeezing stocks and cutting customer credit entitlement. Provided competitors are not offering superior terms which place the leader at a competitive disadvantage, this is money tied up for no good purpose. Such actions should both improve profits by restricting interest charges, and could also have a significant direct impact upon cash flow.

The milk cow syndrome

Thus far, the management of a cash cow seems relatively straightforward. If a competitor is attacking, it is rational to spend money on the defence of market position, if not then expenditure levels should be reduced and greater profits taken. To say that the management approach adopted depends on whether or not a competitor is attacking would seem so obvious to many managers as to be scarcely worth saying. Unfortunately, the actions companies take in real life often do not reflect what is theoretically obvious, and consequently cash cows are sometimes gravely mismanaged.

The first flawed approach runs along the lines of 'it's a cash cow, so let's milk it'. This is to think one dimensionally down the right hand side of Figure 6.2, and can be characterized as the milk cow syndrome. This is of course a mistaken approach, since a consistent failure to re-invest in a cash cow will weaken it, maybe to the point where it becomes vulnerable to competitive attack. The most simple minded of farmers knows that if you fail to feed a cow, the flow of milk will soon dry up, yet many senior managers seem unaware of this basic point.

The sacred cow syndrome

Perhaps even more dangerous is the second flawed approach, which places a company's cash cows on a pedestal with the message 'this is a flagship product, and it must be supported in the marketplace come what may'. In other words, traditional levels of advertising budgets and sales force time are allocated to the product regardless of the circumstances. This is the sacred cow syndrome, and is just as blinkered an approach to cash cow management as the milk cow syndrome. It is rather like an aeroplane flying along at 30,000 feet with its throttles wide open. Like a new product, full throttle is needed for takeoff, but once the plane is into its cruise, the throttles only need to be opened to the level which will maintain its altitude, otherwise valuable fuel will be wasted. It is essential with a cash cow to find and sustain a 'cruising velocity' rather than allocate excessive resource. To do so will deny valuable resources to other parts of the business, which need them to grow and so become the next generation of cash cows.

The task for senior management

The sacred cow syndrome happens far more widely in practice than many, managers recognize. The signs to look for are systems which allocate advertising budgets by a historical proportion of sales revenue, sales forces which are maintained at historic levels regardless of circumstances, and line managers who always 'fight their corner' in budget meetings, determined to secure continuance of historic levels of funding. To implement a maintain strategy, resources should only be allocated with regard to the circumstances, not regardless of them. This means that each year, a detailed competitor activity review should take place prior to budget levels being set. In the case of demonstrated aggressive competitor activity, plans should be laid to defend share, but in the absence of it, every opportunity should be taken to increase profits and cash flow. Allocating funds and manpower to a cash cow on a historical or percentage basis is potentially a waste of precious resources; expenditures on them should be justified just as rigorously as on any other product line, and the basis of the justification is competitive activity. The key is to sustain sufficient competitive advantage to maintain market share, and it is impossible to make rational judgements about competitive advantage without an in-depth understanding of the competition.

Competitive analysis

Key to the question zone

So far we have examined two broad approaches to competitive strategy, strategies for growth and strategies for defence. Situations where these are appropriate are normally quite clear cut; in most cases they will be leaders in growth markets and mature markets respectively, and their position on portfolio analysis models will similarly be clear. However, leadership is enjoyed by only a minority of companies, any given market has only one leader, all the rest are followers. As anyone who has ever tried using portfolio analysis techniques in real life will confirm, a lot of products seem to end up as dilemmas, or in terms of the Five-Zone Business Screen, in Zone 3 — the question zone. For these, portfolio models fail to deliver any real clues about future management action except to say that you can build, maintain or harvest, which is hardly enlightening! For products in the question zone, the market is attractive but the competitive capability really to succeed is lacking.

Understanding how to proceed in such cases is a central issue in strategic marketing planning. As with many other strategic issues, the route to resolving it is to develop a thorough understanding of the competition, or more specifically in this case the market leader, its resources, its strategy and its psychology. If the leader is relatively weak in resource terms, or historically has been somewhat passive in the face of market challenges, or alternatively is just plain bureaucratic and slow to respond, then it is vulnerable to attack. However, if it has a strong resource base relative to the challenger, and if it responds rapidly and aggressively to market place challenges, then mounting such a challenge would probably prove fruitless. Competitive analysis, leading to an understanding of the character of the leader is the key to understanding competitive strategy in the question zone.

The passive leader

British Leyland sadly provides an excellent example of a weak, passive, slow market leader which paid the penalty. During the 1970s, Leyland saw its UK market share halved and its leadership lost. Popular mythology blames an apparently unstoppable tide of Japanese imports, which Leyland were unable to compete with, since the manufacturers were allegedly either propped up by subsidies or 'dumping'. This is in fact quite distant from reality, since

Ford also increased its share during this period to emerge eventually as the new leader and even Vauxhall, once the butt of motoring comedians everywhere, transformed its position and gained share. Nor should it be imagined that these two companies had been massively subsidized by their US parents; on the contrary, Ford UK was consistently one of the largest contributors to its Detroit head-quarters during the 1970s. Leyland was not beaten by 'unfair' com-petition, but by the fact that its competitors consistently worked to improve the offer they were making to their customers, and Leyland failed to respond adequately. The actions of Leyland's competitors added up to a successful challenger strategy, implemented against a weak, passive, slow leader.

Paradoxically, some leaders can be passive about a given market, even though objectively they would be regarded as strong. Indeed, this occurs in some of the best managed companies and often for very sound reasons. The fact is that two different companies may view the same market in different ways. A market which one company sees as relatively attractive may be seen by another, perhaps because of a lack of synergy with its other businesses, or superior invest-ment opportunities elsewhere, as relatively unattractive. These ap-parently contradictory conclusions could thus be perfectly rational to the companies concerned. If the leader felt that the product concerned did not fit with the rest of its portfolio, it might quite reasonably decide to manage it for cash flow, and *de facto* would have less resources available to fight competitors.

Therefore, it is dangerous to make assumptions about a company's attitude to a particular market on the basis of its general reputation or its attitude to other markets. The fact that a leader is a well-known multinational with a reputation for strength and responsive-ness does not necessarily mean it will act that way in every market in which it is active. Indeed, such companies are likely to be stra-tegically managed businesses, and as such will inevitably be harvest-ing some markets while building others. After all, if they were not strategically managed businesses, they would be fighting on all fronts! Managers should try to assess the leader's resources and attitude in each specific market, and be wary of making sweeping generalizations about entire corporations. Even the best managed companies are passive about some markets.

The responsive leader

It is relatively easy to see the justification for challenger strat-egies against a weak, passive or slow leader. However, it must be acknowledged that the vast majority of market leaders do not fit this profile; they tend to be relatively strong compared to their competitors and, having achieved a profitable dominant position, they want to hold on to it. Put simply, most companies will fight hard to defend their cash cows. Managers contemplating an attack on the leader must therefore undertake an in-depth appraisal of the potential opposition first, and analyse carefully a range of factors. Among the more important of these are the size and professionalism of their sales force; the spread of their distribution coverage; the strength of their brand with distributors and customers; the capability of their research and development effort; and the scale of their production resources and buying power. In other words, the manager contemplating a strategy which involves challenging the leader would be well advised first to make an objective assessment of all the attributes that make that company a force in the marketplace. If this is combined with the right psychological attitude, the will to use this muscle to repel challengers, and a history of being quick to respond to threats, then challenges by weaker competitors are likely to involve high costs and little chance of reward.

Force and defence: the leader's weapons

When sizing up a market leader as a potential opponent, it is worthwhile remembering two of Von Clausewitz's principles of warfare, the principle of force and the superiority of defence. The first is easy enough to understand, that if two armies face each other on similar territory with similar weapons the larger is more likely to win. The principle of superiority of defence holds that where the defending side is well entrenched it requires overwhelmingly superior numbers to attack that position successfully. Translated into marketing terms these two principles make the outlook for challengers appear bleak. Firstly, all things being equal, the side with the most resources is likely to win; secondly, it is easier to defend an established position than to attack it. Challengers must be prepared not just to outspend defenders but outspend them massively.

Thus, classic theory tells us that it is folly to attack a strong leader in a well-established position, and in the vast majority of instances an alternative strategy should be found. However, as always there are exceptions, times and circumstances when even the strongest leaders can be attacked. Von Clausewitz, in his research on past military battles, found that superiority of defence could be invalidated if one side had a secret weapon, a new type of siege machine which the defenders had not seen before, and against which they had no defences prepared. The medieval siege machine equates in marketing terms to an innovation. Equally, Von Clausewitz said that the principle of force could be overcome if the smaller side were better trained, fitter and, critically, better organized than their opponents. This is how the relatively small Roman legions consistently overcame the numerically superior domestic opposition. In other words, if one side can find a way of doing a better job with fewer resources it can overcome superior size; perhaps using a new and innovative channel of distribution could have this effect in marketing terms. In short, innovation in products, processes and methods can be used as an effective route to attack a strong leader.

Classic theory about the entrenched strength of leaders is also less compelling when the business environment is changing. A successful strategy is one which fits the environment; if the environment in which the leader operates changes, then the company must change the strategy which brought it success. However, changing a successful strategy in favour of something which is less familiar is something which leaders often find difficult to do. Frequently they prefer to stick to the strategy they know, despite the changes in the external world. Thus, in a changing market, it is often true that 'nothing fails like success': change creates opportunities for challengers who are better able to adapt quickly to the new circumstances. In his article *Strategic Windows*, Derek Abell argues persuasively that environmental change creates windows of opportunity, and that the time to invest in a market is when it is changing. The concept of strategic windows goes hand in hand with innovation, since environmental change can create the conditions where an innovation can flourish. Sometimes an innovation may itself set off a change in the market; innovation and the ability to adapt to change go together.

Choice of competitive strategy

All this leads to some fairly straightforward conclusions for companies with a product in Zone 3, facing an attractive market, but with a relatively low level of competitive strength compared to the leader. Firstly, is the leader weak, passive or slow; or, even if the leader is strong, is the environment changing faster than the leader can adapt, making it vulnerable, and is there a potential innovation available? If the answers are positive, challenger strategies can be contemplated. However, if they are negative, and competitive analysis shows the leader to be responsive and in a highly defensible

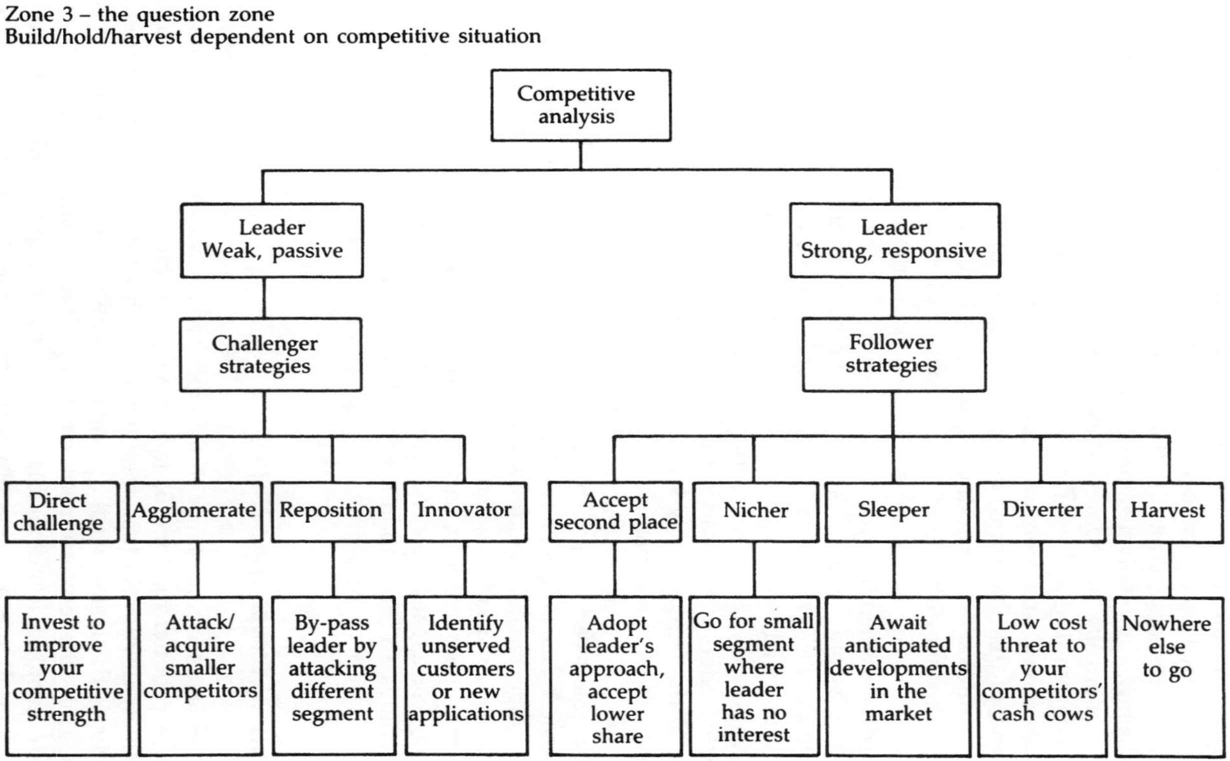

Zone 3 – the question zone
Build/hold/harvest dependent on competitive situation

Figure 6.3 *Competitive strategies for Zone 3*

position, such a strategy is likely to be costly and fruitless, and a better alternative is likely to be found in adopting follower or harvesting strategies (see Figure 6.3).

This may seem common sense, but in reality it is one of the most difficult aspects of strategic thinking for managers to come to terms with. The reason is human nature; managers tend to see following and harvesting as dreadfully negative, lacking excitement, and even career potential. By contrast, challenging seems positive and exciting, and is seen to offer a better prospect of career development moves. In any case it is often argued that management is all about accepting challenges, taking risks, succeeding against the odds, and fighting for your product.

While it is right that managers should be motivated to think positively, they should also bear in mind that sound strategic thinking does not mean attack regardless of the circumstances, nor does it mean attack simultaneously on all fronts. A general who fought like that would hardly be likely to win the war. Thus, before advocating or supporting challenger strategies, managers should take time to examine the circumstances carefully; if they are not right, follower or harvester strategies should be adopted. In Zone 3 more than any other, it is essential to define a well-thought-through competitive strategy before it is remotely possible to draw up a focused marketing plan.

Challenger strategies

The direct challenge

From the above discussion of competitive analysis, it can be seen that challenger strategies are appropriate where the market is attractive and where either the leader is weak, passive or slow relative to the challenger, or where the challenger can benefit from the effects of environmental change or innovation. The four main types of challenger strategy are the direct challenge, agglomeration, innovation and repositioning (see Figure 6.3). Making a direct challenge is potentially the most costly and highest risk option, and it should really only be contemplated where there is hard evidence or substantial experience that the leader is weak, passive or slow. British Leyland (BL), already referred to above, was the victim of such a strategy at the hands of firstly the Japanese and subsequently Ford. At the dawn of the 1970s, Japanese cars were really no better than their BL counterparts, but already the Japanese were evaluating the leader, looking for weaknesses which could be exploited.

Initially, they exploited the fact that traditionally, British manufacturers did not fit many extras; for example, one often had to pay more for items such as a radio, a carpet or even a heater. Indeed, the manufacturers and dealers used to regard such items as useful sources of additional profit. The Japanese chose to offer radios, heaters, carpets and other refinements as standard, an additional attraction for the manufacturers being that the incremental cost of fitting such items on the production line was relatively small, yet the incremental value to the customer was high. Of greater consequence was that they also invested heavily in research and development, to make their cars more reliable and less prone to rusting than those of the competition. However, the basis of the Japanese success was not merely that their cars worked better, but more fundamentally because BL permitted it to happen by a total failure or inability to respond adequately. It cannot even be explained by mystical references to some obscure source of oriental superiority, since Ford, a US firm established for many years in the UK, and with its own fair share of industrial relations problems at the time, also did extremely well.

Basically, there is only one rather mundane explanation. The dethronement of BL as market leader provides an excellent example of the nature of a successful direct challenge strategy. It is a matter of examining the leader's weaknesses, determining the best basis on which to attack, then investing selectively to improve your own resources in that area. The early Japanese challengers made no attempt to steal BL's strong dealer network, neither did they indulge in excessive levels of media advertising in order to build their brands. To attack on those bases would have been more difficult, more costly, and far easier for BL to repel. Instead they attacked where they knew the leader was weak, initially by fitting extras as standard, and subsequently by improving reliability and rust-proofing. The intelligent direct challenge does not involve an all-out assault on every parameter of the customer's purchase decision, it involves a selective assault on areas in which the attacker can perform effectively but where the defender is likely to experience difficulty in responding. Once again, it involves careful strategic thinking, since it involves precise focusing of resources into areas of attack which are likely to prove most fruiftul, rather than spreading them across the board.

A direct challenge essentially involves challenging the leader in his existing market, with basically similar products and technology, targeted at similar customers. The justification for doing this should be the belief that the leader will not respond in like manner; it is the lack of response that fundamentally explains the success of such a strategy. As such, it is really only appropriate against a leader which is weak, passive or slow. If, as in the vast majority of cases, the leader is strong and responsive, an attack on the same market position, aimed at the same customers, is likely to fail. However, it is still possible to challenge even a strong leader, provided some new territory can be found, where the challenger can build a strong position without making a direct challenge initially. This involves the strategies of agglomeration, innovation and repositioning.

Agglomeration

Where a market is fragmented between several competitors, it may be possible to agglomerate share from smaller followers as an alternative to directly challenging the leader. This approach is intuitively appealing, since it avoids the risks of attacking a strong leader head-on. However, the opportunity may unfortunately arise only rarely in practice, because smaller competitors tend to fall out anyway at the shakeout, as a market matures. If a mature market is in effect controlled by three or four companies, there is limited scope for further agglomeration. Any small companies which survive will tend to do so because they are specialists focusing on a market niche with specific needs, and it may be almost as difficult to target this kind of position as it is the leader. The time when the agglomeration approach really comes into its own is at the shakeout, just as the market is maturing. This is precisely the time when the weaker companies fail as the stronger seek to continue their own growth, and achieve this by gaining market share at the expense of their weaker brethren.

Looked at from a broader perspective, planning any challenger strategy involves making an assessment of how a company can improve its competitive capability most effectively relative to the leader; in other words, how it can move from relatively weak, to adequate, then to strong most easily. In pictorial terms, this may be represented as how to achieve a shift from east to west across the Five-Zone Business Screen, so as to move from Zone 3 into Zone 1. An alternative to enhancing one's own resource base is to make an acquisition or form a strategic alliance. Such partnerships are often the practical manifestation of an agglomeration strategy, and are particularly relevant during a shakeout. Indeed, an intensive level of acquisition activity is often a sign that a shakeout is taking place, since an acquisition offers the stronger companies a potential means to strengthen their position quickly, and the weaker ones the opportunity to salvage at least some reward. Of course, acquisitions and alliances are not only relevant to an agglomeration strategy, indeed they may be useful in implementing a number of competitive marketing strategies, both aggressive and defensive.

Although acquisition can be used as a fast track route to improving the strength of a resource or customer base, the difficulties of both retaining and absorbing the skills from the acquired company, as well as retaining their customers, should not be underestimated. Acquisition may also be significantly more expensive than growing your own resource base, since they are by their very nature a package, and the acquirer has to pay for the less desirable elements as well. Strategic alliances seem to be in fashion at present, perhaps because they are much favoured by Japanese companies. An alliance is an agreement to pool two complementary sets of resources, and to share future profits in some equitable way. It is rather like being able to improve the resource base now but defer payment. Where interests are truly complementary alliances may work well, but rather like a successful marriage they require continuing benefits for both partners in order to keep them harmonious. As in one's private life, it is inadvisable to rely solely on some aged legal contract to ensure a continuing good relationship.

Thus, from a viewpoint of strategic thinking, acquisitions and alliances can both be seen as alternative routes to strengthen the resource and customer base. This is not to say they are unique to an agglomeration strategy, they may also be a source of innovations or be used as a form of defensive strategy. However, the basic rationale is similar, that is to build a resource base quicker than would be possible through organic investment. The problem is managing the joint resource base, ensuring the hoped-for improvements are achieved in reality, and retaining the loyalty of the acquired company's customers.

Repositioning

Targeting at a different customer segment can also be a viable strategy for a Zone 3 product. The basis of a successful repositioning exercise is to shift the market territory so that the leader does not perceive the repositioned product as a threat, since it is not seen to be making a direct attack on his traditional territory. The new position may then be used as a base on which to grow company skills, resources and credibility, which subsequently may grow sufficiently to support a more direct attack on the leader.

The early Honda motor cycles were not aimed at the traditional customers of the British manufacturers, but at rather more sober citizens who wanted a reliable, clean and economic means of transport. The British manufacturers did not see Honda's entry into the market as a threat, since such customers were not felt to be an important market segment. Moreover, the machines themselves were small, cheap and low powered, and were not seen technically as a threat to the traditional British bikes. However, Honda used this position to build a distribution system, a reputation for reliability, and brand credibility with trade and public, then on the back of that launched progressively larger machines aimed at the British manufacturers' customers. There was no great technical innovation early on, the initial success was due to effective positioning avoiding an early confrontation with the existing leaders.

Innovation

Innovation is the most positive challenger strategy to use against a strong leader, because it is the route to offering a new and superior competitive advantage. Innovation is not only a way of developing entirely new growth markets, it is also a route to overturn established leaders in mature markets, in Richard Foster's words, it can 'turn leaders into losers'. There could have been fewer market leaders stronger than the mighty Xerox corporation at the height of its powers, yet even this titan became a victim of innovation at the hands of a much smaller Japanese optical company called Canon.

Xerox made large photocopying machines, and sold them through its own direct sales force, which concentrated mainly on people responsible for office services in large companies. Because the machines were large, they tended to be located in a central services department, somewhat remote from the users who required photocopies. While the machines themselves were extremely fast in operation, the central location meant that for the user, obtaining a photocopy was often a time consuming business. Canon saw the opportunity to sell small machines, which could be located beside the user's desk. There was no great technical innovation, in fact Canon's machines were rather slow in operation compared to Xerox's. However, to the user, they saved the time taken to walk to the central photocopying department, so the slower operating time was

irrelevant. But Canon's innovation was in the distribution channel
rather than the hardware. They did not bother selling to the office
services people, they talked direct to the users, managers and sec-
retaries, using advertising and brochures rather than salesmen. They
also established a chain of local high street dealers to distribute
their products, where Xerox had concentrated on direct distribution.
Once again, Xerox did not perceive the small machines as a threat
until it was too late, by which time Canon had established its
product, its brand and its distribution.

It can be seen that Canon succeeded because it offered the customer
a new competitive advantage – convenience – which Xerox was
unable to match without changing its entire approach. To match
Canon's user convenience, Xerox would have had to change its
entire product strategy and switch to small machines. This in turn
would have meant totally reorganizing its factories, and re-orienting
its entire research and development effort. In addition, it would
have needed to change its former sales approach aimed at office
services managers, and instead train and manage a network of local
dealers. Apart from the sheer operating problems such a shift in
strategy would have caused, Xerox would have found it hard to
overcome the sheer inertia which makes it so difficult for large
companies to abandon the very strategy which made them so successful. Again, Xerox provides an example of the maxim that nothing
fails like success.

Lessons for the leader

Repositioning and innovation are of course closely related, the technical distinction being that repositioning is more about targeting a
different customer target segment, whereas innovation in a mature
market is more about finding a means of delivering a new competitive
advantage to the existing customer target group. However, in practice
the two approaches tend to overlap, because they are concerned
with finding either new territory over which to fight the battle, or
finding a new weapon with which to fight it: fundamentally, finding
something new or different is the key. It also goes without saying
that both strategies are likely to be far more effective if the leader
finds it difficult to respond owing to the inertia inherent in its
existing structure, and does not in any case perceive it as sufficient
of a threat to warrant a response. Indeed, this is a feature of any
kind of challenger strategy; its success will depend to some extent
on an initial lack of response from the leader. The longer the response

is delayed, the greater the chance to build skills, credibility, and distribution.

In addition to the time factor, all challenger strategies are assisted inestimably if the environment is changing. Change creates threats for some and opportunities for others, and often it is the leader which faces the greatest threat. The time to invest in a market is when that market is changing, inevitably that is also the optimum time to embark upon a challenger strategy. The corollary is that challenger strategies are more risky when a market is stable. Thus, challenger strategies are likely to be more successful firstly in times of environmental changes, and secondly, where there is reasonable evidence that the leader will allow sufficient time for them to work. There is a converse lesson for leaders here – do not allow challengers that time. As soon as you hear managers saying 'it won't affect us', it is time to start worrying!

Follower strategies

Accept second place

Following the discussion in the previous section, it is clear that to mount a successful challenge to a strong leader, the circumstances must be right, and where they are not, challenging is likely to be costly, and offer an uncertain chance of reward. In this case it is preferable to adopt follower strategies; these implicitly accept a lower level of potential market share, but involve relatively lower costs. The logic of follower strategies is that it is better to accept a lower level of profitable market share, than fight costly and fruitless battles with a strong opponent in a vain attempt to increase share (see Figure 6.3). The most obvious way of following the leader is to accept second place behind the leader, and make it clear to all concerned that your ambitions are restricted to remaining there.

This involves targeting similar customers to the leader and making a similar offer to them, but not making the kind of aggressive moves that would provoke the leader into a defensive reaction. Clearly, a strategy of accepting second place involves lower costs and may permit higher prices than a strategy of challenging the leader; thus it can be a surprisingly profitable approach. It also suits the leader, who can also take the opportunity to spend less on retaining position, so both parties benefit from a harmonious leader/follower relationship. For many years, GM and Ford seemed to enjoy this kind of relationship in the US car market: their market shares hardly changed at all, and both companies were highly profitable, despite Ford only having half of GM's share. Unfortunately for the companies concerned, the applecart was upset by environmental change, in this case a four-fold increase in the price of gasoline and the advent of new competition from Europe and Japan. Harmonious leader/follower relationships rarely last for ever, but while they do, they can be highly profitable for both parties.

Finding a niche

An alternative to accepting second place in the same market as the leader is to adopt a nicher strategy, which involves finding a small specialist market in which the leader is not interested, or at least not sufficiently interested to engage in a costly competitive battle. Niching involves targeting a specialist customer group with a marketing plan geared to their specific needs: it is analogous to the specialization approach to competitive advantage shown in Figure 3.3. Like accepting second place, finding a niche can also be a highly profitable strategy, as it is aimed at building a high share in a relatively less competitive specialist market. In addition, it offers the opportunity to build a defensible market position, by realizing the benefits of specialization. By contrast, accepting second place does not normally offer the basis of a defensible position. Its security rests on hoping that the leader will conclude that having a smaller follower is inevitable, and realize that it is in his own interest to permit a pliant follower to survive, rather than leaving the door open for a more aggressive entrant. This is sometimes known as 'trusting the leader's statesmanship'; cynics would no doubt regard this as an unwritten agreement not to indulge in hostile competition.

Finding niches where the leader is not sufficiently interested to defend energetically can even form the basis of a challenger strategy. This is rather like chipping bits off the leader's periphery one by one until the core is vulnerable: this has been called a flank attack by some writers. The prospect of GM being gradually 'nibbled to death', referred to in Chapter 5, is an example of a leader being attacked precisely in this way. A classic Japanese market entry route is to target niches; in the American car market, this means sports cars, off-road vehicles, pick-ups, second cars, space cruisers and the like. Some commentators feel that GM has given up trying to fight for these specialist markets, and is gradually becoming increasingly exposed in its core large family car business. Whether GM will ultimately be nibbled to death is a matter for conjecture, but it does provide an excellent example of nicher strategies.

Sleepers

The third type of follower strategy is the sleeper. This is the product which is felt to be ahead of its time, and which is placed on the back burner awaiting potential marketplace developments. This may appear to be a classic case of ducking a decision in the name of business strategy, and certainly that danger should be watched out for. Nevertheless, there are sometimes circumstances where a market change is anticipated but has not yet occurred. Recent examples have arisen in the gradual switch which is taking place from solvent based inks, glues, paints and so on, to safer formulations of these products. Frequently, the safer alternatives are far more expensive than the traditional solvent-based products, and it would clearly not be rewarding to indulge in heavy promotional expenditure. However, companies which have developed high performance safer alternatives could take the view that keeping them on the market, albeit with a low profile, will put them in a stronger position when the market for them does start to take off. This may occur perhaps as a result of changes in legislation or by specifiers increasingly insisting that contractors and suppliers cease using solvent-based products.

Thus, the basis of a sleeper strategy is that provided there is some reasonable chance that the market environment will change in the foreseeable future, it is worthwhile retaining products which will fit that new environment as sleepers in the product portfolio. Silk Cut has for some years been a leading brand in the UK cigarette market. It was launched in the 1960s as a mild cigarette aimed at women, and never achieved more than a modest level of success. However, in the 1970s, a fundamental change in the market environment began to take place, as more and more smokers started to understand the health risks associated with smoking. For those who felt unable or unwilling to give up the habit, the less risky option was to switch to a low tar brand, and it happened that Silk Cut offered one of the lowest tar deliveries available. The manufacturers soon realized the potential of the product, and made Silk Cut their flagship low tar brand. Although all their competitors also introduced low tar brands, it was Silk Cut's familiarity and credibility which enabled it to establish the crucial early leadership position. Subsequent effective management of the brand enabled it to retain that leadership as the low tar market grew, eventually becoming a major element in the cigarette market.

The example of Silk Cut shows that it is perfectly possible to grow even in declining markets, provided the environment is changing and you have a product which fits that change. Whether or not the brand was intended to be a sleeper at its initial launch is unimportant; the point is that it illustrates the value of having a product positioned ready and waiting, acquiring some market awareness and credibility, if a change in the environment is anticipated. It could also be argued that the sleeper strategy is a kind of advance innovation, and thus should be classified as a challenger. However, this is for the future, in terms of current management action, a sleeper strategy is fundamentally a non-aggressive approach and is thus classified along with the other follower strategies.

Creating a diversion

The point had already been made that it is easier to defend a well-entrenched position than it is to attack it, but there is one important exception to this. Take the hypothetical case of a large commodity market worth £100 million in total, with Company A having a 70% share and Company B a 20% share. To offer a 10% price cut to all its customers would cost B £2 million, but it would cost A £7 million to respond. In other words the cost of defence is greater than the cost of attack. This apparent contradiction of the theory presents a leader in a commodity market with a potentially significant problem. The underlying reason for this paradoxical weakness in an apparently strong market position is that commodity markets are by definition markets where price is main or sole determinant of customer purchase decisions, and hence the only available source of differentiation and competitive advantage. Unless the leader has overwhelmingly superior costs, which is unlikely if the manufacturing technology is also mature, it has no source of defensible advantage.

Indeed in the absence of much lower costs, a lower price is the least defensible of any form of competitive advantage because it is the easiest to copy. It is this inherent lack of defensible advantage in commodity markets that makes them so volatile, and it also explains why such markets are often the domain of a small oligopoly of producers of approximately equal size. A disproportionately large market share is not sustainable, because it is not underpinned by a defensible advantage, therefore the market shares of the leading companies tend to equalize. It follows that the less sustainable the leader's advantage, the more difficult it is to hold on to a large share. Leaders in this position are vulnerable to a diverter strategy, where the cost of defence exceeds the cost of making the attack. An analogy may be found in guerilla warfare, where a mere handful of guerilla fighters can keep an entire army occupied. The objective is not so much to win the war by military means, as to commit the defenders to such a massive level of resource input that in the end their commitment to continue the defence fails. A classic example in the late 1980s was the war in Afghanistan, where a few thousand guerilla fighters tied up the might of the Soviet army, who were nevertheless still unable to win. In the end, the Soviets gave up the struggle.

While guerilla warfare is not an exact analogy, the principles of a diversion strategy are similar, to make a low cost threat to a competitor's cash cow, where the cost of defence is greater than the cost of attack. The objective is not so much to overthrow the leader, as to deny it the ability to make large profits. One very good reason for doing this is that the profits from a cash cow may well be used to fund new products in other areas; thus, reducing the level of profits generated by a cash cow will restrict the leader's ability to launch potentially more threatening innovations. Other writers have referred to this as 'profit denial' or, predictably, 'guerilla tactics'. While it may appear at first sight to be a highly aggressive strategy, it must be remembered that the basic aim is to deny the leader the chance to make large profits, rather than a bid to secure leadership. Accordingly, it is classified here as a follower strategy, although as in all classification systems, the point is debatable.

Understanding the nature of a diversion strategy provides leaders with a valuable insight into their own strategy, since it is essential for leaders to avoid becoming vulnerable to a diversion strategy themselves. Diversion works best in commodity markets, that is markets where everybody offers essentially the same product, and the only real element in the customer's decision process is price. It follows that the nearer a market is to this model, the better a diversion strategy works; equally, the further away it is the less well such a strategy will work. In other words, the best protection against becoming vulnerable to a diversion strategy is to build and sustain an array of defensible competitive advantages. No competitive advantage lasts for ever, and this underlines the need for leaders constantly to seek new sources of advantage to sustain their position as competitors catch up.

Understanding the diversion strategy also underlines the fact that dominant leadership positions which are not underpinned by a defensible competitive advantage are not sustainable. Only as a member of a benign oligopoly, or in other circumstances which ensure the absence of effective competition, can such a position be sustained. A company which finds it has a commodity product under attack in an unsustainable position is better off recognizing that fact, and managing the product concerned for cash flow, re-investing that cash into areas where defensible advantages can be built. To fight on, attempting to sustain the unsustainable, will only result in a long and costly battle of attrition. Sir John Harvey–Jones recognized this when he set a mission for ICI to become a speciality chemicals business.

Harvesting strategies

When to harvest products

Few products continue in a state of maturity indefinitely, inevitably they sooner or later start to decline as new products take their place, or as the market itself dies as a result of environmental change. The direct cause of decline is normally that the customer base progress-ively shrinks, as customers which abandon the product or die are not replaced by new ones. When decline sets in, it may be appropriate to plan a major shift of strategic objectives from maintain to harvest, and manage the product for cash flow. The reason is simple, if the product is dying, and if that death is being caused by external circumstances over which the firm has little control, it is better to recognize that there is no point in trying to maintain its current level of sales in the long term. Surely it is preferable to extract the maximum cash flow we can while the product still has at least some life, so that the cash can be re-invested in new growth opportunities.

Therefore, the most clear cut circumstance where harvesting strat-egies are appropriate is in the case of structural decline driven by external factors. Such products will invariably fall into Zone 4 of the Five-Zone Business Screen (see Figure 6.4). However, as always in strategic thinking, there are some important exceptions to this. It may be that a declining product can be repositioned into a new, growing customer segment, where its attributes are seen as positive. A remarkably successful example of this is the way Lucozade was repositioned from its declining traditional market into the fast growth market for sports drinks. It is important to recognize that this was not simply a case of an exciting advertising campaign reviving the fortunes of a flagging brand, it was the shift into a growing market which underlay the success. Too often, so-called repositioning is used as justification for supporting a declining brand, when there is no segment shift involved. Opportunities for genuine repositioning of a declining product occur fairly infrequently in practice, and senior managers should be wary of bogus repositioning being used to justify continuing expenditure.

A second exception to the automatic harvesting of a declining product can arise when everybody else in the industry is also harvesting, particularly if they seem to have overestimated the speed of decline. If everybody is getting out fast, this clearly creates opportunities to pick up incremental business at little cost, and in addition reduces the level of competitiveness. Provided there is a reasonable level of expectation that the market will not die quickly, such conditions can create good profit opportunities, even in a declining market. It must also be acknowledged that a number of the other strategies outlined in this chapter may in particular circumstances be appropriate to declining products, so it is not the case that harvesting is the only viable strategy available to declining products. However, having said all of that, it is nevertheless true that harvesting will be the preferred strategy for the majority of Zone 4 products.

In addition, harvesting may be appropriate even in attractive growth markets, where one's relative competitive strength is exceptionally weak. This takes us back to the question zone, where the strategic objective can be build, maintain or harvest. It can be seen from previous sections that a range of possible challenger or follower options exist for the management of products with a relatively weak market position. However, in some cases, none of these will be viable, nevertheless such a product can still play a valuable role in the overall portfolio by being managed purposively for cash flow.

There may also be circumstances where a company will decide to harvest a product with a strong position in a mature market. This is somewhat unlikely, because it sacrifices the prospect of sustained long term cash flow in exchange for a limited period of more intensive short term cash flow. Nevertheless, this may be rational if the company concerned has superior investment opportunities available elsewhere, which will be lost unless additional resources are found quickly. In other words, if a company has a particular pressing need for cash in the short term it may be justified to harvest a product that would otherwise be maintained. Similarly, companies make strategic decisions from time to time to exit certain markets, possibly owing to lack of synergy with the rest of the business. This can be another reason for harvesting a product which another organization might quite rationally decide to maintain. The exit route often chosen in this case is divestment, selling off the business as a going concern, but strategically this is no more than a very rapid method of harvesting.

Harvesting strategies therefore may be appropriate in a variety of circumstances: for Zone 4 products in declining markets, although not invariably; for Zone 3 products with a very weak position; where there is a need for rapid cash flow to finance new product opportunities; and finally, in the case of products which do not fit with the rest of the company's portfolio. It is therefore important to remember when consulting Figure 6.4, that while this applies to most Zone 4 products, it does not apply to all; equally, it may be perfectly rational to harvest products in other zones. However, before a plan to implement harvesting can be drawn up, it is first necessary to define how fast the cash flow is to be taken, because the desired speed of the harvesting process will significantly influence the plan for implementation.

Slow harvest

Where a market is declining slowly, it makes sense to plan for a slow harvest, otherwise the product may die before the market dies, and the opportunity for a longer term cash stream will be lost. The potential rate of decline can be predicted to a certain extent by

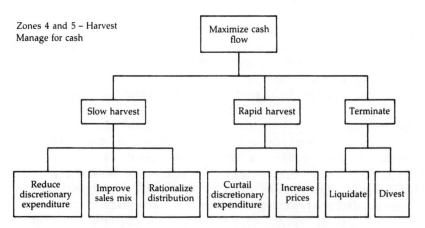

Figure 6.4 *Competitive strategies for Zones 4 and 5*

looking at how fast the customer base is shrinking. Some decline processes last for many years, and the products concerned can be good profit and cash generators over an extended period. If on the other hand the decline has been caused by technical obsolescence, or a far superior alternative becoming available, it is likely to be a fast decline, therefore a rapid harvest is appropriate.

The art of harvesting is to restrict expenditure on the product without proportionately damaging sales. The first step to take is to reduce discretionary expenditure: this means undertaking a thorough review of the product support budget, and cutting down on areas where you are not forced to spend money. For example, advertising budgets can be reduced so as to focus on the most important media, discounts can be reduced, development expenditure should be restricted to safety and legislative issues only, and asset replacement should be kept down to the bare minimum. In addition, the sales mix should be improved if possible; this means focusing on higher margin versions such as de-luxe models, perhaps eventually taking the basic version off the market altogether, and continuing with only the higher margin lines.

A further method of harvesting is to rationalize distribution by concentrating on higher throughput outlets, and cutting out marginal ones. This will save distribution costs while affecting sales proportionally less, and more importantly, will enable sales force time to be reduced. Sales time is a valuable resource, and taking it out of products being harvested will enable it to be redirected towards growth products. Each of these actions will produce a fall in expenditure and thus an increase in profits, whereas in a slowly declining market, sales should fall proportionally less quickly. In addition, cash can be liberated by squeezing stock levels and customer credit entitlement. This process can go on for surprisingly long periods in the case of a long gradual decline, and if it is done skilfully, the declining products can be a source of significant profit and cash flow.

Cash traps

Contrast this with the situation in a company which is not strategically managed, where managers responsible for declining products often appear to try to stave off a product's death by allocating more resources. The fact is that declining products do not have an inherent ability to generate cash regardless of the way they are managed. Inappropriate management decisions can result in their making losses or more likely just breaking even, while tying up valuable cash and human resources. This is the 'cash trap' syndrome, where resources which could be used more effectively elsewhere become trapped in a product with no long term future, and potential invest- ment funds are misdirected into an ultimately futile attempt to keep a dying product alive. So long as it is not actually making losses senior management may not get too concerned, unfortunately they would be overlooking the fact that profit or loss is only half of the story. The real question is whether company resources are being locked up in an ultimately fruitless fight for survival.

It should also be borne in mind that while reducing costs and thereby increasing profit is an important source of additional cash generation in harvesting strategies, it is by no means the only one. Purely by a planned reduction in the scale of the operation, cash will be released in the form of working capital, as stocks and debtors are squeezed down, in line with falling sales. In addition it may be possible to sell off assets or redeploy these into growth businesses. Rather than merely being a profit improvement exercise, harvesting is a way to create an enhanced flow of the cash and other resources tied up in businesses which lack a long term future. This is the reason it is so important to avoid the cash trap syndrome.

Rapid harvest

Slow harvest is appropriate in cases of slow decline, however, where a fast rate of decline is predicted, then a rapid harvest should be undertaken. Again, it is the rate at which the customers are likely to desert the product which is the key to understanding the potential speed of decline. Fast decline is normally caused by technological obsolescence or a very obvious environmental change, and as such is relatively straightforward to identify. However, rapid harvesting may also be appropriate in circumstances where there is a critical need for fast cash flow to finance growth opportunities, even in the absence of fast market decline. The principle is the same as for slow harvesting, to increase profits faster then the corresponding fall in sales, but of course to do it more quickly. Rapid harvesting may be accomplished by curtailing discretionary expenditure, for example stopping all advertising and other non-essential items. If this is combined with increased prices, profits should rise sharply, but only for a short period, as the lack of product support combined with higher prices will soon cause even lagged customers to switch.

It goes without saying that slow harvest and rapid harvest are not so much alternatives as points on a continuum. Any of the suggested harvesting strategies may be combined to produce the desired speed of decline. However, the key point is that the rate of decline is something which can be controlled to a certain extent by management action. It is another instance where strategic focus must be determined before an operating plan can be drawn up. The decision to harvest slowly or rapidly will have an immediate impact upon advertising expenditure, price lists, sales force time, distribution policy and all other aspects of the operating plan. Once again, until the strategic focus has been determined, no rational decision can be reached about the operating marketing plan.

Termination

Terminating a business can take one of two forms; either liquidation, where the business is broken up and the parts sold off separately; or divestment, where it is sold as a going concern. The decision as to which approach to take will turn on issues such as which approach will deliver the best cash flow, whether there are key resources which must be retained, whether a buyer can be found, whether it is appropriate to sell out to a competitor, and so on. However, from a strategic viewpoint, termination by either route can be seen as the fastest possible approach to harvesting and thus, to a certain extent, as a distinctive variant of harvesting strategies in general. Consequently, termination is included along with the other harvesting strategies in Figure 6.4.

The most obvious candidates for termination are those products which fall into Zone 5, where an unattractive market is combined with a weak competitive position. The assumption behind this is that there will be little economic gain to be made from conventional harvesting, and that the remaining resources left in any such product should be released to more productive areas as quickly as possible. It goes without saying that this assumption should be tested before terminating a Zone 5 product, just in case there is still some worthwhile gain to be realized from retaining it.

With Zone 4 products, termination may be sequential to the other harvesting strategies, and carried out after a period of harvesting has taken place, and it is no longer viable to continue. With some Zone 4 products, the market position may be so weak that it is not even worthwhile harvesting in the first place, and again termination is the route to take. Of course, if there is a need for rapid cash flow and a buyer can be found, a divestment of an otherwise healthy product may be in order. Thus, termination may be appropriate in a number of different circumstances, and should not be seen as relevant solely to Zone 5 products. However, just like the other harvesting strategies, the basic purpose is to free up resources which can be transferred into other areas of the business with a better long term future.

Defining a clear cut competitive strategy is an essential element in translating the strategic objective of build, maintain, or harvest into an actionable operating plan. Until we have defined a focused competitive marketing strategy, it is impossible to draw up a focused operating plan. The next stage in the process therefore is to show how all the elements fit together to result in the desired objective of a marketing plan which achieves all-round market focus.

7 The operating marketing plan

So far this book has examined the four key elements underlying the achievement of market focus. The first is customer orientation, and the need to focus on specific customer segments, while the second is competitive advantage, which leads to a focused market position. The third element is the allocation of resources to enable them to be focused on strategic investment priorities, and the fourth is defining a focused competitive marketing strategy. The discussion of these elements, the basic building blocks of market focus, has encompassed some fascinating and absorbing marketing theory. However, this would be useless to a practical manager if it did not result in an actionable plan. This chapter therefore shows how these four key elements fit together to result in such a plan.

The core of the market focus planning process is shown in Figure 7.1, where it can be seen that the operating marketing plan follows from a consideration of the elements outlined above. The first stage is to define the strategic objective, and determine whether the product is to be a cash consumer or a cash generator. Once the strategic objective has been established, then the basic approach to how that objective can be achieved can be considered and, in the context of the stance adopted by competition, the competitive strategy defined. But, as was stressed in the last chapter, it is impossible to determine an appropriate competitive strategy until the strategic objective has been established.

Following on from this, market positioning, the interplay between customer targets and competitive advantage can be determined. But again, it is impossible to make a rational decision about positioning until the previous stages have been thought through; for example, a nicher strategy will require a very different approach to market positioning from a challenger strategy, and so on. The operating marketing plan follows after the positioning decision, since it is impossible to reach conclusions about what is the appropriate advertising, pricing, product design, or distribution until the customer to be targeted and the competitive advantage to be offered have clearly been specified. This outlines the essence of the market focus planning process, a series of logically linked stages, the outcome of which is a focused operating plan.

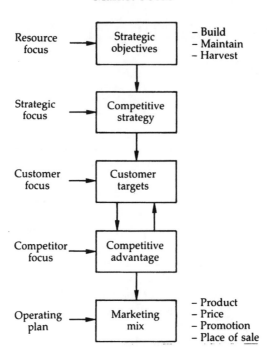

Figure 7.1   *From strategic objectives to the marketing mix*

The marketing mix

Classifications of the marketing mix

The operating plan itself is a conglomeration of management decision
and action areas which is commonly called the marketing mix,
a useful and widely adopted term which encompasses all the variables which manifest the company's offering in the marketplace.
Various classifications of the numerous variables of the marketing
mix have been suggested by academics, the most widely used of
which is McCarthy's 4 'P's; product, price, promotion, and place
(see Figure 7.2). Other classifications have inserted a fifth 'P' –
people, often particularly relevant in service businesses; or a sixth
'P' – packaging, which is split between product and promotion
under the 4 'P' system; some are yet more complex, for example 6
'P's and 2 'S's – sales and service. Which system to use is certainly
not a case of the more 'P's the better, after all, a classification system
is only an aid to good order. Which to use is largely a matter of
personal choice. The McCarthy system of 4'P's has the virtues of

simplicity and widespread adoption to commend it, and seems to have become the accepted 'market leader'.

The only slight difficulty with McCarthy's system is that to achieve a neat 4 'P' approach, he suggested the rather vague term 'place' for the fourth 'P'; it would have been clearer to refer to this as 'distribution', but clearly this would have destroyed the symmetry of the 4 'P's. The precise meaning of 'place' frequently baffles beginners, and hence some writers have suggested 'physical distribution' instead. Unfortunately, this is only one of several aspects which McCarthy included under 'place', so using it as a heading only results in more confusion. A better alternative is 'place of sale', which emphasizes the importance of outlets used and the policies adopted to manage and motivate them, as well as the physical distribution arrangements which feed them. Since this is more all-embracing than physical distribution and less vague than 'place' alone, it is adopted here, resulting in a 4 'P' marketing mix classification into product, price, promotion, and place of sale.

Figure 7.2   *The marketing mix: classification by the 4 'P's*

Elements of the marketing mix

More important than the classification system used is to understand the detail which the marketing mix embraces. For example, 'product' is a clear enough term, but in fact a product is only a conglomeration of a series of other decisions including materials, design, functions and so on. These are tabulated in Figure 7.3, which includes packaging as a product variable, whereas there is clearly a strong alternative case for including it under promotion. Of course, the information and display aspects of packaging must be consistent with promotional messages, so pack design is also listed under promotion. In many products, styling in an aesthetic sense is distinct from design in an engineering sense, and thus is listed separately. The range offered among a family of closely related products is another important decision area.

The interplay of all these variables will in turn have a significant impact on decisions about manufacturing methods, with subsequent knock-on decisions relating to factory layout, materials purchasing, stockholding policy and a myriad of other non-marketing decisions. Product decisions will also have a decisive impact on research and development, since they drive in a very direct manner major R&D programmes. Service and warranty policy is another potentially crucial marketing decision, but again this is often organized in an

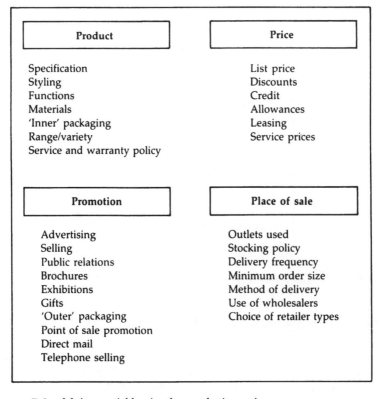

Figure 7.3 *Major variables in the marketing mix*

operational sense by a separate functional unit. Herein lies the danger of seeing the marketing mix purely as something which only affects the marketing department: while this is understandable given its name, it nevertheless drives and influences all the other functions in the business.

'Price' again appears to be a fairly easily understood term, but it also covers a wide variety of decision areas. Credit terms may be an important factor in some customer purchase decisions, yet often these can be set, and varied, in a fairly arbitrary manner by a company's finance department. In fact, this is a marketing decision, but one which it is impossible to divorce from the finance angle. Leasing, or the provision of other financial packages may be a crucial aspect of a company's overall pricing strategy in some businesses, and the company which offers the best range of financing options may gain a competitive advantage. Once again, this is very much a marketing variable, but it is often the responsibility of a separate function. Similarly, the other pricing variables like discount structures, service prices and so on, go together to make up the total price offer. While technically this is all part of the marketing mix, its decisive impact on many other company functions is clear.

'Promotion' encompasses a great many potential variables, and most of these are normally, though not always, the direct responsibility of the marketing department. Indeed, in many organizations, marketing becomes confused with promotion, because the department concerned is called marketing, but in fact spends the majority of its time on promotion. This is in effect the functional aspect of marketing, the whole range of methods used for communicating what the company has to offer to its customers, including the obvious approaches such as advertising, brochures, public relations, direct mail, and so on. Promotion also includes the decorative, informational and styling aspects of packaging, referred to as pack design in Figure 7.3, as well as aspects of communications which are not specific to any one product, such as corporate identity.

From a theoretical perspective, sales is clearly a form of promotion, and is thus included under this category in the classification. Sometimes, the sales function is part of the marketing department, however many companies feel that sales is so important that it is a completely separate function with board level representation. The endless debates which go on about whether sales should or should not be part of the marketing department really seem to miss the point: sales is no more or less a marketing function than service, R&D, manufacturing, or even finance. All management functions are part of the marketing effort, and there is no more or less sense in sales reporting to marketing than there is in any of the others doing so. Even under the heading of promotion, the marketing mix can never be regarded as solely a marketing department responsibility.

The fourth 'P' is 'place of sale', and this encompasses everything to do with distribution channels, including outlets used, the way these are managed, and the physical distribution systems adopted. Spin-off decisions include outlet stock holding policy, delivery frequency and so on. Again, this is frequently the responsibility of a separate function, perhaps reporting ultimately to marketing, but operationally discrete, except at a senior level. Place of sale, like the other 'P's, therefore encompasses a wide range of management decisions, many of them the responsibility in practice of a non-marketing function.

This review of the elements of the marketing mix is intended to emphasize firstly the wide ranging nature of the mix, secondly the fact that it has a significant impact on many other management functions, and thirdly that it cannot successfully be planned or implemented without the full hearted contribution of those functions. Indeed, the term marketing mix is something of a misnomer, implying that it is mainly the responsibility of one function. Perhaps 'management policy mix' would be a far more accurate description from an operational standpoint. However, provided this point is understood by all functions, it is better to stick with 'marketing mix', not only because it is a widely accepted term, but also because it does communicate the essentially external orientation of all the decision variables involved.

Market focus and the marketing mix

The marketing mix is the expression of the company's policy and philosophy to its customers specifically, and to the outside world generally. It embodies all the tangible and intangible factors which the customer considers to reach a purchase decision, and which competitors are likely to consider to reach their own strategic decisions. A customer purchase decision is not one dimensional; no customer buys on product features alone regardless of price, or on price alone regardless of product. Similarly, to believe that marketing success is largely a function of advertising or sales activity is to dangerously underestimate the customer. Customers buy a package of benefits, a package comprised of a balanced blend of many of the elements of the marketing mix; this is why the mix is sometimes referred to as the 'total offer'.

Every element making up the total offer should play its part in enhancing, communicating, and reinforcing the competitive advantage which will lead the target customer to select the company's offer rather than that of the competitor. In addition, each element must be consistent with the others; if the price is inconsistent with advertising claims or product features customer confusion will result. Thus the marketing mix should be a consistent total offer, designed to enhance and communicate the company's competitive advantage to its target customer. Various company functions have to deliver different elements of the total offer, so they all need to understand clearly the nature of both the target customer and the competitive advantage to do this effectively and consistently.

It is beyond the scope and objectives of this book to cover the operating management of all the elements of the mix, such as how to design a brochure, sales force management, media buying, physical distribution management, the theory and practice of pricing, product design, and so on. The list of management action areas which arise from the marketing mix is almost endless, and they are covered in a wide range of specialist texts which it would be impossible to reproduce here. Nevertheless, the marketing mix is the practical manifestation of market focus, and every management action within the mix must be referred back to the target market position, which itself depends on the chosen strategic objective and the competitive strategy adopted.

Thus, without reaching a prior conclusion about the desired market position of a given product, it is impossible to reach rational and consistent decisions about any element of the marketing mix. For example, it is impossible to design an advertising campaign without first specifying the customer target to be reached and the competitive advantage to be stressed in the message. Similarly it is impossible to determine a distribution strategy without first understanding the target customer's buying habits, and his attitudes to the trade-off between cost, convenience, and service. Every management function which has any kind of responsibility for marketing needs to know exactly which kind of customers it is supposed to be serving and the competitive advantage being offered to them. Only then can every function be sure that it is focusing on the correct customers with a consistent package.

This underlines the fact that the marketing mix is anything but a uniquely marketing department responsibility, it is the guiding light for all company functions. The market focus planning process establishes a template against which all functional managers can judge whether they are playing their role in satisfying the target customer, emphasizing the agreed competitive advantage, and satisfying the overall strategic objective. Without such a template, each function is forced back into the approach of managing to traditional functional criteria, rather than customer oriented criteria. Only the common template will enable all functions to participate in implementing a truly focused operating plan.

Setting the marketing budget

Traditional financial planning

A budget is nothing more than a financial plan setting out projected income and expenditure over the next period, normally a year. Operating managers await the agreement of a new budget with high anticipation, because it determines how much of the company's money they are likely to be able to spend next year, and thus has a significant impact on their activities. Marketing managers are no exception to this; the annual budget lays out how much may be spent on advertising and promotions, and what level of sales are expected in return. It is no exaggeration to say that the agreement of the budget is the start of the manager's year; it permits plans to be made, targets to be agreed, and will later form the basis of the control system which monitors income and expenditure throughout the year. Furthermore, a manager's performance against the standards set in the budget is a key factor in determining his or her personal career progress in most large organizations.

However, the effect of this system is that no firm operating plans can be made until the budget has been settled, and the result in many organizations is that the planning process in practice starts with the agreement of budgets. For example, it is impossible to draw up a confirmed advertising schedule until the size of the advertising budget is known. Under this system, the company makes its best projection of its likely sales revenues over the next year, then sets its discretionary costs at a level which will ensure that the overall level of profit desired will be achieved, provided of course that all the operating managers meet the forecasts set in the budget. If it appears, say, half way through the year, that the desired level of profit is unlikely to be achieved, then costs can be trimmed until the profit outcome once again looks acceptable. This approach to planning is clearly organizationally convenient: everyone knows in advance that provided the sales projections come true, they have projected a level of costs which will result in a profit. In addition, operating managers know how much they are likely to have available to spend, and can go ahead with operational planning on that basis.

This outlines the traditional approach to financial and business planning and superficially it is all very neat; unfortunately, however, the underlying logic is fundamentally flawed. The problem is that marketing plans, if they are to be truly market focused, must be driven by the market place, whereas in the traditional system they tend to get driven by the company's budget. A market focused advertising plan should be based on the amount and type of advertising required to secure and sustain the desired market position. In real life by contrast, advertising plans are too often driven by the exigencies and constraints of a budget drawn up to satisfy internal criteria rather than external strategies. This does not only mean that advertising budgets may be set at too low a level; indeed, the traditional system can just as easily result in an advertising appropriation larger than is necessary to secure strategic aims. Financially driven planning may be organizationally convenient, but it results in an essentially arbitrary allocation of resources from a strategic perspective.

Therefore, in a genuinely market driven approach to planning, it is impossible to make rational decisions about budgets until the marketing mix has been determined. For example, how can a sales revenue budget be set until pricing decisions have been taken and numbers of target customers identified; how can an advertising budget be set until the appropriate message and media have been determined; and how can a distribution budget be set until decisions about distribution methods and operations have been taken? The list could go on and on, and the same logic applies to all areas of the marketing mix, which by implication means all of the company's major management decision areas.

While it is thus impossible to take rational decisions about the marketing budget until decisions have been taken about the marketing mix, it is in turn also impossible to take rational decisions about the marketing mix until the desired market position has been determined. This is the approach to marketing planning laid out in Figure 7.4, and experienced managers will quickly realize that it runs counter to prevailing practice in many organizations, particularly in large ones with sophisticated financial control systems. The customary practice is to set the budget first then plan the mix by reference to its inherent financial constraints and freedoms. This may be organizationally convenient but regrettably it is both illogical and arbitrary, and what is worse, it will frustrate all attempts to achieve genuine market focus. Starting the planning process with the budget is the single biggest barrier to market focus: companies which wish to achieve market focus must first resolve to do away with this practice.

Market focused planning

In order to achieve a plan which is market driven, the logical place
to start is with the market. However, given that every organization
has different strengths and weaknesses it follows that they will be
better able to compete in some areas than others. The central idea of
portfolio analysis is to match market areas with attractive investment
potential to the company's competitive strengths; the outcome is to
determine a strategic objective for each product/market unit. Of
course, before the company can even do this, it needs to determine
which business it is in, the business where it can best compete, or
in planning jargon, its business mission. This should be based on
an assessment of the organization's distinctive competences or 'core
skills', leading on to an identification of the broad business areas
where it has a realistic opportunity to compete effectively. Taken
together, business mission and strategic objectives form the starting
point of the market focus planning process, by identifying the
specific market areas in which the company is best placed to compete
effectively.

Once strategic objectives are set for each product/market unit, the
next stage is to determine the best strategy to achieve that objective
in the light of the prevailing competitive situation. As discussed in
Chapter 6, a given objective may be achieved through various
approaches, each one involving choices and trade-offs to be considered relative to the prevailing competition before defining the
most appropriate competitive strategy. Only once this has been
established can judgements be made about which customer segment
should be targeted, again in the light of a thorough assessment of
competition, the segments they are targeting and the competitive
advantages they are offering. This is the process of positioning. The
vital company actions required to underpin the proposed positioning
should now be outlined; these are the key factors for success (KFS)
referred to in Chapter 3. Any proposal to develop and improve KFS
should at this stage be accompanied by a costed plan and realistic
timescale.

Only once the proposed positioning and KFS are clearly understood
can rational judgements be made about how to implement this
in practice through planning and managing the variables of the
marketing mix. Finally, as pointed out above, budgets and targets
can be drawn up, but it is impossible to make rational judgements
about these until the marketing mix has been defined. Taken together,
the marketing mix and the budgets and targets form the framework
for a focused operating marketing plan, to be pursued and implemented by the company's managers in a variety of functions.

Thus, the market focus planning process progresses in a series of logical steps from the business mission to a focused operating plan and budget for each product/market unit, as set out in Figure 7.4. While this approach may seem obvious in theory, it is a complete contrast to what happens in practice, where planning systems are essentially budget driven. Indeed, the financial planning ethos is so deeply rooted in most large organizations, that many experienced managers find it difficult to appreciate that there is any alternative at all. The problem is that when you have been brought up to think in a certain way, and have thought that way consistently for the past twenty years, it is often difficult to think in a diametrically

Figure 7.4 *Elements of the market focus planning process*

different way. This represents a considerable psychological barrier to market focus, and it necessary to understand this before it can be overcome.

Resource prioritization

Balancing the cash budget

While market focused planning may be logical, there is one significant potential problem, in that if plans are made solely on market related criteria, then clearly no allowance is made for a company's ability to finance such plans. It may be all very well in theory to say that to achieve a given competitive strategy and market position will require advertising expenditure of £20 million and a 100-strong sales force, but what if the company is unable to achieve such a level of resource, or if there are other competing projects also with a good case for a substantial resource input? In other words, what should be done where there are several attractive projects, all bidding simultaneously for scarce corporate resources, and, as will almost inevitably be the case, these are not sufficient to fund everything?

In a financially driven planning system, this type of problem is normally resolved by sharing out the resources available on some basis mutually acceptable to the managers concerned. The management emphasis then becomes 'what can I achieve given the level of resources available', rather than 'what level of resource is required to achieve the desired result'. While this may be seen in one sense as a reality of management life, the unfortunate fact is that if a competitor is prepared to invest the optimum level of resource rather than do the best he can with what is available, then the company is likely to be placed at a competitive disadvantage. In short, financially driven planning tends to result in a sharing out of resources, rather than a strategic focusing of resources onto key areas of market opportunity. However, the problem could potentially still arise, even with the market focus approach to planning, and the question remains of how to balance the imbalances.

In any planning system it is inevitable that such imbalances will arise, caused simply by too many projects bidding for too few resources. If anything, a market focused system will exacerbate this, by encouraging managers to focus on what needs to be done regardless of internal constraints, rather than on what can be done given the constraints. Planning in this way will lead almost inevitably to a situation where the budgets being requested exceed the company's financing capacity. The solution to the dilemma is to recycle through

(a) After first round of planning

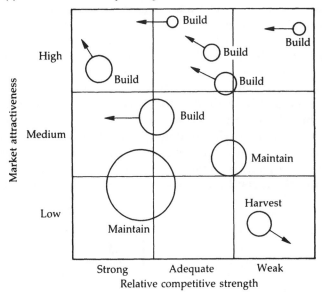

(b) After recycling to balance cash budget

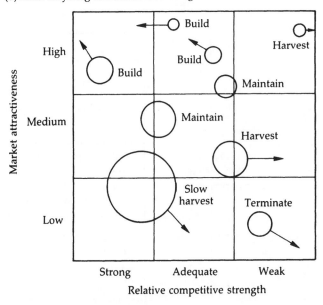

Figure 7.5 *The impact of recycling on a sample product portfolio*

the system, and return to the portfolio matrix. The objective of portfolio analysis is to help managers make more rational decisions about the allocation of resources, and to set priorities for resource input among competing projects. If cash requested exceeds cash available, then clearly priorities have to be looked at again; the only alternative to this is an arbitrary share out of the available resource.

The way to review resource allocation priorities is to recycle to the portfolio matrix and take a tough view of anything marginal or 'on the line'. This process is illustrated in Figure 7.5 by a hypothetical product portfolio showing outline plans before and after recycling. Whereas the company concerned was unable to provide adequate finance for all plans the first time round, the portfolio requires less cash input the second time. However, the 'stars' and the strongest

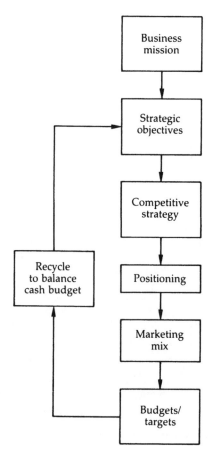

Figure 7.6   *The market focus/cash budget planning process*

'dilemma' are still in a build mode, it is the other units which have been modified to ensure that adequate resource is focused on the best opportunities. If this had been done on a share-out basis, the lesser opportunities would have received more, while inevitably, the best opportunities would have been relatively starved.

The recycle stage

The market focus planning process is completed by this recycle stage, and the final model is shown in Figure 7.6. In order to achieve a proper balance of resource inputs and outputs, as well as the agreement of all concerned, two or more recycles may be involved. As has been pointed out before, strategic marketing planning is in any case an iterative process. For example, competitive advantage is part of positioning, but it will also inherently be linked to the company's strengths and weaknesses; similarly, competitive analysis is input at several stages in the process. While iteration is somewhat inevitable, recycling at least helps to ensure that the iterations are done clockwise around the planning model rather than anticlockwise.

The market focus planning process emphasizes the product portfolio rather than the budget as the centre stage element in management thinking and discussion. A financially oriented system leads to the feeling that if the budget does not balance, the managers debate who gets what so as to make it balance. By contrast, a market oriented system encourages the view that if the budget does not balance, we return to the product portfolio and debate strategic priorities, rather than how to share out the resources. The product portfolio is a unique management tool which combines in one model the key decisions about both the financial and the strategic management of the organization. It allows both the prioritization of resources to key strategic tasks, and the ability to balance the cash budget in line with overall financial goals.

8 Sustaining market focus

No company which achieves market focus can hope to sustain it without continuing effort: like painting the Forth Bridge, sustaining market focus is a never ending task. This many appear daunting, but it is nevertheless inevitable, because as soon as a company has achieved market focus, the powerful corrosive force of environmental change will start to erode it. It is axiomatic that change in the business environment is constant, and that companies have to adapt to this change, or lose out to a competitor which adapts more effectively. After all, the need to adapt to the environment in order to survive is one of the fundamental laws of nature, and it is unlikely that even the strongest company can escape its consequences for long. Market focus is achieved and built in the context of a given set of external circumstances, an effective strategy must be in tune with the business environment. However, this is made up of such a complex mix of factors that constant change is inevitable, and as the environment changes, so the existing market focus needs to be re-defined. This means that sustaining market focus demands constant adaptation in order to ensure that the company's strategy remains focused upon its environment.

The business environment

The nature of environmental change

The business environment consists of all those external factors which make up the world in which companies compete. This is an extremely broad picture, ranging from economic to social to competitive forces, all of which are essentially beyond a company's direct control. For example, an individual business cannot influence economic factors, but they are nevertheless a potent source of environmental change. It seems to be becoming increasingly difficult, even for the experts, to forecast fluctuations in the economy. The onset and the eventual depth of the recession which followed the economic boom of 1987 was foreseen by very few people indeed, in spite of the fact that economic recessions have occurred with periodic frequency over the last twenty years. It left many companies with severe problems, particularly those connected with housing and associated businesses such as furnishings and other consumer durables. One cannot really criticize the managers of the companies which suffered for failing to forecast the recession, even the experts failed to do that. However, some were able to survive despite the problems, whereas others were not.

Economic changes bring with them fluctuations in inflation and interest rates, particularly now that the latter seems to have been adopted as a primary tool of economic management around the world. Different interest rates in different countries bring exchange rate fluctuations in their wake, at least with regard to currencies outside the European Monetary System. Any businessman who has ever been involved in exporting will confirm that it is almost impossible to plan ahead in an environment of fluctuating exchange rates, which can easily turn a profit making contract into a loss making one. While it is possible to insure against exchange rate losses to a certain extent by buying currency forward, there is nothing that will protect an exporter from the potentially far more damaging erosion of a carefully built-up competitive position, which differing inflation and exchange rates can bring.

Social change can produce long term structural changes in markets. One example is the increasing fragmentation of society, so that the traditional nuclear family is now in the minority of households, and the number of single people has in contrast expanded. This, and the steadily increasing proportion of women in the workforce, has led to significant changes for food manufacturing and retailing. One of the companies which benefited from this change was Marks & Spencer, whose approach to food retailing seems particularly appropriate to working and single people. By contrast, other retailers which have failed to adapt to these social changes have failed to match the rapid gains in profitable market share achieved by Marks & Spencer.

An associated factor is increasing customer awareness and education. Consumers are more aware of their rights, more prepared to exercise them, and more able to understand the information companies are providing. A keen interest in consumer issues by the mass media helps to speed up the awareness process about a range of concerns from salmonella in eggs to the use of nitrogen fertilizers by cereal farmers. While the manufacturers involved may feel that the public debate is sometimes rather ill informed, it is nevertheless a fact of life. Like it or not, we have to accept that public perceptions about products which were once believed to be entirely wholesome, can change rapidly. This creates both problems and opportunities for companies: Flora grew from nothing to brand leader on a growing tide of public awareness about the alleged risks associated with cholesterol, while the old-fashioned margarines lost out. Similarly, environmental concerns such as depletion of the ozone layer and atmospheric pollution in general can have a significant effect on businesses, creating a major problem for manufacturers of traditional aerosol propellants on the one hand, but a significant potential opportunity for manufacturers of catalytic converters on the other.

---

1 Slowing economic growth rates
2 Fluctuations in inflation/interest rates
3 Rapid technological change
4 Environmental pressures/'green' concerns
5 Increasing social mobility/fragmentation
6 Faster communications/travel
7 Changing work and employment patterns
8 Increasing consumer awareness/education

The business environment is changing faster

The changes are becoming increasingly less predictable

Figure 8.1 *The unstable business environment*

In addition to social and economic changes, technological change can undermine traditional industries and simultaneously create new ones. But it is not only traditional 'smokestack' industries which are vulnerable to technological change; often, it is high technology companies themselves which seem most vulnerable to changes in their own technology. For years, IBM had the dominant share of the world market for computers, but in recent years it has had to fight increasingly hard to retain leadership as computer systems architecture has shifted from central to distributed processing. In turn this has created opportunities for companies like Digital and Data General. If technological change can undermine the mighty IBM, it can happen to anyone.

Problems in forecasting change

Some of the major current forces behind changes in the business environment are summarized in Figure 8.1. Perhaps the most striking thing about this list is that each category seems to be changing progressively more quickly, and that the changes are becoming increasingly less predictable. It is interesting to compare this with the position in the 1960s. Economic growth was steady and easier to forecast, as were inflation and interest rates. Technological change was slower, environmental concerns were almost unheard of, family structures and work patterns were still traditional, everything about the business environment was slower changing and easier to forecast. Most significantly, this was before the days when the 'new competition' from the Far East had become a global force to be reckoned with, except in a minority of basic industries.

These were the times when many of our best known management concepts were established. Managers who spent their formative years in the 1960s are in many cases now occupying the most senior positions, while even those who started their management careers in the 1970s have inherited the same ideas. One of the most significant management concepts to emerge from this period was so-called corporate planning. The underlying logic of this is that a company should forecast the future, then put resources in place to meet the anticipated future picture. A very simple example is that a company would forecast the demand for its product in three years time, then start building a factory now to meet that future demand. While this may have been logical in a stable, and therefore reasonably forecastable environment, it becomes progressively less appropriate as the rate of change increases.

It has been argued above that in the 1990s, changes in the business environment are for various reasons happening faster, and are being driven by a more complex array of forces than before. The problem is not that forecasting as such is a waste of time, but that forecasts are becoming increasingly unreliable. Managers should try looking back over the last five or ten years in their business, and assess whether the changes that occurred during that period could reasonably have been foreseen. It is a safe bet that the changes over the next five or ten years will be at least as great. Thus, it is not that it is wrong to attempt to take a view of the future, but that accurate forecasting is almost impossible. Indeed, some events are totally unforecastable. Given the inherent unreliability of forecasts, and the general unpredictability of the business environment, businesses need to find an alternative method of coping with change. To understand the nature of this alternative, we first need an insight into the traditional way in which businesses respond to change.

Delays in the response to change

The onset of environmental change

Changes in the business environment rarely have an obvious and immediate effect on company performance in their early stages. The initial impact on sales of a new development tends to be small and slow to show up, but then it imperceptibly gathers force and momentum, like a snowball rolling down a hill. The reason is that in order to impact upon sales levels, a market change needs to affect customer attitudes and perceptions. As we know from Chapter 4, this occurs as the result of the gradual social learning process which leads to the diffusion of new ideas, and this process starts in just a small niche of people, the innovators, rather than affecting everybody at once. The result is that initially a company may not see a change happening, or may dismiss it as too small or insignificant to be of concern.

A well-known example of this is the way the Swiss watch industry responded to the threat from electronic watches. The silicon chip at the heart of the electronic watch was invented in California in the early 1970s, and the first thing the Swiss market leaders would have heard would have been weak signals from this far-off land. The early digital watches were produced in very small quantities, and were thus very expensive. Furthermore, they were somewhat impractical owing to their light emitting diode (LED) display: this required large amounts of power, consequently the user had to push a button to illuminate the time display, the numerals themselves were very small, and the watch had to be very bulky to accommodate the large and heavy batteries required. It is not surprising that the Swiss market leaders were initially dismissive of these products, which seemed to appeal only to a tiny segment of very rich techno-freak customers.

But this case is not so far distant from what frequently happens. The first examples of many new revolutionary products often are very crude compared to what they ultimately become, and all social changes start with an insignificant small niche of customers rather than the mass market. It is hardly surprising that companies respond to such apparently unimportant events by ignoring them. This may take a variety of guises; it may be dismissed with a time honoured management cliche like 'it won't affect us' or 'it's only a small niche'. A small fall in sales may equally be blamed on the sales force, who are then told to 'try harder' (see Figure 8.2). Managers will recognize these forms of response to change from their own experience: it is all too easy to dismiss something which is apparently insignificant, but unfortunately this contributes nothing to solving the problem. Worse still, there may be a lack of urgency in this initial period as the rate of sales erosion is relatively slow, however it allows the new product the invaluable asset of time.

Management's response to change

Of course, this cannot go on for ever, at some time the sales decline reaches a level where management becomes concerned. One might

think that at this stage, positive action would be taken, but paradoxically companies often indulge in the appearance of action rather
than the reality. The first response might be to commission a market
survey, which might take several months to undertake, and then
involve endless meetings subsequently to analyse and digest the
results. This satisfies the need to be seen to be taking some action,
but unfortunately does nothing concrete to respond to the change,
and the decline in the sales goes on; worst of all, the threat is
allowed more and more time to become established. Often the
market survey serves merely to confirm what people already know,
but in a bureaucratic organization one has to go through the process.
And of course, the more bureaucratic the organization the more
time it takes to organize meetings and discuss findings with various
interest groups, and obtain approval from various boards and
committees. It takes some large organizations a year or more just to
arrange a marketing training programme for senior executives, so it
is hardly surprising that it can take even longer to reach a really
important decision.

Bureaucracy may rear its head in other ways than carrying out
market surveys, for example, extended R&D feasibility studies,
lengthy pilot projects and so on. It is not that these things should
not be done, but that they should all be done much more quickly
and decisively, with standard procedures being short circuited in
the interests of a rapid response. So much of this type of activity is
merely procrastination, delaying something which we all know we
have to do eventually. The worst aspect of this bureaucratic procrastination is that it does nothing to solve the problem; all this goes on
internally, while in the real world, the snowball continues to roll
unchecked downhill. Sales continue to decline, but at a faster rate as
the change gathers force. As the process of change continues, concern
increases until finally it is perceived as a problem.

It is well known to accountants, because of the way fixed and
variable costs behave, that a relatively small fall in sales produces a
larger fall in profits. When profits start falling, the natural tendency
is to try to restore them to previous levels; the quickest and surest
way to do this is by cutting costs, and the retrenchment phase
begins. Projects seen as expensive, or with essentially long term
benefits, are shelved or cut back, often despite the fact that these
may be the very things needed to respond to the changing market.
Recruitment is reduced, making it difficult to take on new staff with
new skills. Investment in new plant is reduced, along with R&D
expenditure and new product launch costs. This kind of retrenchment
may well boost profits in the short term, but it is wholly negative as
a means of coping with a changing market. The right response
might be to close a major plant or division making outmoded

products, but this is a much tougher management decision than declaring a moratorium on recruitment and investment. Retrenchment may well be convenient in the short term, but it does nothing to stop the snowball rolling on.

PHASE 1   *Ignore it*

   It won't affect us
   Only a small market niche
   Tell the sales force to try harder

PHASE 2   *Bureaucratic delays*

   Appoint a study team
   Do some market research
   R&D feasibility study

PHASE 3   *Retrenchment*

   Cut discretionary expenditure
   Cut recruitment
   Workforce redundancy a last resort

PHASE 4   *Fundamental management changes*

   New deal with shareholders
   Money to finance restructuring
   New ideas

Figure 8.2   *Company response to environmental change*

Crisis and turnaround

The final stage of this process occurs when things reach crisis point, and it is at that stage that the shareholders step in. For public companies, this may possibly involve direct pressure for management changes from the large institutions which own the shares, resulting in top level resignations. More often, it may be manifested simply as a steady downward drift in the share price, as the market progressively loses confidence in the management, until it reaches a point where the company becomes an attractive takeover target. Following a takeover, the same thing happens, the previous senior executives are replaced by new people chosen by the successful bidder. Even for a subsidiary of a large corporation a similar process occurs. A gradually failing performance is tolerated for so long, until eventually top management changes are instituted by group headquarters.

The key point is to understand what happens after the shareholders have stepped in and the new management team has been installed.

Firstly, the new management negotiates a new deal with the share-holders, after all, they cannot be held responsible for the past. New money is made available for restructuring and investment in new products. The new management may also be able to develop different relationships with the workforce, and perhaps a new attitude from trade unions, customers and suppliers. Most importantly, the new team should be able to introduce new ideas. If all this is successful, the decline will be arrested, and the fundamental restructuring, new investment, changed attitudes, and new ideas will result in a turn-around of the company's position. Of course, if it does not work, the decline will continue towards insolvency.

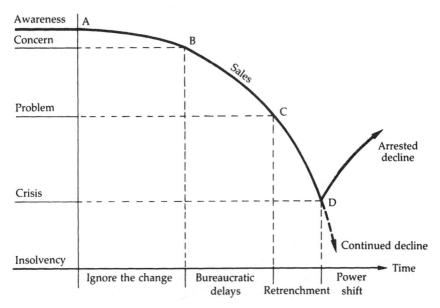

Figure 8.3 *Impact on sales of environmental change*

The fast response organization

This process is mapped out in Figure 8.3; the turnaround stage is shown at point D. The logic of a fast response organization is to shift point D as far as possible backwards towards point A, in other words to ensure that the response to change occurs rapidly, and as soon as possible after the change has started. From the organization's viewpoint, this means not ignoring even minor changes, but making great efforts to understand and monitor them. The identification and understanding of change must then be followed up by taking appropriate action quickly; this means cutting out procrastination by having a constantly updated marketing information system, and shortcutting bureaucratic organizational procedures to push through market related changes fast.

If this can be done effectively, the company will be able to respond to change rapidly, and thus avoid the need for retrenchment and fundamental management changes. The ability to sustain market focus can only be ensured by building an organization which is far better able to respond rapidly to changes in the business environment. Although everyone recognizes that accurate forecasting of the future is notoriously difficult, it would be excessive to claim that forecasting has no role. However, the reason that companies fail to adapt to external change is not fundamentally a lack of ability to forecast it, even 'experts' cannot do this with any certainty. The cause is rather a lack of ability to respond to change quickly and effectively once it happens, and being able to adapt rapidly to external change is the essence of the art of sustaining market focus. Thus, the remainder of this chapter is devoted to a management agenda for the actions and adjustments necessary to build a more flexible and responsive organization.

Tracking environmental change

Environmental awareness

It goes without saying that an organization cannot hope to respond to external change unless it makes every effort to understand its business environment by monitoring it on a regular basis. Therefore, the first fundamental step to take in building a more responsive organization is to create a constant flow of marketing information, and more importantly to ensure that it is used and acted upon. The most basic means of improving environmental awareness is to establish a culture where managers, of whatever function, are encouraged constantly to update their understanding of the market in which their company operates. This may mean something as simple as encouraging managers to read more widely about the activities of the company's customers and competitors. For example, there is no reason why only sales or marketing managers should read the trade press regularly; how many company accountants or engineers would also feel it was relevant to them? More likely, the accountants would read accounting journals and the engineers engineering journals, but these would probably contain relatively little about the markets and customers that it is their firm's job to serve.

One way of assisting this process is to try to provide managers with a weekly digest of important published information on the marketplace. Many companies already do this, but frequently it is too long, too generalized, or both. One major corporation issues all of its senior managers with such a digest which frequently runs to 100 or more pages, most of which feature press articles about the company itself, often the same story from several different newspapers. The circulation is limited by the sheer expense of sending out a weekly document of such size, while the value for many operating managers is limited by the fact that most of the material is just not relevant to their particular operating subsidiary, not to mention the sheer volume of material which needs to be read. If such a news sheet is to be useful, certain parameters need to be set: firstly it should be short, say a maximum of six sides unless there are exceptional circumstances, and it must be relevant to the market and industry in which the recipient operates. The emphasis should be on the external world of customers, competitors and applications, articles about the company itself should be infrequent. Most importantly, it should be circulated very widely to all functions and levels of management.

Finally, it should be seen as the responsibility of a top level senior manager, who should oversee its editorial direction and prepare a short covering note for each issue highlighting important items. It should not become seen as the product of an anonymous 'information department'; however the job of scanning publications and making up the digest can be carried out by a specialist editor, perhaps a relatively junior though enthusiastic person. It is important to foster good working links between the editor and senior management, because not even the most diligent of editors can read everything, and managers should be encouraged to submit items from their own reading for inclusion in the news sheet. It is also important that the editor should never be seen as a mere clerk, but as a key element in the company's attempt to respond to its environment, while the job itself should be seen very much as a step on the management career ladder.

Of course, production of a focused, relevant, weekly news sheet is just the first step in building awareness of the external world, although it is a very important one in that it takes the message to every manager directly. Another method of building environmental awareness is to try to involve a wider spread of managers in visits to customers to improve their understanding of real market conditions. While one clearly has to be careful about the extent of such activity, it is misguided for the sales force to believe customers are uniquely their territory. Although it would be dangerous to overload customers with too many visitors, occasional calls by non sales department personnel can be very positive, especially when accompanied by the regular salesman and when there is a particular customer problem to solve. Customer visits therefore need to be well controlled, but the opportunity to use them as a means of building awareness among other functions should not be passed over lightly. Visits to exhibitions by managers who do not strictly need to be there can be looked at in the same way. While a lot of time can be wasted by non-essential exhibition visits, it would seem a missed opportunity to abandon them altogether.

The marketing information system

While it is important to take every opportunity to build the environmental awareness of every manager, it is equally important to back this up by establishing a more formalized marketing information system. This involves firstly the constant scanning of competitors, by monitoring their advertising and product literature, as well as obtaining any other information which can be gleaned about them from exhibitions, salesmen, customers and the trade press. Secondly, developments at major customers need to be tracked and regularly updated to review any possible impact on company products. Thirdly, developments in the wider environment which impact on both customers and competitors also need to be monitored including trends in technology, the legal framework, changing social attitudes and economic circumstances. This key task is primarily one of organization, since it involves receiving, scanning and prioritizing large quantities of data, sorting and storing it to permit easy review, and finally, setting up a system to ensure that action is taken where necessary.

The sources of incoming data include firstly all the external published information, such as articles in newspapers and journals, published market studies, official statistics and so on. Secondly, every company generates internal data which may have a market research application, such as sales statistics, invoice records, exhibition visit reports, and most importantly sales force call reports, an invaluable source of market information all too rarely used to its full potential. The third source of information is specially commissioned market research surveys, such as those designed to assess the market for a proposed new product. Market surveys are most frequently carried out on an *ad hoc* basis, being undertaken as and when required for special purposes. However, the real value of market research surveys in a marketing information system is when they are done regularly and consistently, in order to enable the company to track changing customer attitudes. This is perhaps the single most important early warning system for the impact of environmental change. This year's attitudes drive next year's sales: looking at sales records provides only an historical picture, whereas attitude tracking can give us an insight into next year's sales based on this year's attitudes.

It is clearly beyond the scope of this book to give a full and detailed account of marketing information systems, besides there are many specialist texts available. Suffice it to say that provided one takes the trouble to look for the information, it is not the quantity of data available which is normally the problem, rather, it is the way the data are processed, presented and used. Any marketing information system will be useless unless its output is valued by senior management, and regularly monitored and reviewed. For this reason there should be a small senior group which meets regularly to review and assess key information uncovered by the marketing research effort. They should identify key concerns, and ensure that these are given particular attention by tracking their development, and recommending company action where appropriate. The important thing about managing a market information system is not maximizing the quantity of incoming data, nor is it improving the sophistication of the handling and processing techniques. Ensuring regular identification, monitoring and updating of evidence of changes in the business environment, and stimulating a response by the company, is the key to the effective use of a marketing information system.

Company criteria

In Chapter 2, traditional financial control systems, and efficiency oriented performance criteria, were identified as perhaps the biggest single barrier to customer focus. In the context of environmental awareness, the problem is that the customary measures of company performance are internal and financial, rather than external and related to the market. Inevitably, this means that the majority of managers spend their time focusing on internal rather than external criteria, and this of course does nothing to emphasize the need for environmental awareness. The managerial emphasis inculcated by the demands of the management control system is a critical issue for any company wanting to achieve and sustain market focus. It needs to be examined and re-evaluated for all sorts or reasons; improving managers' perception of the need for environmental awareness is just one of them.

In order to examine traditional company financial criteria, the same question should be asked as the one outlined in Chapter 2. Senior managers need to evaluate whether each measure is crucial to nurturing the long term health of the business, whether they really do need to monitor it weekly or monthly, and if not, what are the reasons why they perpetuate it. But having swept out non-essential financial criteria, it is necessary to build in a range of market related measures to serve as alternative goals and yardsticks. This involves establishing criteria which measure external effectiveness rather than internal efficiency. Which to use will be related to the circumstances in the particular market concerned, but some of the more widely applicable externally oriented criteria include, for example; the level of customer awareness *vis à vis* competitor brands, perceived product quality relative to competitors, recall of promotional messages, and awareness of distribution channels and availability. In trying to measure the company's performance on external criteria, it is necessary to focus on the most important of the complex range of issues which drive customer purchase decisions in that business.

Only when managers clearly recognize and accept that external factors are the real criteria on which company success is built, will they fully accept the need to improve their level of understanding of the company's broader operating environment. Building awareness of the business environment is the first step in building a responsive organization, clearly a company cannot respond to changes in the environment unless it is aware of them and understands their character. But once awareness has been created, the next stage is responsiveness, and this means building an organization which is sufficiently flexible to adapt to change quickly. Company flexibility can be viewed from a number of angles including product range, financial structure, management skills, and the level of commitment to innovation: all of these need to be addressed in the search for company flexibility and responsiveness. A flexible organization can adapt and respond to change, an inflexible one cannot.

Building a flexible and responsive organization

Product flexibility

Rapid adaptation to change will always be assisted by having several product choices available, rather than only one. However, the problem is that maintaining a wide range of products in order to retain flexibility in the face of change, appears to be the antithesis of focus, in that it must involve spreading rather than concentrating resources. This is partly a question of balance, that is finding an acceptable compromise between a wide enough range to provide flexibility, but not one which is so wide that it leads to a lack of the ability to focus resources. But to say it is all a question of balance is to duck the real issue, because it is more important to understand how the product range should be managed within the product portfolio.

The need for product flexibility underlies the significance of the question zone, location of company's dilemma products. One of the alternative names for dilemmas is 'wildcats': the derivation of this term is not widely understood outside North America, as it refers to the speculative sinking of oil wells, particularly in the early pioneering days of the US oil industry. This is indeed a high risk business, since only one in ten boreholes may yield worthwhile quantities of oil, and only one in a hundred may be a million dollar gusher. The entrepreneurial risk takers who carried out this activity were called 'wildcatters', and they either became millionaires or went bankrupt. This emphasizes the nature of wildcats, or dilemmas, in the product portfolio – high risk ventures that might just lead to significant commercial success.

Environmental change can sometimes change the prospects for such dilemmas quite significantly, perhaps providing the stimulus for what has traditionally been a niche market to grow into a major segment, or to create the circumstances for a sleeper to come to life. One of the reasons for maintaining a reasonable spread of dilemmas is because they form a 'product flexibility bank', which the company can turn to when environmental change dictates. However, it is important to recognize that such products should be maintained on a low budget until required for development, since the whole idea of portfolio management is to focus the investment emphasis onto the growth of stars and the maintenance of strong cash cows. In addition, the range in the product flexibility bank should not be allowed to escalate out of hand; regular reviews and harvesting should be undertaken to keep it down to a manageable size.

Dog products are also, perhaps surprisingly, part of the process of product flexibility. Even a dog may be capable of being repositioned into a new fast growing segment, and more importantly, the role of dogs in generating cash to help finance the stars and dilemmas is a key element in any well-managed portfolio. Thus, product flexibility means having a truly balanced portfolio. It is not as simple as having stars for growth and cash cows for cash flow, every company needs a range of dilemmas and even dogs in order to maintain a balance between current and future opportunities, and between cash users and cash generators. A commitment to R&D investment also goes hand in hand with the concept of a balanced portfolio and product flexibility, so as to generate a constant stream of new opportunities. Resource focus is indeed achieved through portfolio management, but it does not automatically follow that resources are denied to everything except sure-fire stars.

Financial flexibility

It is an inescapable fact of management life that a small fall in sales will produce a proportionally larger fall in profits, and that the higher the level of fixed costs relative to variable costs the greater this effect will be. Variable costs are those which vary directly with output, such as purchases of raw materials; indeed, they are some-times called direct costs. By contrast, fixed costs are those which do not vary with output, such as the salaries of people employed in the accounts department; they are also called indirect costs or overheads. The two categories may run side by side; for example, in the sales force, salaries are fixed costs, whereas commissions are variable costs. In a theoretical company all of whose costs were fixed, a £1 fall in sales would result in a £1 fall in profits, but whereas that might represent say 1% of sales, it could represent 10% of profits. On the other hand, if a high proportion of the company's costs were variable, a £1 fall in sales would also result in a significant fall in costs, and profits would fall by much less than 10%. Thus, the organization better able to withstand a sudden fall in sales caused by unexpected environmental change, is the one with the higher proportion of variable costs.

The practical implication of this is that companies with a high fixed cost base are far more vulnerable to external change, and are therefore inherently less able to respond to it, than companies with a lower fixed cost base. This is the concept of financial flexibility, and it is of course particularly significant for companies involved in fast changing markets; the faster and less predictable the changes, the more important it is to maintain financial flexibility. Even if a company has developed other aspects of the ability to respond to change, this will be of little use if it is driven rapidly into bankruptcy before it even has the chance to adapt to the changed environment. It follows that all things being equal, it is worthwhile trying to reduce a company's fixed cost base, and the greater the possibility of unforeseen external changes, the greater the imperative to do this. But to interpret this as a call merely to reduce fixed costs would be superficial, since the reduction of needlessly borne fixed costs is a good idea in any case: rather than mere fixed cost reduction, the principle involved is to make fixed costs variable.

Distribution and delivery costs are a good example. Most of these costs are fixed, in that it is difficult to fire drivers and close distribution depots simultaneously with a fall in sales, and certainly it is impossible to keep the size of a delivery operation exactly in tune with a constantly fluctuating sales picture. Of course, some costs are variable, fuel and vehicle maintenance costs should fall as distribution activity falls, since these depend ultimately on the level of vehicle usage. Even this is not a clear cut case of costs which are unequivocally variable, since lower sales may be manifested by smaller order sizes, which would lead to little reduction in vehicle mileages. Thus, although some elements are variable, most distribution department costs are fixed, or at best only semi-variable. Contrast this with the cost picture if distribution is handled by a contract distribution service company. The user only pays for delivery when something needs to be delivered, and if the number of deliveries falls, then so too do delivery costs, and they fall simultaneously. By contracting out its delivery function, the user has made fixed costs variable, and has thus helped to protect itself from a future unexpected sharp fall in sales: whereas this would still cause a problem, it would be less likely to be a catastrophe.

Looking around most organizations it is not difficult to find numerous examples of fixed costs which can be made variable. For example, the in-house computer department could be replaced by a bureau, the in-house printer's work could be done outside, telephone sales, and market research can be subcontracted, just like the catering staff. In reality, there are few things which cannot be sub-contracted, perhaps even manufacturing. The problem is that while some of these areas, such as catering, are relatively non-contentious, others, such as computing, tend to generate a great deal of emotion; and a few, like manufacturing, induce an 'over my dead body' attitude in their supporters. The arguments used to support the retention of fixed cost areas in a business are broadly twofold, firstly that the company can do it at a lower cost than subcontractors, and secondly, that it would not be possible to obtain the necessary quality or control by using subcontractors.

The first of these arguments is often difficult to sustain: external specialists like computer bureaux and delivery contractors have to operate in a tough market for their services, so there is a pressure for competitiveness which their feather-bedded in-house brethren are not subject to. Moreover they have the potential to achieve high standards of performance, by focusing on a clearly defined business, and are thus far more likely to be able to do the job well than a company doing it as an add-on extra to its main task. That is not to say that all computer bureaux and delivery contractors do an excellent job, but at least if they do not, the customer has the sanction of the marketplace, a discipline not available to the user of an in-house service.

However, the second argument, about the level of quality and control, is more relevant, and it is normally on these criteria that judgements should be based on whether functions should be contracted out or not. Perhaps a better way of looking at this is to assess whether the function concerned is a key factor for success, crucial to the commercial health of the business, and whether it is true that nobody outside could do it better. For some organizations, manufacturing is indeed a key factor for success, an essential element in achieving competitive advantage, whereas for others it might involve a relatively straightforward assembly process which can safely be contracted out. For manufacturers of perishable foodstuffs such as bread, in-house distribution could be a key factor for success, whereas for many organizations it can safely be subcontracted; it is impossible to generalize.

The advice for chief executives must be to take a hard look at every function in the business to evaluate whether it could be done as well or better outside, and whether it is crucial to competitive advantage to retain it in house. Clearly cost will come into this, if the company can do it at much lower cost in house, it would be silly to take it outside. In addition, security is a factor, both in the form of access to sensitive information, and in ensuring that a competitive market for the service exists to avoid over commitment to one supplier. But the fundamental reason for the retention of any fixed cost which could be made variable must be whether it represents a key factor for success, an indispensable element in the achievement of competitive advantage.

The arguments in favour of making fixed costs variable fit well with the concept of the so-called clover leaf organization. This has been observed in many Japanese companies, and involves identifying three overlapping groups of employees like the three parts of a single clover leaf. The first group comprises the people who embody the company's core skills, those skills which are difficult to replace or substitute. In market focus terminology, these people would be the fountainhead and the guardians of the company's key factors for success. The second group comprises employees who support and contribute to the company's overall efforts, but whose skills are easier to replace or substitute, and do not lead directly to the achievement of key factors for success. The third group comprise a loose-knit group of contractors who are used only on an 'as and when required' basis.

The obvious implication of the clover-leaf organization is that the three groups should be treated differently in terms of salary and other conditions of employment. The first group in particular should be 'locked in' to the organization as far as possible by a long term benefits package which would make it very difficult for them to leave. It is less important to lock in the second group, as their skills are easier to replace, and in any case, looser ties are easier to sever if circumstances demand it. Regarding the third element of the clover leaf, a well-known feature of Japanese companies is their extensive use of subcontract manufacturers for basic assembly work, retaining their own factories for high technology processes, or operations where control of quality is critical. The clover-leaf organization offers a high level of flexibility, since a higher proportion of the people in the business are tied in with relationships that are relatively easy to break if the market changes. However, this flexibility is combined with the benefits of being able to hold on to, and develop in the long term, people with identified core skills.

From a somewhat different but no less important perspective, the level of debt in a company's financial structure has a significant impact on financial flexibility. Borrowing money is a good thing to do, provided it can be invested to produce a higher rate of return than the level of interest payable. Thus, in one sense it is rational for a company to continue to borrow for as long as it can invest in projects which yield more than the interest charge. Unfortunately, interest charges are a fixed cost: they do not fall when sales revenues fall, since it may be difficult to liquidate funds previously borrowed, as fast as sales fall. Indeed, the very circumstances which lead to falling sales often cause commercial interest rates to rise, so exacerbating the problem. Highly geared companies get into trouble when profits fall below the level required to service the debt, and this can happen quite quickly with just a small decline in sales. The moral is that companies in potentially fast changing markets should keep their gearing and hence their fixed interest commitments in very close check, otherwise they may fall victim to a rapid shift in the market which they may otherwise have been able to survive.

Management flexibility

When a company's environment changes, its strategy may have to change, and a change in strategy may require a change in skills. One of the reasons why the Swiss watch companies were slow to change to electronic technology was that they knew absolutely nothing about it. This meant that they lacked a knowledge base on which to make judgements and implement changes, and their lack of understanding itself induced a kind of psychological recoil from

the unknown. It would indeed have been a big step for the acknowledged world leaders in micro-mechanical engineering to throw it all
overboard, and embrace a new technology that required none of
their traditional skills. Worse still, if new people with electronics
knowledge were to be hired, and if the company was to shift its
strategy, would there even be a role for micro-mechanical experts?

This may seem a dramatic example, but many companies have
faced precisely this kind of issue. Adapting to environmental change
has a human as well as a financial dimension, and it is not only
shop floor workers who have to be able to adapt; the same principle
applies to all levels right the way to the top. Indeed, the onus to
adapt to changed products, alternative distribution channels and
new technology weighs particularly heavily on senior managers.
After all, if they do not adapt, it is unlikely that those down the line
will be willing or able to do so. Moreover, the ability of people to
adapt is highly variable; some are temperamentally more adaptable
than others, but even the most adaptable may find it difficult when
the changes are profound, and the new skills difficult to acquire. So
human adaptability is not easy and cannot be taken for granted, the
challenge is that without it, building a flexible and responsive
organization is impossible. Perhaps more books have been written
in the last ten years about the issue of people adapting to change
than any other single management topic, and many new ideas have
been put forward. However, three main themes seem to emerge;
management development, systematic training, and the use of change
agents to stimulate others.

Management development is something which most companies
would claim to do but which in reality, far fewer do seriously. It
may take the form of the 'star system', where a bright young manager
catches the chairman's eye, and is moved at bewildering speed
through a succession of jobs, finally emerging at the top. An alternative is the bureaucratic approach, where central personnel department recommends people for new posts, but the real decision is
taken by a senior line manager. This is defended on the grounds
that line managers have to be free to choose their own people,
regardless of the fact that this does not seem to be put forward as an
argument against the star system. Neither of these approaches is
genuine management development; the bureaucratic system does
not work effectively, while the star system can only apply to a few
individuals who in any case rarely spend enough time in each post
to gain any worthwhile experience.

Management development is one of the key tasks in any chief
executive's overcrowded programme. Having access to a stream of
widely experienced younger managers, with new ideas and the

willingness to acquire new skills, is a crucial element in developing a company's ability to adapt to change. However, the management development system has to work effectively, and this requires the commitment to make it work. In organizations where this happens, part of the culture is an expectation that senior line managers will accept the recommendations of those with a professional responsi-bility for management development, or will have excellent reasons for rejecting them. This should not be seen negatively as imposing staff on line managers, but it does mean accepting that there are wider viewpoints than narrow departmental ones or mere personal opinion. Of course it is easier to let the line managers make the decision, but this is abrogating the responsibility of the chief execu-tive for ensuring a continuing management resource to meet the challenges of change.

Training is another area which most companies pay lip service to, but often do not seem to take really seriously. It is clearly a way of acquiring new skills, but perhaps more importantly, it is a potent source of new ideas. Trainers are often dismissed as lacking practical experience, and therefore the knowledge to help senior managers to manage the business. However, a skilled trainer can provide both a wider perspective, based on insights into a number of different businesses, and an in-depth understanding of a specialist area of management which no practising manager could ever hope to achieve. By its nature, management is a general purpose subject, based on an understanding and experience of a wide range of human and economic phenomena. A manager is a polymath, whereas a trainer is, or should be, a specialist; hence their role in providing additional insights into specific areas of the overall management task.

However, training should be systematic and frequent to be of real use, and it should extend right to the top of the management hierarchy. Ensuring that managers maintain a personal commitment to training is not easy, and that is why an increasing number of companies are insisting that all managers undertake a set period of off the job training each year, some as much as two weeks. This may seem like overkill, but it does help to ensure that everyone, at all levels, does not forget that part of every manager's responsibility is the constant acquisition of new skills and ideas, as well as deepening one's personal understanding of the many fields that comprise management. Norms are nearly always a bad thing in companies, but perhaps training is one of the few exceptions where there is no alternative to a norm, backed up by personal example at the top level.

As well as the acquisition of new skills and ideas, training can be an excellent vehicle with which to foster a change in attitudes. At the core of any attempt to create a market focused organization, there must be an effort to establish a set of market oriented values which are shared by all managers from whatever function. Building new values means displacing old ones, and while most people can do this given time, they must be given the opportunity to evaluate the new ideas rather than having them forced into place. This idea of building a market focus culture among the management team is discussed in more depth in the next chapter, suffice it to say here that one of the most effective ways of starting this process off is a training programme in which managers can share new ideas, contrast these with old ones, and establish a set of common values which everybody in the company can share.

After management development and training, the third aspect of management flexibility is the impulsion to change, that is providing a stimulus to change for people who would rather remain the same. Research has shown that the impulsion to change comes from a few individuals initially, and that they are at first resisted and even ridiculed by their colleagues, but eventually in a successful change process everybody gets carried along. This is totally consistent with what we know about the diffusion of innovations in a market, except that the small band of pioneering early users in a market are known as innovators, whereas in organizations they are known as agents of change. Just like innovators, these people are vital to instigating a change process. However, they are often not well received by their peers. It follows that it is the role of senior managers to recognize, nurture and support their agents of change, since without them, no change process can start.

Managing change agents effectively is one of the most difficult tasks any senior manager will face. Change agents tend to stick out from the crowd, but they have to be encouraged to develop some affinity, to submerge their own personality to a certain extent, or they may be totally rejected. They tend to want to go it alone, but change is ultimately moved forward by coalitions rather than individuals, and it is crucial for change agents to develop alliances. This of course means being prepared to adapt their own ideas and take on board the ideas of others in order to form the alliance, but unfortunately change agents find this difficult to do as they can be very single minded. They also tend to react emotionally to objections, and this obviously antagonizes their colleagues; instead they need to be encouraged to acquire facts and data to enable them to deal with objections rationally. Furthermore, positive change is achieved by finding and building on areas of agreement, whereas the natural starting point of change agents is 'if you are not with me you must be against me'. These are the fundamental characteristics of change agents, and they go a long way to explain why these potentially valuable people can so often be squeezed out of an organization.

However, overlaying all these traits is one dominant theme; change agents are people in a hurry. The problem is that implementing change in any organization that runs essentially on agreement rather than edict takes time and patience. The alternative is to fall back onto autocratic methods of management and force people to do it. This is not really an option in most large businesses; even the chairman in a complex organization has to work by persuading others, and in any case, the best people can easily vote with their feet. It may be an option, and often is, in smaller entrepreneurial organizations. Indeed, this is one of the primary reasons why such organizations can often respond so much more rapidly. But even this depends on one gifted individual having infallible insight, and thus is not totally reliable, even if it were desirable. For most of us therefore, change in organizations is hard work and takes time. It is a question of managing the internal adoption process that gradually moves an idea from the agents of change, through coalitions of early adopters, and on to the majority. It is also true that every organization has its laggards, and dealing with them can be just as testing as managing the change agents.

Commitment to innovation

The singular importance of innovation to any company wishing to achieve market focus has been stressed throughout this book. Not only is innovation the most positive route to competitive advantage, it is essential as a means of coping with environmental change. When a market changes, the first company with an innovation which fits the new circumstances has a clear capability to adapt, indeed, an innovation can frequently initiate the process of environmental change itself. Furthermore, a flexible organization is inherently better suited to handle innovations than an inflexible one, particularly if the innovations demand changes to established corporate norms and practices. For all these reasons, innovation and company adaptability are indivisible.

The task for the senior manager is not merely to espouse a commitment to innovation but to embody it: this means avoiding the three broad behaviour patterns through which managers, sometimes unwittingly, can stifle innovation. The first is to be suspicious of new ideas from below, and to act accordingly. The second is to insist that anybody who needs approval has to go through many levels of bureaucracy to obtain it. The third is to criticize freely, withhold praise, and instil a sense of job insecurity. Any chief executive who operates in this way will not only stifle innovation, but will effectively demonstrate his lack of commitment to it to everyone else in the organization. Ultimately, his company will be the loser. By contrast, the senior manager who wants to show a genuine commitment to innovation should try to create an environment where people are freer to come forward with new ideas, and where praise is more frequent than criticism. It is also important to recognize that new ideas, like any form of change, are moved forward by motivated individuals who need to build coalitions of supporters to provide resources such as money, people, research facilities and market test capability. Senior managers should constantly be trying to identify the individuals and helping to build the supporting coalitions.

Of course, success is rarely instant, it is normally the result of enormous amounts of time and work, and needs persistence and effort to bring it about. Senior managers should recognize this, and be prepared to support their innovators when success appears elusive, rather than pressing for quick results. Encouraging innovation depends on overcoming the barriers outlined in Chapter 4; it means establishing an innovation fund free from the pressures of normal corporate financial norms, and setting up a system to ensure that good ideas are identified, prioritized, reviewed and pursued. But perhaps most importantly it demands leadership. Martin Luther King was one of recent history's great leaders: he proclaimed, 'I have a dream.' He did not say 'I have a few ideas, let's form a committee to report back in six months.' King inspired his people, and led them in pursuit of his vision. As well as ensuring the right corporate framework, leadership in innovation is about providing inspiration.

Organizing to sustain market focus

Environmental change is the biggest single threat to market focus. Change in the market can undermine and destroy even the most highly focused market position, and an organization has no practical means of coping with it other than to adapt to the change effectively. In this chapter, the management actions necessary to sustain market focus have been established, all of which contribute to making the company more flexible, and thus better able to adapt and respond to environmental change. These are the measures which organizations need to implement in order to move point D on Figure 8.3

back towards point A, and so avoid the need for retrenchment by ensuring a more rapid response. The key elements are; improving the company's ability to understand and track environmental change; building product and financial flexibility; encouraging management flexibility; and ensuring a commitment to innovation (see Figure 8.4).

1. *Environmental awareness*
   Measure external variables
   Regular market research
   Formal system to report/discuss/track

2. *Product flexibility*
   Portfolio of products to reduce risk
   Products managed for cash
   Products managed for growth

3. *Financial flexibility*
   Clover-leaf organization
   Make fixed costs variable
   Sensible gearing policy/determine priorities

4. *Management flexibility*
   Management development
   Co-ordinated training at all levels
   Effective use of change agents

5. *Innovation*
   Lead change rather than react
   Recognize organizational barriers
   Formal procedures and goals

Figure 8.4 *An agenda for sustaining market focus*

It should not be forgotten that environmental change brings opportunities as well as threats, and these measures will also make a significant contribution to a company's ability to take advantage of those opportunities before its competitors. Thus, it makes sense to implement them, for both responsive and proactive reasons. This is a wide ranging programme, beyond the scope of any one individual to implement, and it requires a collective effort at the top level to make it happen. In the next chapter, it will be proposed that a Market Focus Council should be set up. One of the key tasks of this team will be to ensure the effective implementation of the measures necessary to sustain market focus.

9 Marketing effectiveness

The first seven chapters of this book reviewed the theory and concepts underlying market focus, and identified the four major building blocks which organizations need to put into place in order to achieve it. Chapter 8 discussed the need for an organization to be able to respond effectively to change in order to sustain market focus. This last chapter will lay out an agenda for marketing effectiveness, a programme for building the attributes which a company needs in order to implement market focus in practice. This is not an easy path to start down, because following it will require changes of attitude from every manager involved, however, the reward will be a truly market focused organization.

Building marketing effectiveness involves three major stages: they are sequential in the sense that one logically follows on from the next, although in effect they are cyclical, as each stage builds on the previous one to form a 'virtuous circle' of good practice (see Figure 9.1). Stage 1 is to start to create a company culture which embraces the major elements of market focus as a total management

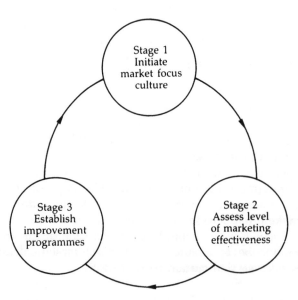

Figure 9.1 *The virtuous circle of marketing effectiveness*

philosophy. Stage 2 is to examine the level of marketing effectiveness the organization is achieving, and to consider the action programmes that need to be put into place to improve it. Stage 3 is to ensure that these programmes are implemented and progress is monitored, so as to improve the company's marketing effectiveness, and thus establish a base to achieve and sustain market focus.

This cannot be done single handedly, it requires the setting up of a Market Focus Council, a top level team responsible for the dissemination and implementation of the market focus philosophy throughout the company. Once this team has got its action programmes under way it should ensure a continuing process of iteration around the virtuous circle. Thus, improvement programmes instituted in Stage 3 will reinforce and build the marketing oriented organizational culture of Stage 1. In addition, Stage 2 should periodically be reviewed, to ensure that marketing effectiveness is being maintained and improved; this will both help to monitor the success of the actions pursued in Stage 3, as well as indicating areas where further action is required. Achieving and sustaining market focus requires a commitment to constant renewal, and the fundamental purpose of the virtuous circle is to stimulate this commitment.

The logical entry point into the virtuous circle is to initiate the development of a market focus culture in the business. Clearly, this cannot be done overnight; culture is about attitudes and values, and it takes time to change these. Creating the right culture throughout an organization could take several years depending on its size, and it is thus unrealistic to propose that this task must be fully completed prior to starting Stage 2. Indeed, a market focus culture will only grow as a result of people seeing tangible changes occurring as a result of Stages 2 and 3. However, setting the tone for what needs to be achieved is the vital prerequisite which starts the virtuous circle turning.

Creating a market focus culture

The fast moving consumer goods paradigm

When interviewed, managers express different views about the nature of marketing, and the problem is that many of these views are serious misperceptions, or at best partial truths. For example, it is widely believed that marketing is basically concerned with selling and advertising, the skills involved in persuading the customer to buy. One very experienced sales manager once told the author 'I'll tell you what marketing is − marketing is selling with knobs on!' It

was of course said partly in jest, but nevertheless does communicate
the reality of marketing in the eyes of some managers, even those in
the marketing department. A slightly more serious quote, which
nevertheless makes the same point, was included by Philip Kotler
in his article *From Sales Obsession To Marketing Effectiveness*. Kotler
quotes a chief executive in one of the world's largest automobile
companies.

> I thought we were doing marketing. We have a corporate vice-
> president of marketing, a top-notch sales force, a skilled advertising
> department and elaborate marketing planning procedures. These
> fooled us. When the crunch came, I realized that we weren't pro-
> ducing the cars that people wanted. We weren't responding to new
> needs. Our marketing operation was nothing more than a glorified
> sales department.

If we want to create a market focus culture we have to understand the kind of bells which ring when managers hear the word
'marketing'. Unless we can clear up misperceptions about the nature
of marketing itself, we cannot hope to create a culture which recognizes that marketing is a total business philosophy. It is worthwhile
taking some time to understand the historical roots of these misperceptions, since this will provide us with an insight into their
nature. Stephen King was a director of a large international advertising agency, and on the basis of his experience there wrote an article
called *Has Marketing Failed Or Was It Never Really Tried*. In it, he
traces the development of modern marketing in the UK.

> It arrived in the 1950s, travelling over from the US and alighting at
> Newcastle. It spread from Procter and Gamble, and has gone from
> strength to strength. More and more manufacturing companies got
> themselves Marketing Managers; and the Marketing Managers got
> themselves bigger staffs, bigger offices, and bigger company cars.

Packaged consumer goods such as confectionery, toiletries, processed
foods, household cleaning products and pet foods are traditionally
known in marketing literature as Fast Moving Consumer Goods
(FMCG). This type of business has been the seedbed from which
marketing has taken root in other areas of commercial life. As a
graduate during the 1960s, one got the impression that a first job in
marketing with Procter and Gamble or Lever Brothers would be an
invaluable passport to success in marketing with any subsequent
employer. Companies fostered this during the 1970s by insisting,
regardless of the industry they were in, that the new marketing
director should have a blue chip FMCG background. Soap powder,

chocolate bars and dog food became the models for marketing excellence. It is worthwhile examining the classic approach which constitutes the FMCG paradigm of marketing. Stephen King identified 'four routes to failure' which are all too readily apparent in many companies.

Thrust marketing

This activity is close to what the general public and indeed many managers call 'marketing'. It involves heavy advertising and promotional expenditure, along with aggressive selling. Managers who espouse this concept of marketing are victims of the megaphone syndrome, the belief that the loudest voice will attract the most customers. This is fine while the megaphone is being used to promote a product which customers feel is better than that offered by competitors, but is merely a means of wasting money when applied to a product with no competitive advantage. This problem is exacerbated in industries with high rates of technological change, where competitors are constantly offering better ways to solve the customer's problems. Nevertheless, where rates of product change are low, and particularly where competitive advantage is based primarily on brand recognition, there is no doubt that Thrust Marketing can work well.

Marketing department marketing

This is the approach which holds that marketing decisions should be taken only on the basis of exhaustive and rigorous market research. There is nothing wrong with this most of the time, indeed to reject it would be to reject the fundamental concept of customer orientation: surely the whole basis of marketing is to find out what customers want and then provide it. Unfortunately, this all falls down when it comes to innovations; market research can report people's views and preferences, but it cannot discover what their views might be once they have had the opportunity to consider, re-evaluate and possibly change them over time. This is exactly what happens during the social learning process which drives market innovation. History is littered with anecdotes about phenomenally successful innovations which market researchers would have strangled at birth: computers, the Jumbo Jet, Perrier Water, the Sony Walkman and 3M's Post-It note; all were pronounced to have no hope of success. Innovation is crucial to long term success, yet it does not seem to fit the classic marketing concept. But just like Thrust Marketing, Marketing Department Marketing may well be relatively more appropriate where there is a low rate of innovation and change, however, it can be positively dangerous if applied too rigorously in fast changing markets.

Accountant's marketing

This approach holds that marketing is basically a cost, and like other costs, the secret of success is control. This has led to the still ubiquitous advertising to sales ratio method of setting advertising budgets, and to a whole range of efficiency ratios to monitor and control marketing and sales activities. Of course, control is fine, a company which fails to control its costs is unlikely to survive long. However, while tightly managed financial controls are admirable in stable conditions, they lead to an inability to adapt to change in a dynamic environment, since they encourage managers to make financially rather than market oriented decisions. This is the efficiency syndrome, and excessive pursuit of efficiency damages marketing effectiveness. Thus, once again, while Accountants Marketing may be appropriate where changes are slow, it does not appear to work well in conditions of innovation and change among customers and competitors.

Formula marketing

This approach is based on the application of experience gained in other industries or societies, or in earlier times. It can often be observed in large international companies, and is manifested by a marketing philosophy which appears to be based on the belief that 'if it works here it must work there'. While there are undoubted benefits to be gained from international marketing, it is only in a tiny minority of cases that it can be interpreted as the slavish cloning of a single marketing strategy across national boundaries, regardless of economic and cultural differences. Formula Marketing in a slightly different form, is sometimes adopted by chief executives as a means of rejecting ideas they do not support; 'we tried that ten years ago and it didn't work'. These are formulae for ensuring success or avoiding failure, formulae based on experience of success or failure elsewhere. Of course, there is nothing wrong with experience, companies and managers must use their experience to aid decision making. The problem arises when the business environment is changing: what was a good decision in the 1980s may be a very bad decision ten years later. It is not necessarily that the previous decision was wrong, it is just that the circumstances have changed.

Basing ideas on success formulae from a previous era may be fine in conditions of stability, but it can never be relied on in conditions of change.

Does the FMCG paradigm work?

King's four routes to failure are the tenets of classic FMCG marketing: heavy investment in advertising and promotion, extensive and rigorous market research, tight financial controls, and a significant dependence upon approaches which have been shown to work in the past. When a director of a major advertising agency describes the approach adopted by the majority of his clients, and indeed by the majority of advertising agencies, as 'routes to failure', it is a criticism which should be taken very seriously. Could there really be such a dichotomy between marketing as it should be practised, and marketing as it appears to be practised by the very companies which are held up to be the models of marketing excellence? But perhaps the paradox can be explained: while the approaches adopted by FMCG companies do not seem to be appropriate in markets characterized by high levels of innovation and a rapid rate of change, they may nevertheless be somewhat more sensible in slow changing markets.

The soap powder market is a classic example: in the UK it is dominated by two major competitors, and, as in most oligopoly markets, the competitive pressures are somewhat muted by the absence of small aggressive entryists, and the fact that both contestants realize that all-out war would only lead to mutual destruction. Soap powder, like confectionery and dog food, is basically a mature technology, and accordingly has a rather low rate of technological change. Consumers also tend to be conservative about the food they eat, the powder they wash their clothes in, and what they feed their dogs: accordingly, the speed at which innovations are adopted is relatively slow, and manufacturers have plenty of time to study trends before deciding to make a major new investment. This pattern of relatively slow change is bolstered by heavy and extremely professional advertising, which produces levels of customer loyalty which are unparalleled elsewhere: consumers do not merely prefer their favourite brands, in many cases they are hard core loyalists for life.

To a lesser or greater extent, these characteristics are shared by many branches of the FMCG industry. It is odd that businesses characterized by such slow changes should have become known as 'fast moving'. In reality, the only thing which is fast is the speed at

which the packs of the more successful brands move off the super-
market shelves. From a strategic perspective, it would be far more
appropriate if we called them slow moving consumer goods, and
herein lies the explanation of the paradox. In markets where an
oligopoly has led to a relative lack of competitive pressure, or those
characterized by low rates of technical change, long innovation
adoption cycles, and very stable consumer preferences, King's so-
called 'routes to failure' are in fact a sound basis for success. The
FMCG paradigm of marketing makes a great deal of sense in such
circumstances. On the other hand, gearing up a business to cope
with constant change is expensive, even inefficient, and it could be
argued that there is little point in trying to make an organization
more adaptable than it needs to be given the market in which it
operates.

Thus, there is a trade-off between full blooded adoption of the
market focus paradigm and slavish commitment to the FMCG
paradigm: each organization needs to find its own place on the
continuum between the two, and the key determining factor is the
rate of change in its markets. However, while companies in slower
changing markets have a less pressing need to adopt the market
focus paradigm than those in fast changing markets, it would be
foolish for any organization to ignore it altogether. All businesses
are subject to the pressures of external change, some admittedly
more so than others. The FMCG paradigm only really works in
situations of very slow and predictable change, and few organizations
have this luxury today, particularly with the spectre of world-class
organizations increasingly penetrating national markets as historic
barriers to international business continue to fall.

Therefore, Stephen King was only partially right in his criticism
of the classic FMCG approach: it may well be the right approach in
the circumstances outlined above, indeed it has been shown to
work well over a long period of time in some very large consumer
goods markets. The problem arises when these methods are trans-
planted to other less stable, more competitive, more innovative
industries. It is unfortunate that many UK companies have attempted
to achieve just such a transplantation in the belief that they were
introducing 'marketing' into their organization, and it is small
wonder that so many of these attempts have failed to live up to
their promise. Every company has to find its own marketing paradigm; we should not be surprised if the attempt to bolt on someone
else's, from a completely different industry, ends in disappointment.
It must also be underlined that even apparently secure and slow
changing markets will increasingly be subject to the pressures of
international competition and environmental change: no business

can afford to rest on its laurels, in the belief that a secure position will last for ever.

The market focus paradigm

The misperceptions involved in the FMCG paradigm are a significant barrier to introducing market focus into an organization. After all, if managers do not even understand what marketing really is, how on earth can they be expected to embrace it as a business philosophy which will drive the entire company, including their own function? In order to break down these barriers, current and future managers need to be provided with an insight into what marketing really involves for the majority of industries in our fast changing, competitive and innovative world. Certainly, for many companies, even some FMCG companies, this will involve a significant shift away from the traditional FMCG paradigm. The market focus paradigm involves three fundamental elements; customer and competitor orientation, innovation and adaptation, and a commitment to the long term. This model is like a three-legged stool, take one leg away and the whole lot collapses.

Customer and competitor orientation

Customer orientation is the starting point of market focus, and must be the guiding light for all functions, not just the marketing department. This itself is difficult enough to achieve, but customer orientation alone is not sufficient, there must also be a sharp focus on competitors, because marketing involves providing something better than the competition in the perception of a given target customer. Only by building a sustainable competitive advantage will a company be successful, and this has to be an advantage which is valued by the customers and which the competitors will find difficult to copy. Thus, customer and competitor orientation is the first leg of the market focus paradigm.

The basis of successful customer focus is effective market positioning, the interplay of the three 'C's, customer needs, company skills, and competitors' offerings. In order to achieve an effective market position, managers need to assess the needs of target customers, the company's offering and the skills it has available to produce it, compared with the competitors' offerings and skills. Focus on the customer is all about achieving a defensible market position through the achievement of a sustainable competitive advantage. But how does a company achieve a competitive advantage? It is not something which can be pulled out of thin air. This leads on to the second leg of the market focus paradigm – innovation and adaptation.

Innovation and adaptation

The most effective means of achieving a sustainable competitive advantage is to be the first to offer it, the least effective is to wait until market research tells you it has already been successfully offered by everybody else, then hope to jump on board. The successful pioneering innovator gains the dual rewards of lower costs through greater experience and scale, and crucially, higher customer awareness, wider distribution and lower perceived purchase risk. However, it is difficult for market research methods to spot genuine innovations, often it is necessary to rely on the judgement of the managers concerned, something which bureaucratic organizations are often ill equipped to do.

In addition to innovation, organizations need to adapt to changes in the business environment. A variety of measures has been suggested in order to help companies do this, the fundamental idea being to build the company's ability to spot the early signs of environmental change, and give it the flexibility to act quickly, rather than waiting until the change is showing up as a significant variable in market research reports or is making an impact on profits. The problem with early adaptation is of course that it is risky. Responding to a change in the environment involves being prepared to adapt the organization's strategy and structure accordingly, when everybody knows that it would be less costly in the short term to stay the same. Conceptually, innovation and adaptation are inextricably linked, one feeds off the other, and both require a long term rather than a short term perspective of the management task. This leads us on to the third leg of the market focus paradigm.

Taking the long view

It is axiomatic that marketing is a long term activity. Just as it can take leading products many years to decline, so it takes them many years to achieve their pre-eminence, because the acceptance of an innovation is rarely an overnight phenomenon. Innovation is a slow, sometimes painfully slow, social process, by which people gradually change their attitudes and values. Any company looking for quick rewards is unlikely to be a successful innovator, and is thus likely to find it difficult to build long term competitive advantage.

However, in the real world there is constant pressure for short term results, and more specifically for steady growth in earning per share. If some external event should threaten this year's profits, the easiest method of maintaining earnings stability is to cut costs such as research, training, advertising, new ventures and recruitment. The market focus approach recognizes that taking the long view is essentially a selective process; it would be totally unrealistic for any organization to take a long view of everything. Unfortunately, doing this requires some fundamental changes in management attitudes, if we are managing selectively for the long term, not everybody can have more resources every year: resource allocation means that if one project gains, another is denied.

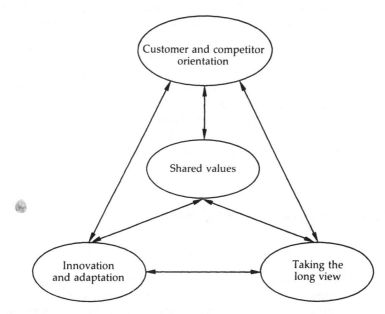

Figure 9.2 *Key values in a market focus culture*

Building shared values

Stephen King asked whether marketing had failed or whether it had merely never been tried. He was quite right to pose this rhetorical question, because it is not that marketing has failed, but that businesses have not fully understood the implications of introducing a genuine marketing orientation. The fundamental problem lies in the belief that being a marketing oriented company means adopting the FMCG paradigm. Aggressive selling and promotion; extensive and rigorous research before any decision is taken; tightly managed controls and norms applied to marketing expenditure; and following proven formulae which have stood the test of time. Some or all of these are good ideas in the right circumstances, but by themselves they fail to encapsulate the essence of marketing.

Unfortunately, the process which has created these misperceptions of marketing has probably gone too far, and become too deeply ingrained in society to easily be changed. It is likely that most new graduates will continue to see FMCG as the most interesting and challenging area of marketing, and the one which will provide the best professional training. And in the world of business itself, perhaps too many managers still perceive the FMCG giants as the paragon of sound marketing practice. Building a market focus culture is about reversing some of these deeply rooted attitudes about the nature of marketing. The market focus paradigm is the basis of the shared values to which every manager should subscribe in a marketing oriented organization (see Figure 9.2). Establishing these values demands that a significant education programme be undertaken in the company, and more importantly, that an example be set, and leadership provided at the very top level. Providing the vision and the leadership is the single most important task of the Market Focus Council, for without it, the rest of the Council's effort will largely be wasted.

Assessing marketing effectiveness

The marketing effectiveness checklist

Once we have started to create a culture in which market focus can thrive, the next stage is to assess whether the organization is in the right condition to achieve market focus and hence competitive success. Building marketing effectiveness means getting into shape to achieve market focus, and is best undertaken after understanding the level we are starting from, and identifying which areas need particular attention. This is done by examining the company's current position on each of the attributes which characterize an effective marketing organization: the marketing effectiveness checklist is a way of carrying out a self-administered assessment of this. It is reviewed here on the assumption that it will be undertaken internally by the company's managers, although it must be said that a skilled external assessor may carry out a more impartial initial analysis.

The checklist is shown in Figure 9.3, and asks the user to make an overall assessment of the company's current performance level on each of twelve attributes. Respondents should be asked to check the numerical rating which most closely reflects what they feel is the company's current position. An overview of the meaning of each

Please check each of the twelve boxes using a 1–5 rating scale

not at all				completely
1	2	3	4	5

1 *The marketing environment* ☐
All of our managers have a good and regularly updated understanding
of the marketing environment in which the company operates

2 *Customer orientation* ☐
Every functional manager understands his/her role in enabling the
company to satisfy its customers better

3 *Customer targeting* ☐
Each product/business sector manager issues clearly defined
customer target statements for the guidance of other managers

4 *Measures and controls* ☐
The management control system measures internal efficiency criteria
and external market criteria with at least equal emphasis

5 *Competitor orientation* ☐
Every manager understands the importance and the nature of
sustainable competitive advantage

6 *Innovation* ☐
The company makes a structured formalized effort to encourage
and nurture commercial innovation

7 *Competitive analysis* ☐
We undertake regular competitive analysis studies and circulate
the results widely among the management team

8 *Resource allocation* ☐
Our planning system results in the ability to focus resources onto
the best market opportunities

9 *Product portfolio* ☐
The company has a well-balanced product portfolio in both cash flow
and product strategy terms

10 *Strategic objectives* ☐
Product/business sector managers are set clear strategic objectives
which recognize the trade offs between growth, profit and cash flow

11 *Organizational flexibility* ☐
We make a specific and adequate effort to create a flexible
organization which can adapt rapidly to a changing market environment

12 *Long term vision* ☐
We ensure that selected parts of the business are managed
purposively for long term growth rather than current profit performance

Total score ☐

Marketing effectiveness ratings
12–20   none
21–28   some
29–36   fair
37–44   good
45–52   very good
53–60   excellent

Figure 9.3 *Marketing effectiveness checklist*

attribute is given in the sections below, while a more detailed interpretation is given in previous chapters as indicated. One manager can complete the checklist alone, although this will clearly produce a biased result, and a better overall picture will be gained by involving a number of managers from each function. The checklist is not a scientific tool, it is driven by opinions and perceptions, and some answers at least are likely to be a reflection of each individual's personal agenda. However, it is difficult to envisage a truly scientific tool for measuring marketing effectiveness; this self-assessment process is intended both to stimulate debate about critical issues, and point out the key areas for subsequent management action programmes. Nevertheless, it remains essentially a structured survey of management opinion, and the limitations inherent in this should not be overlooked.

The twelve numerical assessments add up to result in a total score, and the checklist gives some qualitative interpretations of this score from nil through good to excellent. However, a more important exercise is to look carefully at the score for each section, particularly the average score taking all respondents into account. The low scoring sections are those where particular action is likely to be most warranted, and the checklist may thus be used to indicate areas for more or less urgent attention. But the main purpose of the marketing effectiveness checklist is to provide a collectively derived and agreed basis for planning subsequent action programmes. Indeed, this is a primary reason for not relying solely on an external assessor: while external people may offer impartiality, participation in the assessment process by the company's managers can only be beneficial in securing ownership, or at least acceptance, of the resulting action programmes.

The actions should be aimed at making a deliberate effort to improve the company's performance in identified areas of weakness. At the end of the assessment process, all respondents should be invited to participate in a review session. This should involve a discussion to identify clearly what action needs to be taken to improve the company's score by, say, 10 points in the next year. This creates clear goals; an action programme, a performance target, and a timescale. Naturally the specific goals will depend upon the circumstances; it is easier to improve 10 points from a base of 15 than it is from a base of 50, but essentially the management team should set itself a goal, establish an action programme, then repeat the assessment process at the end of the period to evaluate whether the goal has been achieved.

The checklist highlights twelve specific areas where a co-ordinated programme of management action will deliver significant improvements in a company's marketing effectiveness. Unless continuing attention is paid to maintaining and improving performance in each dimension of the effectiveness package, it will be impossible to realize the benefits of market focus. The following paragraphs summarize the twelve key organizational attributes involved. From a practical management viewpoint, this provides an overview of what a company needs to implement in order to achieve and sustain genuine market focus.

Environmental sensitivity

The first fundamental element of marketing effectiveness is to recognize that companies need to respond to the outside world in order to survive and prosper. This means firstly that every manager needs to be aware of the shape company's external environment and how that environment is changing. Only then can individual managers fully play their part in helping the company to respond. Environmental sensitivity means more than just awareness of the changing market environment; it also means having the capability to adapt to those changes. The company should therefore establish a programme to build the awareness level, and set up a small team to stimulate and monitor the company's response (see Chapter 8).

Customer orientation in all functions

Every function in the business has a role in serving the customer effectively, thus functional decisions cannot be divorced from customer criteria. This means the customer should be at the centre of every functional manager's decision process (see Chapter 2). This in turn requires an understanding of the company's customer targets, and a control system that emphasizes external as well as internal performance measures, and these aspects are examined in more detail below. But it also requires a change in philosophy from functional managers, a shift in emphasis from purely functional objectives towards customer satisfaction objectives: reinforcing this latter point is an educational task, and should be part of the effort to build a market focus culture.

Tight customer targets

In order to ensure that every manager can focus on customers, and that marketing plans are focused on well-defined target customers, everybody needs to understand the company's specific customer targets. This means that not only do customer target statements need to be drawn up, they need to be as tightly defined as possible: accurate segmentation is the route to focused marketing plans (see Chapter 3). Drawing up and disseminating tightly defined customer target statements is a key element in market positioning, and without it, real customer and competitor focus is impossible.

Externally focused control systems

Detailed financial control systems are the most significant practical barrier to market focus in large organizations. These systems are based on the pursuit of short term gain and internal efficiency, and can often lead to the sacrifice of long term external effectiveness. All such measures need to be reviewed, and any which are not essential to the overall direction and survival of the business should either be abandoned, or treated as operating early warning systems, rather than management goals and yardsticks. They should be replaced by monitoring systems which encourage managers to make customer rather than financially oriented decisions. In short, we need to ensure that the control system encourages rather than penalizes customer orientation (see Chapter 2).

Understanding of competitive advantage

While it is axiomatic that companies need an advantage over their competitors in order to compete effectively, the message of competitive advantage is somewhat more subtle than this. Firstly, a given competitive advantage may only be perceived as an advantage by a particular customer target group; this is the whole basis of the concept of positioning. Secondly, an advantage needs to be sustainable, and, in the absence of overwhelmingly superior costs, price is the least sustainable source of advantage. Understanding the real nature of competitive advantage is as essential to all managers as understanding the need for customer orientation (see Chapter 3).

Commitment to innovation

Innovation is the positive way to benefit from environmental change, building new competitive advantages calls for innovation, and without it companies will stagnate and die. Yet large organizations seemed geared up to squeeze it out rather than encourage it. A real commitment to innovation means far more than merely saying 'it's a good thing', it means establishing a special innovation fund, encouraging the innovators with time and facilities, and setting up a system to identify, monitor and drive forward new ideas in the business. The barriers to innovation may well prove insuperable unless specific steps are taken to overcome them (see Chapter 4).

Competitive analysis

Undertanding competitors is essential to market focus, given its role in firstly assessing the value and sustainability of competitive advantage and secondly in helping to define competitive strategy, whether to be a follower, a challenger, a defender, an innovator, or whatever. Only with rigorous and regularly updated competitive analysis can these tasks be carried out effectively, and this involves understanding competitors' products, their organizational strengths and weaknesses, and of course their psychology, how they are likely to respond if attacked. Competitive analysis is the basis of both understanding competitive advantage and defining an effective competitive strategy (see Chapter 6).

Concentration of resources

An integral element of the market focus approach is that scarce resources should be concentrated where the firm has the best opportunities rather than spread thinly. In addition, sufficient resource should be applied to create leverage in the market, since an insufficient effort compared to competitors is likely to be dissipated through lack of critical mass. Resource focus is achieved by using the product portfolio to identify investment priorities and ensure that sufficient resource is applied to achieve the task required, rather than spreading the available resource over a wide range of targets (see Chapter 5).

Balanced portfolio

A well-managed product portfolio will have a spread of product or market units across all the zones rather than a cluster in just one. Stars (Zone 1) are the key investment area for the company's future growth; cash cows (Zone 2) generate current profits and help to finance the stars; dogs (Zone 4) can be powerful cash generators if properly managed; and dilemmas (Zone 3) include potential sleepers and innovators, possible challengers, and profitable followers and nichers. A balanced portfolio permits a balance between cash generators and cash consumers as well as a balance between different strategic approaches to product management (see Chapter 5).

Clear strategic objectives

It is impossible for a product manager to make rational operating decisions about any aspect of how a product is to be marketed until the strategic objective has been clearly defined in terms of the emphasis to be placed on growth, profit or cash flow. The choice is between build, maintain and harvest, and until that strategic choice has been made it is impossible to draw up a focused marketing plan. Setting a clear strategic objective will ensure that marketing action programmes are strategically rather than financially driven. However, this can only be achieved after setting clear product line strategic objectives (see Chapter 7).

Flexible and responsive organization

In order to adapt to the environment, an organization firstly has to understand its environment and then respond to it. Getting an organization to respond to change requires more than mere exhortation, a high level of flexibility needs to be built into the product range, the financial structure, and the attitudes and skills of the managers themselves. Without building a flexible organization, sustaining market focus will be impossible (see Chapter 8).

Long term orientation

The concept of market focus is indivisible from longer term management thinking, the whole package is a commitment to a continuous long term process. While this is easy to say, it is undeniably difficult to do in a world where shareholder assessments seem to be driven largely by short term considerations, and this gets translated into management pressure for short term results. However, in an investment sense, long term orientation can never be a company wide creed, no organization could invest across the board in a long term basis. The long term view can only sensibly be applied selectively, to those priority investment areas which warrant it, and this means that other parts of the business need to be run even harder to provide the short term results. This is the central purpose of the portfolio approach, to identify priority areas for long term investment, and allocate company resources accordingly. But a long term philosophy underlies all the elements of market focus, each one requires an essentially long term orientation in order to flourish. It is one of the shared values which should be inculcated as part of the effort to create a marketing culture (see Chapter 9).

The Market Focus Council

Building marketing effectiveness

The twelve areas discussed above are the attributes of effective marketing organizations, and as such, represent the final overview of what this book has set out to establish. However, the book would be incomplete if it did not consider how the market focus philosophy should be implemented in practice. This means examining who might be responsible for managing and monitoring progress on each of the twelve marketing effectiveness attributes (see Figure 9.4). The various tasks involved require a continuing effort from several people, and are best overseen by a small sub-group drawn from the existing board of directors. It must be made clear to all concerned that this is not to be some kind of superior decision making body over and above the existing board, but rather that its role is to facilitate the process of achieving and sustaining market focus within the company. Calling this group the Market Focus Council communicates the nature of its role, and emphasizes that it is not some kind of superior corporate strategy committee.

```
1   Environmental sensitivity
2   Customer orientation in all functions
3   Tight customer targets
4   Externally focused control systems
5   Understanding of competitive advantage
6   Commitment to innovation
7   Competitive analysis
8   Concentration of resources
9   Balanced portfolio
10  Clear product line strategic objectives
11  Flexible and responsive organization
12  Long term orientation
```

Figure 9.4 *Attributes of effective marketing organizations*

The Council should be led by the chief executive, but responsible to the board. As regards the make-up of the membership, three people in addition to the chief executive are probably sufficient, although it could be one more or less, depending on the circumstances. The primary qualification for membership is the necessary enthusiasm to ensure the success of market focus, rather than any particular functional background. Indeed, it would be undesirable to have too much of a sales or marketing bias, as this might tend psychologically to exclude the other functions. At the same time, it is desirable to limit the membership in some way, otherwise it becomes a board meeting by another name. Individual members of the Council should be given specific areas of responsibility, and a four way division of the key tasks of the Council is discussed below. This is summarized in Figure 9.5, although clearly this allocation of responsibilities could be modified to suit a larger or smaller group.

Tasks of the Market Focus Council

The first key task of the Market Focus Council is to track and understand the business environment, and to ensure that regular reports about this are made available to every manager. This includes managing the marketing information system, and ensuring that its output is regularly monitored, prioritized and followed up. Fuller details of what needs to be done are given in Chapter 8. A coordinated marketing information effort will help to ensure that every manager is aware of the nature of and the changes within the company's business environment, and that regular rigorous competitive analysis is carried out. Customer analysis is also essential to the tasks of customer orientation and the specification of customer targets. A marketing information system may already be in existence within the marketing department if one exists, and if so, it would be silly to start an identical parallel system. Hence, there will be close links with the existing marketing function, but over and above that, there is no reason why any functional director should not take it on.

The second task to be allocated is that of managing the market focus planning effort. This involves overseeing a structured strategic planning system as set out in Figure 7.6, whose outcome will affect every function in the business. It follows that it needs a senior manager to organize it, and ensure that it operates to timetable. Here we come to a difficult area, because the marketing director will see the product portfolio as his responsibility, whereas the finance director will see the budget as his. After all, this is the way planning is managed in most organizations, product planning is separate from financial planning. One of the great strengths of the market focus planning system is that product and financial plans are inseparable, so it really makes sense to put the management of the system under one individual.

A well-managed planning effort will help to ensure a balanced portfolio, clear product line strategic objectives, and concentration of resources. The positioning element of the planning process should also ensure the adoption of tight customer targets, and the need to identify sustainable competitive advantages. Provided the process outlined in Chapter 7 is followed rigorously, it should lead also to market driven marketing plans. One member of the Market Focus Council should be responsible for organizing and overseeing the planning process, incorporating the above tasks within it.

Managing the market focus planning system is an ideal remit for a market oriented finance director, and making it his responsibility in any case offers the best chance of doing away with budget driven marketing plans. But whoever manages the planning system, it should not be the same person that has responsibility for understanding and tracking the environment. This information is the vital external data upon which the entire market focus planning process depends. External information underpins the accuracy of the whole portfolio planning process, the determination of viable competitive strategies, effective positioning, and the drawing up of customer focused plans. It is essential to separate the management of the system itself from the provision of the basic input information which drives that system, otherwise the whole thing may lack credibility in the eyes of other board members.

```
1  Track and understand the business environment
2  Manage the market focus planning effort
3  Ensure financial and management flexibility
4  Provide leadership for innovation effort
```

Figure 9.5 *Tasks of the Market Focus Council*

A further member of the Market Focus Council should be responsible for the management and financial aspects of company flexibility. This includes organizing the search for fixed costs which can be made variable, and identifying areas for contracting out. This member of the team should also take on the task of ensuring that the control system encourages managers to take customer oriented decisions. This means evaluating the current system and taking out unnecessary measures, along with the associated bureaucracy. It also involves the introduction of new externally oriented control criteria as suggested in Chapter 2. A further important responsibility is to identify the people who represent the company's core skills, and to ensure that the right packages are available to lock these people into the organization as far as possible. In addition, this team member would oversee the management development and training function, and ensure it is working effectively. This includes taking personal responsibility for managing the educational programme to build shared values, referred to earlier in this chapter.

While aspects of this series of tasks appear to fit the personnel function, again there is no reason why it cannot be undertaken by any director. Perhaps the most important feature of this role is that it involves work in every function and department, and it may well involve reaching and implementing decisions that functional heads do not welcome, at least initially. Overseeing these areas is likely to involve delicate discussions about the structure and role of management functions and the careers of individuals, and it is thus a task requiring the utmost tact and diplomacy. It is consequently an ideal role for either the chief executive or the most experienced member of the board, someone whose judgement is trusted by all, and whose impartiality is doubted by nobody.

This brings us to what is perhaps the Market Focus Council's most difficult task in a large organization – innovation. Managing the innovation effort can again be the responsibility of any functional director, since it crosses many functional boundaries, although there will inevitably be close links with R&D. At the level of the Market Focus Group, it is particularly important to ensure that there is a proper structure to identify, encourage, and provide resources for innovations, as outlined in Chapter 4. Regardless of which member of the team looks after innovation, it must be given the closest personal support by the chief executive, because it is so vital to the company's future, and yet is so easily squeezed out. It is thus essential to demonstrate that there is absolute top level commitment to it. Leadership from the top will give the innovation effort real teeth, ensure the allocation of adequate resources, and inspire the company's innovators to try just that bit harder to push their ideas through.

Involving every manager

Market focus will only be sustained through management effort, and the Market Focus Council is suggested as the major vehicle for the expression of that effort. However, over and above their individual responsibilities, it is the job of every member of the Council to ensure that all managers understand and live by the market focus ethos. While the four sets of tasks summarized in Figure 9.5 represent specific management responsibilities which can be assigned to designated members of the Market Focus Council, each individual element will require the contribution and co-operation of many managers from different functions to ensure its successful implementation. Therefore, while it is sensible to allocate particular tasks to identified senior managers, the whole process will only work with the active involvement of every manager.

It is also clear that some of the attributes of marketing effectiveness are more general in nature, and cannot be made the responsibility of any one person: these must be part of the effort to build shared values. Therefore, while all of the twelve items on the marketing effectiveness checklist are relevant to every manager, there are some which should explicitly be built into the programme to achieve a wider marketing culture. Creating a market focus culture is an integral element of the virtuous circle outlined at the beginning of this chapter, however, it requires a specific educational effort to question existing values and raise awareness of the alternatives. The shared values which form the basis of an organizational marketing culture are customer and competitor orientation, innovation and adaptation, and taking the long view, as set out in Figure 9.1. Of course, these are inseparable from the other points on the checklist, however, they form the basis for the educational effort to build a genuine market focus ethos across all functions, and thus encourage every manager to support actively the work of the Market Focus Council.

Building shared values, and developing the company's competence in the twelve attributes of marketing effectiveness, is the route to achieving and sustaining market focus. These goals will not be realized by training programmes alone, however inspirational they may be, nor will they be secured by exhortation, however eloquent or high powered. Both of these will help, but ultimately, market focus will only be achieved by individuals and teams being prepared to put in the necessary effort. However, by implementing a series of targeted action programmes, it is possible to improve the level of a company's performance on each of the marketing effectiveness attributes. Market focus is not merely an unattainable theoretical dream, but it does require managers to change their values, to look at the world in a different way. Given that, plus the hard work necessary to implement the nuts and bolts, market focus is within the grasp of any organization.

Index